Hyperborea and the Aryan...
(Natural-scientific aspects)

N.K. Roerich. Moses is the leader

Russia is a country of eternal changes and completely non-conservative, it is country beyond conservative customs, where historical times live, and do not part with rituals and ideas. The Russians are not a young people, but the old ones - like the Chinese. They are very old, ancient, conservatively preserved all the oldest and do not refuse it. In their language, their superstition, their disposition, etc., one can study the most ancient times. Victor von Hyun. 1870.

Alexander Bykov
Should we be afraid of climate change?

Many years ago, in the smoking room of the Vologda Museum of Local Lore, S.V. Zharnikova, a person in the museum who was unloved for freethinking and oppressed by the director Novozhilova (the grandmother of the famous Vologda showman Kirill Panko), spoke about the impending global warming based on the historical experience of 5,000 years ago.

Then the climate in the Northwest was akin to what is now in western Ukraine, in Poland and the Czech Republic. Deciduous forests grew everywhere, inhabited by deer, bison, and, they say, even some varieties of large feline predators. Here lived the ancient Indo-Europeans, who are usually called arias.

Zharnikova said that there was a climatic optimum. Then came the cooling, not immediately and suddenly, but gradually the climate began to change in the direction of the cold. Deciduous forests were replaced by conifers, and even further north by the "white-fronted sea", where the forests used to grow, the tundra appeared. The species composition of life has gradually changed.

The Aryans also left here and settled widely on a vast territory from the Baltic to India, preserving in the legends and monuments of folklore information about their northern ancestral home. Others came to the liberated territories - Finno-Ugric tribes. At the end of the first millennium of a new era, a part of the Indo-Europeans - Slavic tribes returned to the north, assimilated or mixed with the local Finno-Ugric peoples (alright and all) and gave rise to the modern population of the North of Russia.

They did not believe Zharnikova, she studied the ornaments of some village towels, the names of tracts, rivers and lakes, compared them with the names of Southern Europe and Northern India and found parallels. Some allowed themselves to laugh openly at the arguments of the researcher ...

A little over 30 years have passed. Svetlana Vasilievna is no longer with us, but her lectures on the Internet, articles and books have made in the public mind a researcher with a modest academic degree, Academician, unquestioned authority in the field of ethnography.

The climate is also changing, we are predicting low snowy warm winters, scare, shout about the death of the northern fauna. But is it really bad when there are no 30-degree frosts, fruit trees do not freeze, and forest dwellers do not die from a nonsense.

As for the polar bears, the Arctic is great. The benefits of warming are much greater. You will talk about the cold summer of last year. This is a reality, forests are cut down, winds from the north rush non-stop to the Ural Mountains. This is certainly bad ... But man is to blame for this, not nature.

We conclude that a warm winter is not a reason to be upset, but those who miss the frost and huge snowdrifts can be moved to Vorkuta, Yakutsk or other places where everything is in order with this matter.

Jan 13 2020

A. A. Seibutis

Indo-Europeans: Paleoecology and Natural Plots of Myths

For more than a hundred years, scientists have been investigating the problem of the origin of Indo-European peoples. However, there are still too many unresolved issues: "Those constructions on ethnogenesis that scientists arranged to some extent several decades ago now no longer satisfy ethnogenetic science," wrote a few years ago, the Soviet archaeologist V. V. Sedov wrote about the current situation in Indo-European studies. . And what is proposed to be considered in this article is also, of course, preliminary. Rather, it is a material for reflection.

Since the processes of ethnogenesis occur in a specific environment, there can be no doubt that much valuable information about the past of ethnic groups is captured in the annals of natural phenomena. The attraction of data from

4

the natural sciences should, to some extent, revitalize ethnogenetic research.

The consequences of environmental crises on the Russian Plain

In recent decades, environmental advances have forced a new interpretation of some aspects of the life of primitive man. Sections that study the flow of energy in ecosystems, the growth and regulation of the number of populations, and successions help to comprehend the ethno genetic processes of the past. At the same time, one should also keep in mind such an important regularity that A. A. Velichko recently again paid attention to: the deterioration of the ecological situation stimulates the process of anthropogenesis. This allows you to better understand the possible causes of spasmodic shifts in the development of humanity. A radical change in the natural environment in the Late Glacial period, primarily the excessive extermination of large mammals, led to an environmental crisis in the Upper Paleolithic. In response to this challenge of nature, man learned to hunt small, non-gregarious game (bows and arrows were invented), created a higher - Mesolithic culture.

A significant cooling of 4.6 - 4.1 thousand years ago led to the spread of conifers on the Russian plain by reducing broad-leaved. This led to a reduction in the number and diversity of herbivores, since coniferous forests are poor in grass and shrubs, and, as a result, in a new environmental crisis. Herbivores use 1.5-2.5% of the net primary production of mature deciduous forests, about 12% - fallow lands, 30 - 45% - cultural pastures. Ethnographic studies have shown that primitive people noticed this already at the level of the Stone Age cultures and began to reduce woody vegetation with the help of fire long before the formation of slaughter agriculture.

On the Russian Plain, an environmental crisis manifested itself on the eve of the livestock era, when the migration of people to these regions from the south intensified. Trying to overcome the consequences of this crisis, the then local hunter had to artificially maintain the productivity of forest ecosystems, thereby preparing himself to become a breeder. And for this it was necessary first to learn how to increase the reserves of wood (young twigs) and grass feed. In this case, the local hunter was much more experienced than the shepherd who migrated here from the Black Sea steppes, who also underwent a kind of "cultural regression" from the Eneolithic to the Neolithic when moving to the forest zone. The initial phase of the sub-Atlantic period 2.5-1.8 thousand years ago on the Baltic plains was characterized by deterioration in climatic conditions, which led to the decline of agriculture and related grain farming.

Its new rise became possible here only after local farmers "re-educated" the weed-field rye and it became the main cereal in central Russia. This happened already at the time when Roman civilization was flourishing, which, however, did not have any noticeable effect on the economic development of the Baltic countries.

Any advance of "southerners" to the north (in this case by "southerners" we mean not only people, but also cultivated plants, domestic animals) was accompanied by a long period of acclimatization. Not all people, not all species of flora and fauna have overcome the climatic barrier. Not all immigrants from the Black Sea-Caspian steppes were able to develop the already populated forest zone and assimilate the indigenous population.

What are linguists talking about?

6

Ethnogenetic constructions based on linguistic data usually end with the geographical localization of the identified linguistic communities. Often this problem is solved too straightforwardly. In linguistic literature, it is regularly noted that among the Indo-European languages, the Baltic languages are richest in archaic elements (phonetic, morphological, and lexical). In this regard, some scholars consider the Baltic languages to be less distant from the Indo-European parent language: this point of view is reflected, for example, in the model of the interconnections of Indo-European languages, in the centers of which are the Baltic languages. There are even sharper opinions: considering the Lithuanian language as the most archaic, such scholars argue that Lithuania is the ancestral home of the Indo-Europeans.

It goes without saying that linguistic archaisms individually cannot be reliable witnesses to the fact that their speakers are the indigenous (autochthonous) population of the region in question. However, the question of how and why such a language survived in the Baltic States remains unanswered. Nevertheless, now, when carved hypotheses arose of localizing the ancestral home of the Indo-Europeans, it is becoming especially relevant.

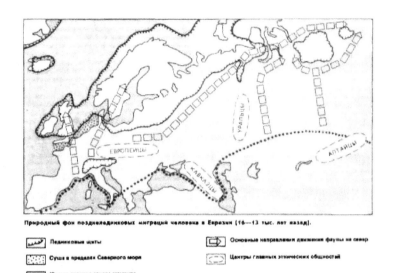

Природный фон позднеледниковых миграций человека в Евразии (16—13 тыс. лет назад).

Ледниковые щиты

Суша в пределах Северного моря

Южная граница ареала мамонта

Основные направления движения фауны на север

Центры главных этнических общностей

At one time, a famous scholar of the history of Indo-Europeans O. Schroeder tried to solve this question, which collected a lot of linguistic material. In his opinion, "the initial limits of the originally Indo-European territories ... and the place of the outcome of the Indo-European folk should be sought within the boundaries of a certain land complex, stretching in a narrow land strip from the Rhine to the Hindu Kush. ...In connection with the more widely developed terminology of forest species of birds, salt, pig breeding in the vocabulary of European languages, I am inclined to think that... the features of each group (in the specific vocabulary of Indo-Europeans of Europe and Indo-Iranians) reflected contrasts of the forest and steppes, found only once in a rather sharp form and size, throughout the entire belt noted above: namely, north and northwest of the Black Sea." Such a statement, however, would be more convincing if the paleogeographic data confirmed that in the indicated region during the collapse of the Indo-European praetnos, the forest really coexisted with the steppe.

Apparently, the ethnogenetic hypothesis of A. A. Shakhmatov is also worth recalling. In 1916, he wrote: "... the ancestral home of the Indo-Europeans should be attributed to such a place in Europe, where there were conditions for the formation of a more or less integral culture ... The original homeland of the Indo-Europeans was located north of the Mediterranean cultural centers. Most likely, we should look for her in Central Europe, perhaps in modern southern Germany and the western regions of Austria. ... Over time, the eastern branch of the Indo-Europeans, apparently the ancestors of the Iranians and ancient Indians, broke up ... the original territory of the eastern Indo-European tribes, including the ancestors of the Slavs, was Northwest Russia, the Baltic Sea basin. I see confirmation of this in the fact that the Baltic people are still sitting on this territory, and we don't have any evidence that they are not autochthonous here, that they came here from the south, from southern Russia ... movement Aryans from the borders of Europe find a satisfactory explanation precisely under this assumption.

More than 70 years have passed since the publication of the Shakhmatov hypothesis, which was extremely rational from an ecological-paleogeographic point of view. Now a similar point of view is again beginning to attract the attention of scientists.

Of all the currently known geographical localizations of the ancestral homeland of the Indo-Europeans on the basis of linguistic materials, the latest scheme proposed by T.V. Gamkrelidze and V.V. Ivanov should undoubtedly be considered the most thorough. Its linguistic basis is favorably supported by paleobotanical, biogeographic, paleozoological data; Support for geographical localization of the ancestral home of the Indo-Europeans is landscape landmarks. "The first thing that can be argued with sufficient certainty regarding the Indo-European ancestral homeland is that it was an area with a mountainous landscape ..." the authors emphasize. "This picture of the pra-Indo-European landscape naturally excludes those flat areas of Europe where there are no significant mountain ranges, that is, the northern part of Central Eurasia and all of Eastern Europe, including the Northern Black Sea region."

As you can see, this scheme completely refutes the previous one! And yet, in our opinion, to abandon it until all its aspects have been studied — not only linguistic ones — are early. Apparently, nevertheless, in the studies of ethnogenesis is a theory that is fruitfully developed by ethnographers. Yu. V. Bromley, for example, believes that it is advisable to "consider an ethnic group and its environment as certain integrity - an ethno-ecological system." Actually, our task is to study the paleoecological situation, which does not, however, claim comprehensive coverage of the issue.

Warming results

According to A.A. Velichko, during the maximum of the Valdai glaciation's (20-18 thousand years ago), the territory between the Scandinavian ice sheet and the Pyrenees, Alpine, Carpathian Mountains were one natural zone. Under these conditions, there was no clearly coordinated seasonal migration of fauna, animals that were the object of hunting, wandering in search of food any season of the year in various directions. Such haphazard "migrations" of animals contributed to the fact that ethnic uniformity was maintained at the ice border from the Atlantic Ocean to the Ural Mountains.

On the eve of the degradation of the ice sheets, the nature of atmospheric circulation changed, the boundaries of new natural zones outlined in connection with this, unsystematic migrations of the Pleistocene fauna were replaced by purposeful seasonal migrations from glacial tundra to more remote forest areas and vice versa. Paleozoologists claim that clouds of harmful insects forced animals to seek refuge at the edge of the ice sheets. Archaeological finds of the Hamburg culture in the thickness of moraine loam near Lübeck (Germany) undoubtedly indicate that hunters of that time also appeared there.

Eastern Europe on the map of Ptolemy

In late glacial Europe, the formation of seasonal fauna migration paths was dependent on the southern ledge of the Scandinavian ice sheet, and then the southern outflow of the Baltic reservoir. This wedge could well contribute to the fact that the once united ethnic community was divided into two main parts: - western and eastern. This assumption is confirmed by archaeological data. The second half is the maximum largest leveling of the primitive economy from the Atlantic to the Urals, and later (12-10 thousand years ago) two distinctive provinces stood out in this territory - with the Azilian (early Mesolithic) culture in the West and a group of close archaeological cultures in Central and Eastern Europe.

To the west of the Baltic wedge, seasonal migrations of the fauna occurred south-north. Due to the gradual displacement of the border between the forests, they appeared to be at an impasse on the British Isles and on the Scandinavian Peninsula. The West European hunter could not but adapt to such migrations. Once upon a time, the areas of new ethnic communities stretched from south to north were to be laid down: one from Central France to Scotland, and the second from the Alpine foothills to Northern Scandinavia.

On the other side of the Baltic glacial wedge, seasonal migrations had a direction from south-east to north-west, and their routes slowly shifted to the north-east. The Pleistocene fauna of Eastern Europe had a free path to the North and even to Siberia, bypassing the Ural Mountains. The northern part of the Russian Plain during the degradation of the ice sheets for another three millennia (16-13 thousand years ago) was in a semi-closed position. From the northwest it was protected by the Scandinavian ice sheet, from the north - Novaya Zemlya, and in the east the Ural ridge rose. In this cauldron, large mammals and their persistent pursuers retreated northward. Therefore, it was here that the isolation of a new ethnic community could begin.

Later, a corridor between the Ural Mountains and the Arctic Ocean, through which animals penetrated into Siberia, was released from under a continuous ice sheet.

Following them, a certain part of the population of the North of the Russian Plain could also have drifted there.

In the Late Glacial in the expanses of North Asia, natural zones were also restored and seasonal migration routes formed. Fossil remains of the fauna indicate that huge herds of mammoths still grazed in Eastern Siberia about 12 thousand years ago. Nearby was a man.

The patterns of animal migration leave no doubt that in the late glacial period on the treeless expanse of Siberia people of different ethnic groups constantly met. They could not but exchange economic skills, cultural values, lexical borrowings. The late glacial treeless populated part of Asia was quite suitable for anthropological and ethnic mixing. This representation is reliably certified by archaeological data. A.P. Okladnikov wrote: "At the end of the ice age and at the beginning of the post-glacial era, about 15-10 thousand years ago, east of the Urals, throughout the territory of North Asia ... there was the same way of life of stray people, or, half-wandering hunting tribes ... Paleolithic people at the same time entered here not from any center, but from various regions of Europe and Asia, primarily from glacial Europe."

11 thousand years ago came the last significant cooling during the Valdai glaciations. By that time, there were no more mammoths in the Far North either; the number of other large mammals was significantly reduced. The then main inhabitant of the tundra - the reindeer - began to shift south. The vast majority of hunters of Arctic Eurasia had to move in the same direction along the river valleys. As a result, reindeer hunter cultures have flourished on the plains of the middle belt of Europe.

After several centuries, 10.3 thousand years ago, the last cold period of the Late Glacial period was finally replaced by a warm one. The temperate zone of Europe was soon covered with continuous forests. The new environmental situation no longer caused significant relocations of human communities. Further natural factors (for example, transgression of the Baltic Sea 7.5 - 7 thousand years ago) predetermined migrations of only a partial nature. In the northern half of Europe, covered with impassable forests and swamps, tribal communication was significantly complicated. The time has come for the fragmentation of ethnic communities.

What are myths talking about?

Information hiding in traditions, legends, and myths is still little used to study ethnogenesis, although some of their elements have long attracted the attention of many researchers.

Indo-Iranian myths are particularly rich in natural subjects, in particular the myths of the main monument of ancient Indian writing - the Rigveda. The heroes of these myths originally lived where the sun did not set for six months, and then did not rise for the same amount of time, where very slippery mountains rose, and nature abounded with a variety of game. Later, myths testify, in those parts the cold intensified, the trees and grass stopped growing, the "hunting" animals disappeared, and when the water turned to stone, people were forced to leave that fertile land and retreat south along the river valleys. The Indo-Iranian peoples have long lived in the southern regions of the Northern Hemisphere, far from the Arctic Circle, and the mystery seems all the more mysterious - how did the Arctic

14

plots appear in the creation of myths by Indians and Iranians?

The Indian scientist B. G. Tilak was the first to start a thorough study of the genesis of the natural plots of the Rigveda. In 1903 he published his famous work, The Arctic Homeland in the Vedas. His main conclusions: the heroes of the Rigveda lived in the warm interglacial beyond the Arctic Circle, while the new offensive of the glaciers forced them to move south; the position of the stars in the high latitudes of the Northern Hemisphere about 10 thousand years ago according to the Rigveda and according to astronomy is the same. It is significant that Tilak, still not knowing anything about the climatic dissection of the Late Glacial period, comparatively "fell" into the cold period of time.

This mysterious problem is also being investigated by Soviet scientists. Orientalists G.M. Bongard-Levin and E.A. Grantovsky came to the opposite conclusion: the authors of Indo-Iranian myths did not need to dwell on the Arctic Circle, they borrowed Arctic plots from foreign northern neighbors, and this happened on the Russian Plain. The scientific work of Bongard-Levine and Grantovsky is distinguished by a close systematic generalization of the natural plots of all Indo-Iranian myths and thus represents a valuable basis for paleogeographic consideration.

According to Indo-Iranian myths, mountains Meru and Khara once stretched from west to east throughout the north. An important detail: in the most ancient Indian texts Mount Meru is still a long ridge, and in a later one there is already a separate peak "covered with gold". What are the realities underlying this story?

These mountains cannot be the Ural and Scandinavian ranges, since they are stretched from north to south and not from west to east. The mountain ranges of the middle belt of Eurasia do not have polar days and nights. In addition, over the past millennia, these ridges have remained unchanged. The mythical mountains Meru and Hara are, most likely, the mountainous edge of ice sheets, impressively rising from the British Isles to the Urals. In the Late Glacial, long ice ridges disintegrated into residual blocks (peaks), on which, as the ice melted, the moraine was layered. It was she who could give that golden brilliance, which myths mentioned. After the blocks of the so-called dead ice completely melted, the sediments were on the ground, covered with vegetation and the unique sight disappeared without a trace.

Indo-Iranian myths are unanimous in that all rivers originate from the high mountains of Meru and Khara: they flow from ponds located on them or at their foot. That was exactly what happened in the Late Glacial on the Russian Plain - glacial ponds were the source of the main rivers.

Zoroastrian texts narrate that many "golden channels" flowed into the lake at the top of the Khara. This plot is an accurate picture of the formation of subglacial reservoirs. The "golden channels" of the Indo-Iranian mythical rivers were undoubtedly identified with the constant strata of water-glacial deposits, which in the Arctic climate were enriched with limonite, aqueous iron oxide and therefore had a yellowish-brown (golden) color.

Judging by myths, amazing life was in full swing at the northern mountains. Immense clouds of birds lived on the peaks of Meru and Khara, groves grew nearby, evergreen meadows bloomed and tall plants smelled, juicy fruits ripened, and herds of antelopes grazed everywhere.

What could serve as the basis for creating such a picture?

In the strip of adjacent waters there were comparatively productive oases with woody and grassy

16

plants, colonies of waterfowl. With more demanding feed animals. Such productive and resilient ecosystems gave the then man food, raw materials for clothes and other products, fuel, and sheltered from inclement weather. All this according to the Late Glacial "standard" could well be regarded as a blessed life.

From Indo-Iranian myths it is clear that such a life proceeded far in the north, on the shores of the ocean. Over time, the edge of active ice sheets and adjacent water bodies shifted more and more to the centers of glaciations. As a result, the strip of productive glacial ecosystems turned out to be significantly distant from the original mountainous edge of the glaciers - the mythical mountains of Meru and Khara.

In determining the place of origin of the natural plots of Indo-Iranian myths, their hydronyms — the names of rivers — are very valuable. G. Ya. Elizarenkova in the afterword to the translations of the Rigveda notes: "The main river of Vedic geography - Saraswati, which is described as great, full-flowing, fast, flowing out of the heavenly ocean. It's not possible to precisely identify it with any modern river."

Orientalists argue that many of the data in Indian and Iranian myths are interpreted unambiguously. Signs of the celestial ocean of Vedic geography are most suitable for subglacial reservoirs. With a long descent of a powerful stream from a high ice sheet, large circuses are usually generated, covered with sandy sediments. A typical circus of this kind is located northwest of the Rybinsk Reservoir, where the glacier-Volga originates. Within this circus, many names of small rivers with sar / sor- ephemente are known: Kumsara, Samosorka, Sora, Chimsora, etc.

On the Caspian lowland stretches a long hollow of the Sarpinsk lakes, along which one sleeve of the water-glacial

17

Volga flowed. So, cap-topoelement is known both at the source and in the delta of the water-glacial Volga.

The river Sarysu adjoins the northern part of the Sarpinsky hollow. This complex hydronym consists of two words: sary - yellow and su (river) (Turk.). Even today in Semirechye "the Steppe Rivers are usually called," E. M. Murzaev points out, "flowing through clay and loess territories, as a result of which they carry a large amount of suspended material. Their water is really yellowish, muddy. " Therefore, the prototype of the Vedic Sarastvati may well be the water-glacial Volga.

Cartography Information

Let us now see how the Arctic plots of Indo-Iranian myths are reflected in the monuments of ancient Greek cartography (Bongard-Levin and Grantovsky established this at one time).

On the map of Ptolemy there is a long mountain range - Hyperborean mountains. This ridge on the Russian Plain exactly coincides with the edge of the Valdai glacier ice sheet.

The hydrographic network of Eastern Europe on the map of Ptolemy resembles the flow diagram of melt glacial waters restored by D. D. Kvasov. The Ptolemaic river Ra and the water-glacial Volga are strikingly similar. The river Ra, according to Ptolemy, originates in the form of two streams near the Hyperborean mountains, apparently in the areas of Belozersk and Valdai. These two streams are combined into one full-flowing channel, most likely, in the vicinity of Kostroma. Further, the river Ra takes a large river flowing from the Riphean Mountains.

This tributary, undoubtedly, is a section of the Kama from the Ural city of Berezniki to its mouth. In the further course, Ra assumes another left tributary, the route of which coincides approximately with the Urals segment between the cities of Orenburg and Ural and the former northwestern coast of the Caspian Sea during the Khvalyn transgression. On the map of Ptolemy, the Sea of Azov is called the Meotian swamp. It is significant that the swamp is the only sea that was completely lowered in the Valdai glacier due to the lowering of the World Ocean at that time.

The vast expanses of Southeast Europe in Ptolemaic mapping are called Asian Sarmatia. This country coincides with the main loess region of Europe. The areas east of the Vistula, located in the main area of distribution of water-glacial sediments, are called Sarmatia in Europe. Loess and water-glacial deposits differ in brownish-yellow colors. Under the conditions of the Arctic climatic regime, when there was still no dense, continuous vegetation cover, the brownish-yellow color of the parent rocks determined the general color of the landscapes. Perhaps the word "Sarmatia" can be deciphered as "yellow-brown earth (country)"?

The glacial picture of the Earth is even more distinct on the map of Hesiod (VIII-VII centuries BC). The northern hemisphere on it, mainly Europe, is bordered by some coastal mountains, after which a strip of water extends, the ocean, according to the ancient Greeks, is a great rapid river flowing around the Earth.

During the retreat of ice sheets, hill-shaped ramparts of terminal moraines formed along their edge, along which meltwater rivers flowed. Such a powerful water-glacier stream, with a watershed on the Dnieper and Neman interfluve's, bordered northern Europe from the British Isles to the Caspian Sea. The space beyond the edge of the ice sheets, then the man was an inaccessible unknown world, like the edge of the earth (Earth). These parallel stripes of the glacial belt of Europe found a clear schematic image on the map of Hesiod.

Late glacial environment is clearly shown by another important detail - the Eridan River. This is the only channel in the northern half of Europe on the Hesiod map that coincides with the Rhine, flows through a mountain range into the ocean (a river flowing around the Earth).

In the beginning, the Late Glacial Rhine really flowed into a full-flowing river on the mountainous strip of regional formations, along which melt water flowed in the western part of the Scandinavian ice sheet.

The ecological and paleogeographic examination of the natural plots of myths and monuments of cartography opens up a multifaceted picture of the late glacial situation. But do all of these data, albeit artistically transformed, have any true foundations, or is it purely fantastic narratives, only by chance, coinciding with past realities? The first seems true.

Such an assumption may raise a number of new questions, for example, the question of the mechanism for transmitting environmental information. Indeed, the era of writing is separated from the early narratives and the first cartographic experiments by about 13 thousand years. It would, of course, be comparatively simple to rely on a hypothesis according to which tales of late glacial realities were transmitted along a continuous line of related offspring. And if this kind of memories of the ice age had to repeatedly pass through the barrier of translation from languages of different families? In this, frankly speaking - unbelievable, case of the accuracy of a primitive man in transmitting geographical characteristics, modern translators, apparently, could envy. The question, however, remains open.

The paleoecological view of distant antiquity extends to some extent the existing ideas about primitive man, clarifies some moments of the resettlement and isolation of ethnic communities, and reveals some realistic basis for mythopoetic creativity. Over time, some of the achievements of paleoecology will probably become useful for a more successful study of the ethnogenetic aspects of the early history of the Indo-Europeans, in particular for the localization of their ancestral home.

Rigveda about the northern ancestral home of the Aryans

In 1903, the work of B. G. Tilak "The Arctic Homeland in the Vedas" was published in Bombay. Its author is an outstanding fighter for the liberation of India from colonial oppression. Devoting his whole life to studying the culture of his native people, he long and carefully studied ancient legends, legends, and sacred hymns, born in the depths of millennia and brought to the territory of Hindustan by the distant ancestors of the Indians from their ancient ancestral home.

Summing up the phenomena that were described in the holy books of the Vedas in the ancient Indian epic Mahabhara, B. G. Tilak came to the conclusion that the ancestral home of the ancestors of the Indo-Iranians (or as they called themselves - "Aryans") was in northern Europe , somewhere near the Arctic Circle.

E. Jelachich, who published the book "The Far North as the Homeland of Humanity" in the 1910s, also leads to the same conclusions. The time of occurrence of the most ancient parts of the Veda dates back to 4-5 thousand BC, i.e. to the period when, according to some researchers, "Indo-Iranians separated from the Slavs as a community."

21

Linguists came to the conclusion that "the ancient Aryan languages with Slavic have a much more painful number of similarities than with any other language of the Indo-European family." Created in ancient times by the common ancestors of the Slavic and Indo-Iranian peoples, the Vedas hymns, along with the ancient Iranian Avesta, are considered one of the oldest monuments of human thought.

Numerous geographical and astronomical evidence of the Rigveda, the oldest part of the Vedas, speak of the knowledge by the aryans of the circumpolar regions of Eastern Europe. The North Star is described as the axis of the world around which the entire starry sky moves and above all the Ursa Major. Only in the polar polar latitudes during the polar night can you see how the stars describe their diurnal circles near the motionless North Star. In the hymns of the Rigveda and Avesta it is said that in the homeland of the Aryans, the night lasts at least 100 days a year, that "the dawns do not brighten until the end" for thirty days, that with the end of the night and the arrival of the day the ice-bound rivers are released. The ancient Indian epic describes the appearance of the Supreme God to the sage Narada in the form of flashes of the Polar Lights. (It is interesting that the highest peak of the Subpolar Urals is called Narada).

The Rig Veda describes, in connection with the homeland of the Aryans, an ongoing day that lasts six months. One of the main geographical landmarks of the land of the Aryans is the sacred mountains, which are described as stretching from west to east and dividing the rivers into the currents flowing north into the White Sea and south into the warm sea. On the map of Ptolemy (1st century), the sacred river "Avesta" Ra or Rga (i.e. Volga) originates from these mountains. The ancient holy Iranian river flowing north was called Ardvi Sura, which means the mighty

22

double river. These mountains, sung in ancient Aryan anthems, stretching from west to east and dividing rivers into northern and southern, are reliably identified at present with the mountain range of the Subpolar Urals, Timan Ridge and Northern Uvals. The Northern Uvals served as the main watershed of the rivers of the south and north of Eastern Europe during the Carboniferous period, when the ancient sea splashed in the place of the Urals.

The description of the northern ancestral home of the Aryans as a flowering region corresponds to historical reality, because according to the data of modern paleoclimatology in 4-3 thousand BC the temperature rise in the forest and tundra zones coincided with their drop south of 50-55 gr. N. Paleobotanists note that in 4 thousand BC in the north of Eastern Europe, July temperatures were higher than currently at 5 ° C. Such a greatest warming was characteristic of the northern part of the continent (north of 55-60 ° N, i.e., beyond the Northern Uvals, on the White Sea coast), to the south it decreased and approximately at a latitude of 50 gr. N temperatures were close to modern. At latitudes 57-59 ° N the frost-free period was 30–40 days longer than the modern one.

It should be noted that, as academician L. S. Berg noted in 1947, "paradoxically at first glance, the yield of bread in the taiga subzone (as well as in the mixed forest subzone, i.e., in general in the non-chernozem zone) is much higher than in the steppes.» According to the data of 1901-1910, the excess of average yields in the Non-Chernozem region over the chernozem provinces was: oats - 51%, barley - 60%, spring wheat - 33%, winter - 42%. According to the paleoclimatic map, already in the Mesolithic, the territory of the modern Vologda region and a significant part of the Arkhangelsk region were in the subzone of broad-

23

leaved forests. Paleoclimatologists believe that 8-4.5 thousand years ago, "a strip of broad-leaved forests in the west of the Russian Plain reached 1200-1300 km. in the meridional direction, broad-leaved formations in the composition of broad-leaved - coniferous forests spread over 500-600 km. north of their current situation. "

In the Russian North, to this day you can meet such hydronyms as Usa, Uda, Sheaf, Sindosh, Indola, Indosar, Strig, Svaga, Svatka, Varna, Pan, Thor, Arza, Prupt. Hvarsenga, etc., which are explained using the ancient language of the Aryans - Sanskrit. And it was precisely in the places where these ancient names of rivers and lakes were preserved that the tradition of ancient geometric ornamental complexes, the sources of which can be found in the ancient cultures of Eastern Europe of 6-2 thousand, was persistently preserved in the weaving and lace of Russian peasant women until the end of the 19th and beginning of the 20th century. BC. And above all, these are those ornamental complexes, often very complex and difficult to do, which were a peculiar hallmark of Aryan antiquity.

S. V. Zharnikova
История и культура Вологодского края. III краеведческая научно-практическая конференция. Тезисы докладов и сообщений. Вологда 23-24 мая 1990 года.

Plants of the Indo-European Motherland
(Based on materials by V.A.Safronov, T.V. Gamkrelidze, Vyach. Vs. Ivanova)

The problem of localization of the ancestral home of Indo-European peoples has been facing science for a long time. As early as the mid-18th century, the linguistic kinship of European peoples was noted, and in 1767 the Jesuit monk Kerdu noted the proximity of a number of European languages to Sanskrit - the language of the sacred texts of the Ancient India of the Vedas.

Friedrich von Schlegel, the first to express the idea of a single ancestral home of all Indo-Europeans, placed this ancestral home on the territory of Hindustan. "The decisive factor for the emergence of Indo-European studies was the discovery of Sanskrit, acquaintance with the first texts on it, and the enthusiasm that began with ancient Indian culture, the most striking reflection of which was the book of F. von Schlegel "On the language and wisdom of Indians" (1808), writes V.N. Toporov.

However, the fallacy of this assumption was soon proved, since before the arrival of the Aryan (Indo-European) tribes, India was inhabited by representatives of another language family and another racial type - black Dravids.

Assumed at different times as the ancestral home of the Indo-Europeans (and these are today the peoples of 10 language groups: Indian, Iranian, Slavic, Baltic, German, Celtic, Romance, Albanian, Armenian and modern Greek): India, the slopes of the Himalayas, Central Asia, Asian steppes, Mesopotamia , Near and Middle East, Armenian Highlands, territories from Western France to the Urals between 60 ° and 45 ° N, territory from the Rhine to the Don, Black Sea-Caspian steppes, steppes from the Rhine to

Hindu Kush, areas between the Mediterranean and Altai, in Western Europe - currently, for one reason or another, most researchers rejected.

Among the hypotheses formulated in recent years, I would like to dwell on two in more detail: V.A. Safronov, who proposed in his monograph Indo-European Ancestral Homes the concept of the three ancestral homelands of the Indo-Europeans - in Asia Minor, the Balkans and Central Europe (Western Slovakia), and T.V. Gamkrelidze and V.V. Ivanova, who own the idea of the Near Asian (more precisely, located on the territory of the Armenian Highlands and the adjacent areas of Western Asia), the ancestral home of the Indo-Europeans, detailed and argued by them in the fundamental two-volume "Indo-European language and Indo-Europeans".

1

V. A. Safronov emphasizes that on the basis of the Early Indo-European (hereinafter RIE) vocabulary, it can be concluded that "the Early Indo-European society lived in cold places, maybe in the foothills, in which there were no large rivers, but small rivers, streams, springs; rivers, despite the rapid flow, were not an obstacle; crossed through them in boats. In winter, these rivers froze, and in the spring they overflowed. There were swamps... The climate of the ancestral homeland was probably sharply continental with severe and cold winters, when the rivers froze, strong winds blew; in a stormy spring with thunderstorms, heavy snowmelt, river spills, hot, dry summers, when the grass was dry, there was not enough water. The early Indo-Europeans had early phases of agriculture and cattle breeding, although hunting, gathering and fishing did not lose their significance. Among the tamed animals are a bull,

26

a cow, a sheep, a goat, a pig, a horse and a dog that guarded the herds.

He notes that: "Riding was practiced by the early Indo-Europeans: what animals were circled is not clear, but the goals are obvious: taming." Agriculture was represented by a hoe and kidney-fire form, the processing of agricultural products was carried out by grinding grain.

The early Indo-European tribes lived settled; they had different types of stone and flint tools, knives, scrapers, axes, adzes, etc. They exchanged and traded. In the early Indo-European community there was a difference in childbirth, taking into account the degree of kinship, and juxtaposition of friends and foes. The role of women was very high. Particular attention was paid to the "progeny generation process", which was expressed in a number of root words that passed into the RIE language from the boreal parent language. In the RIA society, a pair family stood out, management was carried out by leaders, and there was a defensive organization. There was a cult of fertility associated with zoomorphic cults; there was a developed funeral rite.

V. A. Safronov concludes that the ancestral home of the early Indo-Europeans was in Asia Minor. He notes that such an assumption is the only possible, because Central Europe, including the Carpathian basin, was occupied by a glacier.

However, paleoclimatology data indicate something else. At the time in question, that is, during the final stage of the Valdai glaciation, the chronological framework of which was established from 11,000 to 10,500 years ago, i.e. 9 thousand BC, the nature of the vegetation cover of Europe, although it differed from modern, in Central Europe, Arctic tundra with birch-spruce woodlands, low-mountain tundra and alpine meadows, rather than a glacier, were common. Sparse forests with birch-pine stands occupied most of Central Europe, and on the Great Central Danube Lowland and in the southern part of the Russian Plain, vegetation of the steppe type prevailed.

Paleogeographers note that in southern Europe, the influence of ice cover was almost not felt, especially in the Balkans and Asia Minor, where the influence of the glacier was not felt at all. The time is 8-7 thousand BC, to which the culture of Asia Minor Chatal Guyuk belongs, connected by V. A. Safonov with the early Indo-Europeans, marked by the warming of the Holocene. Already 9780 years ago, elms appear in the Yaroslavl region, 9400 years ago in the Tver region and 7790 years ago oaks in the Leningrad region. Moreover, the presence of a cold climate in Asia Minor is unlikely. Here I would like to refer to the conclusions of L. S. Berg and G. N. Lisitsina, made at different times, but, nevertheless, not refuting each other.

So L. S. Berg, in his 1947 work, Climate and Life, emphasized that the climate of the Sinai Peninsula has not changed over the past 7000 years and that here, and in Egypt, "if there had been a change, it would be more likely to increase rather than decrease atmospheric precipitation". He noted that: "Blankengorn believed that in Egypt, Syria and Palestine the climate in general has remained constant and similar to the current one since the end of the plural period; the end of the latter, Blanquengorn refers to the beginning of the interglacial era "(130-70 thousand years ago - S. Zh.).

In a 1921 paper, Blankengorn writes that "From the Riesz-Wurm interglacial (Mousterian of Western Europe) to modernity (S. Zh. in these territories), dry desert, and in the north, a semi-desert climate similar to the modern one, interrupted by a short wet time corresponding to the Wurm glaciation."

G. N. Lisitsina in 1970 comes to similar conclusions and writes: "The climate of the arid zone in 10-7 millennia BC not much different from the modern one."

We have no reason to believe that the climate of western Asia Minor, where daphne, cherry, barberry, maquis, Calabrian pine, oak, hawthorn, hop-hornbeam, ash, white and prickly astragalus grow, live such animals as mongoose, jackal, porcupine, mouflon, wild donkey, hyena, bats and locusts, and tender cover, as a rule, does not form, in 8-7 thousand BC so much different from the modern one so that it could be similar to the harsh ancestral home of the early Indo-Europeans, which is being reconstructed based on their vocabulary.

In addition, V. A. Safonov writes: "The deep kinship of the Boreal with the Turkic and Uralic languages, according to N. D. Andreev, allows you to localize the boreal community in the forest zone from the Rhine to Altai. From this it also follows that from all areas where RIE carriers could have gone, Anatolia seems to be the only possible one: narrow straits did not serve as an obstacle, since the early Indo-Europeans knew the means of crossing (the "boat" was recorded in the language of the early Indo-Europeans). "

As for the role of the Early Indo-Europeans in the world historical process, it is difficult to disagree with the main conclusions of V. A. Safronov made him in the final part of his work. Indeed: "In solving the problem of the Indo-European ancestral homeland, which has been exciting for two centuries by scientists from many professions and various countries of the world, they rightly see the origins of the history and spiritual culture of the peoples of most of Europe, Australia, and America. "Just as their descendants, Indo-Europeans of the new time, dug the New World, so the Indo-Europeans of the Ancient World revealed to humanity the knowledge of the integrity of the earthly home, the unity of our planet ... These discoveries would remain nameless if the echoes of the great wanderings could not be kept in Indo-European literature, separated from us and from these events for thousands of years ... Indo-European travels became possible thanks to the invention of wheeled transport (4 thousand BC) among Indo-Europeans. " And we add, due to the domestication of a wild horse in the southern Russian steppes already on the border 7-6 millennia BC. As noted by N. N. Cherednichenko: "At present, the spread of a draft horse from the Eurasian steppes is no longer in doubt ... the process of taming a horse is carried out on the distant plains of the Eurasian steppe region ... Thus, at present, we can only talk about ways of penetration of the Indo-European horse breeding tribes of Eurasia on East and in the Mediterranean ... Eurasia, therefore, was the territory from where the chariots were brought by Indo-European tribes to various regions of the Old World, which greatly affected life of the Ancient East. "

V. A. Safronov notes that "The period of the general development of the Indo-European peoples, the pre-Indo-European period, was reflected in the amazing convergence of the great literatures of antiquity, such as the Avesta, Vedas, Mahabharata, Ramayana, Iliad, Odyssey, in the epics of the Scandinavians and Germans, Ossetians, legends and tales of the Slavic peoples. These reflections of the most complex motifs and plots of common Indo-European history in ancient literature and folklore, separated by millennia, are fascinating and await their interpretation. However, the emergence of this literature became possible only thanks to the creation by the Indo-Europeans of the metric of poetry and the art of poetic speech, which is the oldest in the world and dates back no later than 4,000 BC ... By creating our own system of knowledge about the universe, which opened the way for civilization to humanity, the Indo-Europeans became the creators of the most ancient world civilization, which is 1000 years older than the civilizations of the Nile Valley and Mesopotamia. There is a paradox: linguists, having recreated according to linguistics the face of the pre-Indo-European culture, by all signs of the corresponding civilization, and determined it to be the oldest in the series of known civilizations (5-4 millennia BC), could not cross the Rubicon of historical stereotypes that "light always comes from the East ", and limited themselves to the search for the equivalent of such a culture in the areas of the Ancient East (Gamkrelidze, Ivanov, 1984), leaving Europe aside as the" periphery of Middle Eastern civilizations ".

The civilization of the pra-Indo-Europeans turned out to be so high, stable and flexible that it survived and survived despite the global cataclysms.

V. A. Safronov emphasizes that "It was the late Indo-European civilization that gave the world a great invention - wheel and wheeled transport, that it was the Indo-Europeans who created the nomadic economy", which allowed them to go through the vast expanses of the Eurasian steppes, to reach China and India. " And summing up, he writes: "We believe that the guarantee of stability of the Indo-European culture was created by the Indo-Europeans. It is expressed in the model of the existence of culture as an open system with the inclusion of innovations that do not offend the foundations of its structure. "

As a form of coexistence with the world, the Indo-Europeans proposed a model that was maintained in all historical times - the removal of factorial colonies into a foreign-language and foreign culture environment and bringing them to the level of development of the metropolis. The combination of openness with tradition and innovation, the formula of which was found for each historical period of the development of Indo-European culture, ensured the preservation of Indo-European and universal values. " We allowed ourselves such a long quotation, since it is difficult to more clearly, compactly and comprehensively determine the importance of the pre-Indo-European and early Indo-European culture for the destinies of mankind than this was done in the work of V. A. Safronov "Indo-European ancestral home."

2

The next fundamental work devoted to the ancestral home of the Indo-Europeans, the main provisions of which I would like to dwell on, is the work of T. V. Gamkrelidze and V. V. Ivanov's "Indo-European language and Indo-Europeans", where the idea of a common Indo-European ancestral homeland on the territory of the Armenian Highlands and the adjacent areas of Western Asia, from where part of the Indo-European tribes then advanced into the Black Sea-Caspian steppes, develops and is thoroughly argued.

Paying tribute to the very high level of this encyclopedic work, which collected and analyzed a huge number of linguistic, historical facts, data from archeology and other related sciences, I would like to note that a number of provisions postulated by T. V. Gamkrelidze and V. V. Ivanov, causes very serious doubts.

So V. A. Safronov notes that: "The linguistic facts cited by Gamkrelidze and Ivanov in favor of localizing the Indo-European ancestral homeland on the territory of the Armenian Highlands can receive other explanations. The absence of hydronymia in this area can only indicate against the localization of the Indo-European ancestral home. The environmental data presented in the parsed work contradict this localization even more. Almost half of the animals, trees and plants listed in the list of flora and fauna listed by Gamkrelidze and Ivanov are reconstructed in the Common Indo-European (aspen, hornbeam, yew, linden, heather, beaver, lynx, black grouse, salmon, elephant, and monkey) crab). "

It is on these environmental data cited in the work of T.V. Gamkrelidze and V.V. Ivanov, I would like to dwell in more detail. The authors of the "Indo-European language and Indo-Europeans", in confirmation of their concept, indicate the oldest names of trees recorded in the ancient Indo-European parent language.

These are birch, oak, beech, hornbeam, ash, aspen, poplar, yew, willow, branches, spruce, pine, fir, alder, walnut, apple, cherry, and dogwood. And in connection with this, the following is affirmed:

Birch

"Birch species are currently found throughout the temperate (northern) zone of Eurasia, as well as in the mountainous regions of the more southern zones, where it grows to an altitude of about 1,500 m (in particular in the Caucasus, on the spurs of the Himalayas and in the mountainous regions of Southern Europe) . In the subboreal period (about 3300-400 BC), birch was also distributed in the more southern belt ... The presence of a common word

33

for birch in the Indo-European suggests familiarity with the ancient Indo-European tribes, which was possible either in the zone temperate climate (in Europe at latitudes from the north of Spain to the north of the Balkans and further east to the lower reaches of the Volga), or in mountainous regions of the more southern range of the Near East. "

However, Academician L. S. Berg in 1947 emphasized that in the northern part of Eastern Europe 13-12 thousand years ago there were forests of birch and pine. In the warming that began 11-10 thousand years ago, the absolute maximum of birch was noted.

These conclusions are also confirmed by materials prepared by Russian paleoclimatologists for the XII Congress of INKVA (in Canada in 1987), which indicate that in the Vychegda and Upper Pechora river basins in layers 45210 + 1430 years ago pine and birch in combination with cereal forbs prevailed. In the forests, pine made up 44%, birch up to 24%, spruce - 35 to 15%.

In the north of the Pechersk lowland in the postglacial period, i.e. 10-9 thousand years ago, "woody vegetation developed territories" and these were forests of birch, spruce and pine. Data on Belarusian Polesie indicate that $12,860 \pm 110$ years ago (i.e., at the beginning of 11 thousand BC), pine-spruce forests and associations of pine-birch forests with an admixture of broad-leaved: oak, elm and linden trees.

Samples of peat from the marshes of the Yaroslavl, Leningrad, Novgorod and Tver regions, performed in the laboratory of V. I. Vernadsky Institute, confirm that the peak of birch distribution dates back to about 9800 years ago, 7700 years ago - the absolute dominance of birch. L. S. Berg wrote: "A study of the history of vegetation in the post-glacial time, carried out by analyzing pollen from peat, showed that in the central part of the Union, immediately

34

after the retreat of the glacier, first there were a large number of birch and willow, and then called subarctic time, prevalence passed to spruce and birch; in the next boreal era, birch and pine began to dominate."

I must say that birch is one of the most important forest-forming species in Eastern Europe since the time of the Mikulinsky interglacial (130-70 thousand years ago) and up to the present day.

The authors of the "Paleogeography of Europe for the Last Hundred Thousand Years" note that: "Tracing the Holocene history of birch, one might think that primary birch forests are much wider in modern forests of the European part of the USSR than is usually assumed."

At the same time, nothing testifies to the wide distribution of birch in antiquity in the Near East and on the Armenian Highlands. L. S. Berg emphasized that: "The climatic situation of Palestine at the northern border of palm culture and at the southern limit of grape cultivation has not changed since biblical times. As for the Armenian Highlands, at present it is a combination of folded-block ridges and tectonic depressions, often occupied by lakes - closed saline (Van, Urmia), and less commonly - flowing fresh (Sevan). Semi-desert and even desert landscapes are characteristic of the deepest depressions. There is a dry feather grass and steppes, "in some places in the middle course (between 1000 and 2300 m) there are dry rare forests of deciduous oaks, pine and juniper."

In the Iranian highlands, in the mountains of Zagros (on the western slopes and in the wetter northern part, between 1000 and 1800 m.), Park oak forests with elm and maple are common, and wild mulberries, poplar, oak, and figs are found in the valleys. Due to the fact that the period from the middle of 1 thousand BC hitherto defined by climatologists as the period of cooling and moistening with respect to the climatic optimum of the Holocene (4-3 thousand BC) and the previous time (7-5 thousand BC), there is no reason to suppose on these the southern territories have a much more humid and colder climate in 7-3 thousand BC, i.e. the time in question in the work of T. V. Gamkrelidze and V. V. Ivanov.

Further, the authors of the "Indo-European language and Indo-Europeans" write: "The main economic value of birch is determined by the fact that it served in antiquity (and still serves in separate traditions) as material for the manufacture of a wide variety of items from shoes, dishes, baskets, to writing material in certain cultures, in particular among the Eastern Slavs and in India until the 16th century." A. A. Kachalov points out that: "the inhabitants of the Himalayas use birch bark useful for this purpose in our time."

"The connection of trees - birch, beech, hornbeam with the terminology of writing indicates the technique of writing and the manufacture of materials for writing in ancient Indo-European cultures. The emergence of writing and writing is based in these cultures on the use of wood and wood material, on which signs or nicks were applied using special wooden sticks. This writing technique, characteristic of a number of early Indo-European cultures, obviously reflects a typologically more archaic degree of writing development than carving signs on stone, or applying them to clay tablets, or to specially processed animal skin. "

I must say that it is difficult to imagine that a simpler, more affordable, maneuverable and less laborious letter on birch bark was more primitive than an uncomfortable, bulky letter on clay tablets or carving inscriptions on stone. Indeed, if there were both clay and birch bark from the early Indo-Europeans, they would hardly have switched from writing on birch bark to using clay tablets for business correspondence or for business records.

In addition, the question arises why birch bark, as a material for writing, was preserved precisely in the East Slavic and Indian ethnic range. If you follow the findings of T. V. Gamkrelidze and V. V. Ivanov, the Slavic and Indo-Iranian branches of the Indo-European community dispersed even on the territory of their supposed common ancestral home in Asia Minor (where there are practically no birches).

The Pre-Slavs left for Eastern Europe, and the Indo-Iranians moved to Iran (where birch is not common) and Hindustan, where only the Himalayas grows at a height of 2,500–4,300 m, the "useful birch", the "Jacquem birch" and, finally, the birch of the Akuminat section - a tree 20-30 m high with very large leaves. But these trees are not widespread in India and are considered endemic to a very narrow range. But in the Indian tradition, birch bark is not just writing material, but sacred material: on birch bark (and only on birch bark) a record was made of marriage in the higher castes and without this record on birch bark, marriage was not considered valid. This situation could not develop in areas where birch is almost not widespread.

Birch bark could become material only where birch has been one of the main forest-forming species for many millennia - in the forest strip of Eastern Europe. It makes sense to pay attention to the following circumstance. T. V. Gamkrelidze and V. V. Ivanov emphasize that birch bark was used for writing in the most ancient Indo-European cultures and was preserved in this quality among the Eastern Slavs and in India until the 16th century.

But the ancestors of the East Slavic peoples and the Aryan peoples of North-West India dispersed no later than 2 thousand BC and, nevertheless, birch bark, as a material for writing, was preserved precisely among the Eastern Slavs and Indians. It follows from this that birch bark was still on their common ancestral home as a material for writing.

Then the conclusion is also natural that long before 2 thousand BC the ancestors of the eastern Slavs had writing and the predecessors of the Novgorod and Pskov birch bark letters were older than them for many millennia.

It is also interesting that in the North Russian tradition birch bark and in the 19th century (as in India) was precisely sacred material for writing. This is evidenced by the story of an outstanding ethnographer of the 19th century. S. V. Maximov wrote about the Old Believers birch-bark book decorated with miniatures, which the old Pomor man from Arkhangelsk did not want to sell for any money. S. V. Maksimov notes that this book, "written by half-mouth" on birch bark, "finely and successfully stripped, and assembled, sewn into quarters ... The written was disassembled as conveniently as the written on paper, the letters did not spread, but they stood straight, one beside the other: another paper makes letters worse ... the book was somehow bound in a homegrown way into plain, birch bark boards."

"To write such a book: sticky soot is made from a burnt birch peel, which, when diluted in water, gives decent ink, at least those that can leave a very noticeable mark on their own if they are wiped off on the top layer. Eagles and wild geese, which are many on the tundra and which are difficult to fly away from the well-aimed shot of the usual hunters, give good feathers. And here's the henchman, always comfortably peeling over the layers of birch bark, which can be turned into pages and on which you can write soon and, perhaps, clearly, "writes S. V. Maximov.

The sacred nature of birch bark, as a material for writing, is evidenced by the customs preserved in the Russian North almost to the present day. So A. A.

38

Veselovsky in his "Essays on the History of the Life and Work of Peasants of the Vologda Province" describes a rite of "unsubscribing", in which the healer "whispers, writes a note and puts it into the wind and makes the patient easier." They write a petition on birch bark, and the father-wind takes it away. From the same series, it is customary to write conspiracies and letters to the devil - "bondage" - on birch bark, and the text is not written (in the literal sense of the word), but is applied by soot in the form of erratic strokes, oblique crosses, curving lines, etc.

All this testifies to the now anciently forgotten, supplanted Cyrillic alphabet, the ancient Slavic writing system. Perhaps her relics are the mysterious signs on the manure of the North Russian icons and the so-called "ornaments" painted by Dionysius on the arch of the portal of the Cathedral of the Nativity of the Virgin in the village of Ferapontovo.

Oak

T. V. Gamkrelidze and V. V. Ivanov believe that the early Indo-Europeans could get to know this tree only in the southern regions of the Mediterranean (including the Balkans and the northern part of the Middle East), because "Oak forests are uncharacteristic of the northern regions of Europe, where they spread only from 4-3 thousand BC."

However, it is now known that oak forests were widespread in northern Europe (and Eastern Europe in particular) during the Mikulinsky interglacial period (130-70 thousand years ago). During the peak of the Valdai glaciation (20-18 thousand years ago), in a number of regions of the Russian plain there were forests with the participation of broad-leaved species such as oak and elm. At the beginning of 11 thousand BC (12860 + 110 years ago) in the Belarusian Polesie there were widespread associations of pine-birch forests with an admixture of broad-leaved: oak, elm and linden. During the Mesolithic, a significant part of the territory of modern Vologda and Arkhangelsk regions was covered with deciduous forests, which include oak forests.

S. V. Oshibkina notes that at the Mesolithic site Pogostishche in the East Prionegie (7 thousand BC) the forest consisted of birch, pine, a small amount of spruce and mixed oak forest. L.S. Berg noted that as early as 9-8 thousand BC "In the Neva basin separate pollen grains of broad-leaved species and hazel trees appear", and in 5–4 thousand BC here noted "a large, distribution of oak forests with linden, elm and hazel."

Conclusions L. S. Berg is confirmed by data obtained by domestic geochemists in 1965. It is noted that starting from the turn of 7-6 thousand BC "The pollen spectra are characterized by a high pollen content of broad-leaved species ... Here are the climax points of the curves of oak, elm, hazel and alder." We emphasize that the culmination of the distribution of oak in the Tver region dates back to 6945 years ago (i.e., the beginning of 5 thousand BC), and in the Leningrad region - to 7790 years ago (i.e., the beginning of 6 thousand BC. e.). In addition, in the Neolithic and Bronze Age, it was in Eastern Europe that the largest zone of oak forests in Europe was located.

Thus, the thesis about the presence of oak forests in ancient Indo-European time only in the Mediterranean, mountainous areas of Mesopotamia and adjacent areas is completely groundless.

Beech

The authors of the "Indo-European language and Indo-Europeans" note that the name "beech" is not in the Indo-Iranian languages. This is more than strange if we accept the hypothesis. V. V. Ivanov and T. V. Gamkrelidze on the Near-Asian ancestral home of the Indo-Europeans.After all, this tree was in ancient times one of the main forest-forming in the Transcaucasia and Western Asia. The fact that the ancient Indo-European name of beech has not been preserved in Indian languages can still be explained - there is no beech on the territory of Hindustan.

But how could the Iranians lose this ancient Indo-European name if the beech is the main forest-forming not only in the Near East and the Armenian Highlands (the supposed oldest ancestral home), but also in the Iranian Highlands - the new homeland of the Iranians (according to T. V. Gamkrelidze and V. V. Ivanov)?

After all, G. I. Tanfilyev (the chief botanist of the Imperial Botanical Garden, an outstanding phytogeographer and connoisseur of the flora of Russia), describing the vegetation of the Caucasus in 1902, noted that "the forests here consist mostly of beech mixed with chestnut and oak." Currently, in the Caucasus, beech occupies almost half of the total area covered by forests. It is widespread on the northern slopes of the Caucasus, in Transcaucasia it is characterized by almost continuous distribution, and only in the upper reaches of individual rivers gives way to conifers. It runs along the main ridge from the Black Sea coast to the eastern border of forests (Shemakha), along the Lesser Caucasus to the east to the Terter River, and in the east it is again found in Talysh, leaving the foothills of Elburz to Iran.

The same picture was observed in antiquity: pollen analysis of samples from the bottom of the Black Sea, dating from the beginning to the middle of 6 thousand BC, when there was a rapid filling of the freshwater Black Sea with salt water from the Bosphorus, indicate the presence of forests from hornbeam, beech, oak and elm! Apparently, the picture has not changed to this day. But then it is absolutely inexplicable how the ancient Iranian tribes, who came from their supposed ancestral homeland with its beech forests to the territory, where beech forests also prevailed and still prevail, the ancient Indo-European name of this tree was completely lost. Probably, such a situation could only develop if the ancient Iranians came to the territory of the Iranian Highlands from areas where the beech does not grow. And here it is appropriate to recall that, as T. V. Gamkrelidze and V. V. Ivanov: "to the north-east from the Black Sea coast to the lower reaches of the Volga throughout the entire postglacial period" there is no beech.

Hornbeam

And with this tree, whose ancient Indo-European name is in many Indo-European languages, but not in the Indo-Iranian, a situation similar to beech has developed. The hornbeam grows in the Near East, making up a significant part in the forests on the western shore of the Caspian Sea. He dominates with the oak in Karabakh. In the Caucasus, in Southern and Eastern Europe (pure hornbeam forests are known only east of the Vistula and in the upper Bug), in Asia Minor and Iran, the eastern hornbeam or hornbeam growing in the lower, less often middle belt of mountains to a height of 1200 m is common. Like beech, throughout the postglacial period to the north-east of the Black Sea, the hornbeam is absent. And (one can see a certain regularity in this) the name of the hornbeam is absent in the Indo-Iranian languages.

Yew

This ancient Indo-European name also does not exist in the Indo-Iranian languages. "Yew is distributed in Europe from Scandinavia to the mouth of the Danube, its eastern border roughly coincides with the border of beech ... Yew in historical times is not found in Eastern Europe and the Northern Black Sea region." But "yew is especially widespread in the more southern regions of the Caucasus (starting from the North Caucasus), in Asia Minor and some parts of the Balkans," write T. V. Gamkrelidze and V. V. Ivanov.

The situation repeats itself, similar to the situation with beech and hornbeam. Yew is growing in the alleged Near-Asian ancestral homeland, is also widespread in the new Iranian homeland, and there is no Indo-European name for this tree in the Indo-Iranian languages, just as it was not in historical time in Eastern Europe and the Northern Black Sea region.

Fir

"Fir in its various forms is known from the Middle and Late Atlantic period (7-4 thousand BC) in Transcaucasia and Western Asia, as well as in the lower Volga, in Eastern Europe, in the Pripyat - Desna basin. Later, fir is pushed aside by some other types of trees, preserved mainly in the mountainous regions of Europe, the Caucasus, Western Asia and Eastern Europe" T. V. Gamkrelidze and V. V. Ivanov.

43

But I would like to draw attention to the fact that even during the peak of the Valdai glaciation, when, unlike Western Europe, "within the Russian Plain, forests occupied a large area in the form of a wide strip crossing it in the direction from the south-west to north-east", they were represented mainly by birch-pine and spruce-fir forests.

At the same time: "With regard to the non-moral and subtropical types of shrub forests, the following should be noted: the fact that these types were preserved in southern Europe during the glaciation in Valdai clearly indicates the result of flococenogenetic analysis of modern vegetation of the Mediterranean countries."

How in such a situation, when the climate of Asia Minor has not changed from the time of the Valdai glaciation to the present day, fir could be pushed to the mountainous regions of Europe, the Caucasus and, most importantly, Asia Minor, where it is not currently located?

According to modern vegetation maps in the Old World, the range of the genus fir is it is the northeast of the European part of Russia, Siberia, China (northwest), slightly in the Caucasus and the Western Mediterranean.

G. I. Tanfilyev noted that: "In the European taiga they come from Siberian species, except for larch, still fir and cedar. Of these, cedar grows on this side of the Urals in small groups and individual trees among forests and other species, while larch and fir in places form even forests in places. " Currently, fir in our country occupies 12 million hectares. Thus, there is no certainty that fir grew in antiquity in Asia Minor, but the fact that it had and has an extensive range in northeastern Europe and in Siberia is a fact.

Pine

V. V. Ivanov and T. V. Gamkrelidze write that pine and its varieties from antiquity are represented in the mountainous regions of the Caucasus and the Carpathians, as well as in the Black Sea region. But it should be noted that in ancient times, pine was spread by no means only in these territories. So, at the peak of the Valdai glaciation in the Oka basin, spruce-pine forests of the north-taiga type were noisy, in the middle reaches of the Desna forests with spruce and Siberian cedar pine were locally distributed.

According to paleogeography in the ancient Holocene (11 thousand years ago), spruce, pine and alder were present in the forests of the Vologda Oblast. A similar situation was in other areas of the central part and the north of Eastern Europe. In general, conifers began to play a significant role in the vegetation cover of Eurasia since the Triassic period, which began about 240 million years ago. "Among modern conifers, the most ancient families are Araucariaceae, Podocarpaceae, and especially pine ... plant residues (including pollen grains), more or less confidently related to the pine genus, are known from Jurassic deposits."

Currently, forests with a predominance of pine are most pronounced in the northern regions of Eurasia and North America. Pine forests in our country occupy an area of 108 million hectares. The range of the genus pine is all of Europe, Siberia, the Himalayas, the Pamirs, China, Japan, and Asia Minor. In Western Asia there is no pine!

Pine forests are not as significant as T. V. Gamkrelidze and V. V. Ivanov, and in the Caucasus. So G. I. Tanfilyov, describing the forests of the Western Transcaucasia, notes that: "The coastal pine tree, which is found only at the very sea, is very typical of the coastal pine, a tall tree growing in small groups between Novorossiysk and Cape Pitsunda, and only at this last point it forms a large forest." He notes that "in the forests on Talash there are no conifers at all except yew and juniper", and "in the East Caucasus only pine and juniper are found from coniferous species, of which pine, however, goes only to the meridian of Elisavetpol."

Spruce

The authors of the "Indo-European language and Indo-Europeans" argue that: "In ancient times, spruce was represented only in the highlands, in particular in the Caucasus and in the mountainous regions of Central and Southern Europe."

However, L. S. Berg believed that: 11-10 thousand years ago, spruce forests prevailed in the north and in the center of Eastern Europe; 9-8 thousand years ago, the amount of spruce fell slightly; 7-6 thousand years ago, in a temperate, warm and humid climate, the secondary distribution of spruce began; and in 1 millennium BC in colder and wetter conditions, spruce begins to penetrate into oak forests.

The botanical data indicate that at present "most species and individuals of spruce are kept in an area whose southern border does not extend beyond 35 ° N, and the vast majority of spruce stands is located much north".

And, moreover, even during the maximum of the Valdai glaciation (18–20 thousand years ago), 55 N up to 63 ° N meadow steppes with birch and spruce forests.

As for the Caucasus, spruce is distributed here "mainly in the west of the Greater Caucasus, both on its northern slopes and in the Caucasus, reaching almost Tbilisi in the East. The southern and southeastern border of the eastern spruce lies in Anatolia. " Thus, the range of the spruce genus is the north of Eurasia, the Himalayas, China and a few

Balkans, Asia Minor and the Caucasus, i.e. the thesis that: "In antiquity, spruce was represented only in high mountain regions, in particular in the Caucasus and in the mountainous regions of Central and Southern Europe" seems unconvincing.

Dogwood

T. V. Gamkrelidze and V. V. Ivanov write that: "Dogwood is prevalent mainly in the relatively more southern regions of Europe, the Caucasus and Western Asia."

But at present, 15 species of wild dogwood are growing in our country, among them: holly dogwood, reaching in the European part Arkhangelsk, where it bears fruit as well as in Crimea; Cotoneaster, common in Crimea, the Caucasus and Western Asia, also bearing fruit to the latitude of Arkhangelsk; cotoneaster whole or ordinary, growing in the Baltic states, Western Belarus, the Caucasus, Zap. Ukraine, in the Crimea and Central Asia, and also reaching Arkhangelsk; black-fruited cotoneaster, common in Eurasia from Central Europe to China, and from Lapland to the Caucasus and Central Asia, growing everywhere except for the tundra and uninhabited deserts.

But, at that time, about which T. V. Gamkrelidze and V. V. Ivanov is said to be of common Indo-European (i.e. 5-4 thousand BC), there were practically no tundra in Eastern Europe. In addition, dogwood varieties are widely distributed under the general name derain, about 50 species of which grow in temperate climates. This is Siberian white derain growing in the north of the forest strip of the European part of our country, in Siberia and the Far East. This shrub prefers wetter and wetter places along the banks of rivers, lakes, river floodplains and does not grow in the

47

south of the steppe zone. Derain is red, blood dogwood, spread throughout the European honor of Russia, except for the Far North and the Caucasus, as well as central and southern Europe. This shrub lives in floodplains, thickets, undergrowth, and forest edges. And, finally, ordinary derain - dogwood, spread to the north to Orel.

Thus, it is argued that dogwood was 5–4 thousand BC grew only in the more southern regions of Europe, in the Caucasus and in Asia Minor, hardly correct.

Mulberry tree

A very interesting situation is developing with T. V. Gamkrelidze and V. V. Ivanov and with the name of the mulberry tree. They note that "the mulberry tree with dark fruits is a characteristic fruit tree of the Mediterranean and Southwest Asia; Western Asia is considered its ancient homeland. Large fruits ... in a number of highlands of Central Asia and Central Asia (in the Pamirs) are used for food (flour is replaced from dried mulberry fruits, replacing flour from grain), the leaves go to feed livestock, and wood is valued as a building material. But in a number of Indo-European dialects that have lost the old word (like Indo-Iranian languages), the name of the mulberry tree is transferred to blackberries. So in Greece (where both mulberry and blackberry grow) they have one name - mjroi (already at Homer), and in Armenia mor, mori, moreni - blackberry (although the mulberry grows here too), the Latin "morms" - mulberry, morum is the fruit of the mulberry tree and the blackberry. "

The strange thing about this situation is that if the ancestral home of the Indo-Europeans was Asia Minor (the ancient homeland of the mulberry tree), then in the new territories the Indo-Europeans did not make sense to call this

48

name anything else besides the well-known plant growing on their ancestral home. And, nevertheless, in spite of the fact that mulberry is a tree of the "Near Asian ancestral home", that flour is made from its fruits in the Pamirs, Iran is generally the birthplace of a wild mulberry tree with black fruits (morus nigra), as well as Afghanistan that in India (as in China) is an ancient culture, in the Indo-Iranian dialects the ancient Indo-European name is preserved to denote blackberries and only blackberries. But the mulberry tree is characterized by completely different names that have nothing to do with the first ones.

T. V. Gamkrelidze and V. V. Ivanov believe that the tree was given a new name in connection with the culture of breeding silkworms on it. But the whole paradox is that the culture of breeding silkworms is associated with morus alba - a tree with white fruits, whose homeland is China, where it was first used to produce silkworm cocoons. On a tree with black fruits - morus nigra, whose homeland is Iran and Afghanistan, these worms do not live. So it is not at all clear why the tree that grew on the proposed ancestral home in Asia Minor and from the fruits of which they began to make flour in the new homeland, suddenly found a name here associated with silkworms, which have nothing to do with it.

A different conclusion would be logical here. The name of the blackberry - "morus", was primary, and subsequently, when promoting the Indo-Europeans in the territory of its distribution, they began to call the mulberry because of the similarity of its berries to blackberries. The distribution area of the blackberry is huge. Only in our country 52 species of this berry are known: Nessa blackberry, or cumanica, growing in the forest and forest-steppe zone of the European part of Russia; cut blackberry - in the Baltic states, Belarus, Lipetsk region; bluish blackberry or burn, growing throughout the European part of our country, except the Far North, as well as in the Caucasus and Central Asia, etc.

It is possible that for blackberry this name - "morus" - was not at all monopolistic, because together with it the Rosanne family includes such beautiful berries as "polynika" - polar meadow ("mamura" or Arctic raspberry) and "moroshka" - cloudberry. Is the name of this beautiful northern berry, outwardly similar to a blackberry and different from it only in its honey color, connected with the ancient name "morus", although its black and red varieties are found in the north (that is exactly what "morus" is called cloudberry in Sweden).

Grape

The authors of the "Indo-European language and Indo-Europeans" write that the Indo-European term lacks the Indo-European term for wine and grapes.

But! In Iran, Tajikistan, Turkmenistan, wild grapes are growing. It also grows in Asia Minor, and L. S. Berg noted that: "In Palestine, grapes now find the southern limit of their distribution. In Bible times, the Palestinian plateau was famous for its vineyards, but beyond Palestine, to the south, grape cultivation was not common. "

A strange situation is once again emerging with Indo-Iranian languages. Grapes are growing in the supposedly "Near-Asian ancestral homeland", in the "new homeland" - the Iranian Highlands - too, but there is no Indo-European term for wine and grapes. T. V. Gamkrelidze and V. V. Ivanov believe that: "it can be assumed that the place of wine as a cult and household drink in the Indo-Iranian tradition is beginning to be occupied by other intoxicating drinks made not from grapes, but from other plants that replaced grapes in the new ecological conditions of the ancients Indo-Iranians."

But what kind of new environmental conditions are these if, in Asia and Iran, we repeat, grapes grow equally successfully, and even in the wild in Iran? Wild grapes are also growing in Tajikistan, another new homeland of the ancient Iranians. Why look for other plants for making wine as a cult and domestic drink, if the well-known grapes have always been at hand.

It's another matter if Indo-Iranians did not know grapes in their original Indo-European ancestral home, because in the places of their original habitat he did not grow, and they prepared heady drinks using other plants, for example, hops.

But then, Asia Minor was not their oldest ancestral home. And moreover, the initial formation of the Indo-Iranian peoples probably took place in territories much more northern not only in relation to the Near East and Asia Minor, but even to Ukraine, since here it is in Tripoli settlements (4 thousand BC) already cultivated a cultivated grape variety, although it had a small berry. Researchers believe that as early as 4 thousand BC "Viticulture, for which the natural conditions of the Dniester-Prut interfluve were quite favorable, has become a new branch of agricultural production in Trypillian society. Moreover, for thousands of years, purposeful selection of varieties was carried out, as evidenced by 3 thousand years BC, found in the settlement. Varvarovka VIII cereals large table grapes.

Among the plants of the Indo-European ancestral home T. V. Gamkrelidze and V. V. Ivanov are also called ash, willow, aspen, apple, cherry, moss, heather, rose.

Ash

Trees or shrubs today are known mainly in the temperate zone for more than 60 species. Various species of ash are widespread in the forests of North America, in Korea, China, and Japan, in the mountains of the Caucasus, Crimea, the Carpathians, Central Asia, Southern and Central Europe and Asia Minor.

In Russia, 11 species of ash are currently growing wildly. Common or tall ash is common in almost the entire European part of Russia, reaching the Volga in the east. As for its northern border, according to the data of 1897 in the Arkhangelsk province on the Mehrenge River, the forest consisted of pine, bird cherry, larch, oak, ash and maple. And since in the common Indo-European period, as noted earlier, the climate of Eastern Europe, especially at latitudes from 70° N up to 55° N, was much warmer than modern, it can be assumed in antiquity the widest distribution of this light-loving plant here.

Willow

More than 600 species of trees and shrubs in both hemispheres. More than 170 species and many varieties and crosses of willow grow in Russia. These are: white willow; vetla; beloloz, distributed throughout Russia, with the exception of the Far North, the north of the forest zone and the east of Siberia; pear-leaved willow, growing in the forest and forest-tundra zone and in the subalpine zone of the mountains of the North; tree-shaped willow, widespread in the tundra and forest-tundra; goat willow or "delirium"; rakita growing throughout Europe, with the exception of the tundra and subalpine zone; ash willow; chernotal; seudoltosis; Russian willow, etc.

It was the willow, together with the birch, that was the trees that were the first to develop the territories that had just been freed from the glacier. Thus, over the past 13,500 years, willow has been a characteristic tree for all of Eastern Europe.

Aspen

One of the trees of the Indo-European homeland. Today it grows in the European part of Russia, Siberia, the Far East, with the exception of the tundra, in Kazakhstan and the Caucasus, to alpine meadows, as well as in Manchuria and North Korea. Aspen is very photophilous and its gigantic form was found in the Gorky region.

V. A. Safronov emphasizes that: "the aspen argument has not yet been advanced by researchers excludes from the search zone of the Late Indo-European ancestral home all previously assumed Asian territories, including the Near East with the Armenian Highlands, almost all Eurasian steppes, except their northern outskirts and the southern half of Western Europe, including The Balkans, the southern slopes of the Alps, most of France, the Apennine peninsula and the Pyrenees." But, according to the conclusions of V. A. Safronov, on the basis of the "aspen argument", should also exclude Asia Minor from the search zone of the Indo-European ancestral homeland, where aspen did not grow and does not grow. He writes: "The only known instance of aspen in Asia Minor was discovered by V. Sapozhnikov on July 12, 1916 at Erzurum. Paleogeography data on the distribution of plant zones of 4 thousand BC confirm the exclusion of the above regions from the area of aspen distribution. "

But it is precisely in Asia Minor that the settlement Chatal Guyuk is located, with which V. A. Safronov, as noted earlier, connects the ancient ancestral home of the Indo-Europeans.

As for Eastern Europe, or rather its forest zone, the participation in the aspen forest is characteristic here for the entire postglacial period, up to the present day. Thus, the Brockhaus and Efron Encyclopedic Dictionary notes that: "In the forests of the Olonets province, pine and spruce predominate from conifers, and birch, aspen, willow and black alder prevail from deciduous".

Moreover, the "News of the Arkhangelsk Society for the Study of the Russian North" for 1910 reports that: "Since ancient times, Russian aspen has been occupying a very prominent place in foreign markets. Russia directly and indirectly is almost the only supplier abroad of this kind of goods. "

Apple tree

It is well known that the great importance attached to the apple tree and apples in the mythology of almost all Indo-European peoples. Indeed, it is the apple orchard in the pan-Indo-European tradition that is a symbol of paradise.

The apple tree is one of the most widespread fruit crops in the world, it is cultivated on a total area of more than 5 million hectares, including 2.7 million hectares occupied in our country only for industrial production (excluding private orchards), that is about 54% of world space. According to gross production, apples occupy the fifth place in the world after grapes, citrus fruits, bananas, coconuts; world production is from 21 to 25 million tons, of which 6-8 million tons in our country (excluding private gardens).

The vegetative row, built on the principle of increasing heat demand, is very indicative. These are: mountain ash,

54

currants, gooseberries, strawberries, raspberries, apple trees, cherries, hazels, pears, plums, cherries, apricots, walnuts, pecans, hazelnuts, quinces, peaches, almonds, pistachios, sweet chestnuts, persimmons, olives, pomegranates, figs, citrus fruits. It is also interesting that temperatures above 30 ° C lead to overheating of tissues in the apple tree and cause burns to fruits, leaves, shoots, bark, inhibits photosynthesis and other life processes.

The wild ancestor of the domestic apple tree beyond the antiquity of culture has not been established. It is believed that they could be: forest apple, wild, sour. It is currently growing in the forests of Russia south of 60-65 ° N along the Karelian Isthmus - Vologda - Perm line and to the south, as well as in Northern and Central Europe.

Wild forest apple trees are widespread along the banks of rivers, at the fringes. The fruits of this tree are edible, especially after frost. The wild ancestor of the home apple tree could be an early apple tree, a ranetka growing in the forest-steppe regions of the Volga, Dnieper and Don.

It is found mainly in deciduous and mixed forests. By the way, it is the fruits of wild apple trees that are most rich in vitamins "C". At present, in our country, a wild apple tree occupies about 353 thousand hectares. And, about 238 thousand hectares is a ranetka, there are many of it in the forests (mostly oak) of the Voronezh, Tambov, Kursk and Belgorod regions, where one hectare of forest can produce from 5 to 9 tons of wild apples.

Archaeologists note that the inhabitants of the Early Tripoli settlements of 5 millennium BC engaged in intensive gathering in the forests and groves of wild dogwood, wild pears, apples and cherries.

Another alleged ancestor of the domestic apple tree is a low apple tree, closely related to the forest apple tree, growing in the Crimea, Central Asia and the Caucasus;

although it is believed that the central regions of the formation of this species are the Central regions of China.

And, finally, in the millennia-old selection, apparently, took part: the Nedzvetsky apple tree - a wild-growing species of Central Asia and Northern China; Sivers apple tree is a Central Asian species; Oriental apple tree - widespread in the Caucasus and adjacent territories; Turkmen apple tree; berry apple tree - in the wild, spread in the forests of western and eastern Siberia (one of the most frost-resistant species - tolerates a decrease in temperature to 50-55 ° C); slalivny apple tree is a wild-growing species of Northern China.

Thus, the range of domestication of wild apple trees is quite wide. Speaking about the territory of Eastern Europe, as the alleged oldest ancestral home of the Indo-European peoples, it must be emphasized again that already from 7 thousand BC here, from the White Sea coast to the Black Sea coast, mixed and broad-leaved forests spread, the border of which ran 550 to 600 km to the north of the present. In these forests, a wild apple tree was probably represented quite widely, because We recall that hazel in the forests of the Vologda Oblast at that far time was about 5% of all species, and yet it needs more heat supply than an apple tree. Note that even in the climatic conditions of the 19-20 century, much more severe (average summer temperatures are 4-5 ° C lower than during the Holocene optimum), the wild apple tree successfully grows in the forests near St. Petersburg, in the Vologda and Arkhangelsk regions. In the description of the forests of the Olonets province of 1897, it is noted that here: bird cherry and mountain ash are quite common, it is found in the wild form of linden, maple, elm and apple tree, which, crossing Svir, reach their northern limit in Zaonezhie.

Cherry

The northern borders of the cherry culture are currently passing from Lake Ladoga to Vologda, Kirov and Chelyabinsk. The wild ancestor of homemade cherries is steppe or shrubby cherries, which are common in the forest-steppe regions of the Volga region, southern Siberia, the Southern Urals and the North Caucasus. She is the ancestor of the cultivated types of garden cherries, widely used in many temperate countries. In the Crimea, in the Caucasus, in Central and Asia Minor, Magaleb cherry, antipka, or fragrant cherry also grows wild. This is a shrub or tree 4-7 m high (sometimes up to 10-12 m) with a spherical crown. Its fruits are small and inedible, however, forms with edible fruits are occasionally found. Turning to archaeological data, we recall that as early as 5 thousand BC in the south of Ukraine, the population of Early Tripoli settlements in the forests collected the fruits of wild cherries and conducted its directed selection. On the scale of heat demand, cherry is located between the apple tree and the hazel, which suggests the presence of wild cherries far in the north of Eastern Europe during the Holocene climatic optimum (6-3 thousand BC), because we repeat, hazel more demanding for heat at that time amounted to 5% of the total species composition of forests in this zone. Currently, in European Russia, wild cherry reaches 60 ° N and is in second place for frost resistance after the apple tree. And, finally, moss, heather, rose - like plants of the ancestral home of the Indo-Europeans.

Heather

Common heather is common in the forest zone of Europe, Asia and the Atlantic part of North America. It grows on the sand, sometimes forming continuous thickets of heaths, very often in pine forests and sometimes comes to peat bogs. In our country, heather grows in the European part from the tundra in the north to the southern borders of coniferous-deciduous forests. For the Carpathians, heather is already a rare plant, but it is found in small areas in Asia Minor, North-West Africa and the Azores.

Rose (rosehip)

About 400 species and varieties of this plant are distributed exclusively in the Northern Hemisphere. About 60 species of wild rose grow in our country, but it is so widespread that it cannot be an important differentiator in determining the location of the ancient ancestral home of the Indo-Europeans, as, indeed, moss. Concluding the analysis of the names of trees and plants of the Indo-European ancestral home, it is worth noting the significant fact that in the common Indo-European vocabulary there are no names for many trees that are widespread in Anterior and Asia Minor from ancient times. These are: olive; apricot, which was grown in 4 millennium BC even residents of Tripoli settlements; edible chestnut, known in these territories from the Tertiary period; quince, which grows wild in northern Iran, Asia Minor and the Caucasus, where the primary foci of genus formation and foci of introduction to the culture were located; loquat, in the wild, spread in the Caucasus, the Crimea and Northern Iran, the primary focus of shaping and introducing into the culture of which was Asia Minor; almonds, the primary focus of the formation of which was in Asia Minor and surrounding areas; figs or figs; fig tree, found wild in the Near East, Asia Minor and the Mediterranean; date, the primary focus of domestication of which is southern Iran and Afghanistan, where this plant was introduced into the culture in 5-3 millennia BC.

This list can be greatly expanded. But even in such a fragmented form, he confirms that neither Front, nor Asia Minor, nor the Armenian Highlands could be the oldest ancestral home of the Indo-Europeans. And here again I would like to refer to the conclusion of P. Friedrich that: "the Pre-Slavic best of all the other groups of Indo-European languages preserved the Indo-European system of tree designation", and "the speakers of the common Slavic language lived in the ecological Slavic period (in particular, defined by wood flora), similar or identical to the corresponding zone of the common Indo-European, and after the general Slavic period, the carriers of various Slavic dialects continued to a significant extent to live in a similar area. "

S. V. Zharnikova

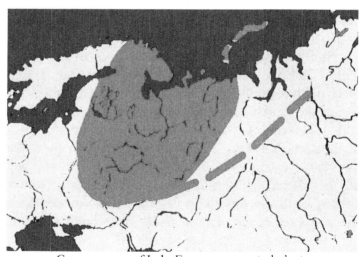

Common area of Indo-European ancestral plants

Fauna of the Indo-European ancient homeland

Let us turn to the typical fauna of the Indo-European ancestral home, reconstructed on the basis of the Early Indo-European vocabulary.

Ivanov V. V. and T. V. Gamkrelizde in their work "Indo-European language and Indo-Europeans" call those animals that were known to the ancient Indo-Europeans. This is a wolf, bear, fox, wild boar, deer-elk, bull-tour-bison, hare, squirrel, ferret, ermine, otter, beaver, leopard leopard, lion, lynx, elephant, mouse, snake, crane, raven, crow, thrush-starling-sparrow, black grouse, capercaillie, goose-swan-duck, eagle, and hawk.

The habitat of the snake, mouse, wolf, bear and fox is quite wide and there is no doubt their presence on the territory of the forest and forest-steppe strip of Eastern Europe from ancient times, as evidenced by the theriofauna of the Late Valdai.

Snakes (Serpentes, or Ophidia), a detachment of reptiles. The body is elongated, limbs are absent. The eyes are devoid of eyelids, have a continuous transparent shell on the outside, which separates during molting along with the entire old layer of skin covering the head. Eardrum and middle ear are absent. The right and left branches of the lower jaw are connected by a tensile ligament. The whole body is covered with scales, the color of which is often in harmony with the environment. Fossils have been known since the Cretaceous. The ancients were large (over 11m long); the largest modern boas reach 10 m. Snakes eat only animal food. Most snakes lay eggs, others (for example, vipers) are ovoviviparous, that is, they lay eggs, from which juveniles immediately emerge. About 2500 species are known. Snakes are common throughout, with the exception of New Zealand, many oceanic islands, and Polar Regions. In the USSR, 55 species are found.

Mice (Muridae), a family of mammals of the rodent order. Body length 5-50 cm.; tail up to 45 cm. It is subdivided into 2 subfamilies - murine (Murinae) and Australian water rats (Hydromyinae). Only 80 modern genera and 12 extinct with more than 400 species. Distributed around the world, most species are in the forests of the tropics and subtropics. Represented in the Americas and many islands. In the USSR, 11 species from 5 genera. Most lead a semi-terrestrial lifestyle, eating seeds, and part - animal food. Mice are natural carriers of a large number of parasites and keepers of the causative agents of many diseases of humans and domestic animals, including dangerous infections. Harm grain and forestry, damage materials and food.

Wolf (Canis lupus), a predatory mammal of the canine family. Body length up to 160 cm. Distributed in Europe, Asia and North America; in the USSR it is absent only on the Solovetsky Islands, in the southern part of Crimea and on some islands of the Far East and the Polar Basin. Most numerous in the steppe; often found in the desert, rare in the continuous taiga. The color is gray. It feeds mainly on animal food: wild and domestic ungulates, dogs, hares, small rodents. The wolf is harmful to livestock and hunting.

Hares (Leporidae), a family of mammals of the order rabbit-like. 8 genera: hares (1st genus), wire-haired hares (3 genera), rabbits (4 genera); unite 50 species. Some species are adapted for fast running, digging, swimming, and climbing. Distributed throughout the globe, with the exception of the island of Madagascar, the southern regions of South America and Antarctica. They live in a wide variety of conditions. They feed on grassy vegetation, bark, buds and tree branches. Some species spread vectors of natural focal infections. Five species inhabit the territory of the USSR: Manchu hare (Caprolagus brachyurus), wild rabbit (Oryctolagus cuniculus), white hare (Lepus timidus), brown hare (L. europaeus), tolai hare (L. Tolai).

Foxes (Vulpes), a genus of carnivorous canine mammals. The muzzle is narrow, ears are erect, pointed. The tail is long, fluffy. The fur is thick, fluffy. The color is predominantly red, of different shades, or gray with red. 6 species are known; distributed on all continents except Antarctica. In the USSR there are 3 species: common fox, or red, fox Corsac and Afghan fox. The ordinary fox (V.vulpes) is the largest species: body length 60-90 cm, tail 40-60 cm, weighs up to 10 kg. The color is variable, but mainly the upper body and sides are yellowish-red, the bottom and end of the tail are white. In the USSR, the brightest, "red" foxes are characteristic of the northern and northeastern parts of the country, the southern races are lighter, sometimes almost gray in color. Pure white or black individuals are occasionally found. Foxes are common throughout the USSR. They feed mainly on mouse-like rodents, as well as hares, birds, carrion. The Afghan fox (V. spapa) is smaller; the tail is very long and magnificent. Distributed in the eastern part of Western Asia; in the USSR comes into the southernmost parts of Central Asia. The fox is an important subject of hunting. Useful extermination of harmful rodents.

Bears (Ursidae), a family from the order of predatory mammals. The head is elongated, the muzzle is massive, the eyes and ears are small. Paws are powerful, five-fingered;

62

stop-moving; claws are non-retractable, very large. The tail is short. The physique is tight; body length up to 3 m., weigh from 60 kg. (Malay) up to 700 kg. (White). The fur is thick, with developed undercoat, relatively coarse; coloration from coal-black to whitish-lemon; some have a bright spot on their chest. Incisors and fangs large, pre-rooted small, radical massive, flattened. 7 modern species - spectacled bear in the mountainous regions of South America, Malay bear, gubach and white-breasted bear in Southeast Asia, baribal in North America, brown bear in North-West Africa, Eurasia and North America, polar bear in the Arctic. They live in a wide variety of conditions - from deserts to highlands, from tropical forests to Arctic ice, in connection with which they differ in their way of life and ways of feeding. Brown is found in a variety of conditions (in the steppes and even in the desert, in the subtropical forests, taiga, tundra and on the sea coasts); food - vegetable and animal. The meat is edible; fat and bile are used in medicine. The object of fishing is mainly brown. The numbers and ranges of all species in the 20th century are sharply declining.

Fossil remains are known from the Middle Miocene deposits of Eurasia (genus Ursavus). The largest number of species was in the Pliocene in Eurasia and North America. Cave bears are known that existed in the Pleistocene in Eurasia. In anthropogen, many species have become extinct.

Wild boar, wild pig, wild boar (Sus scrofa), mammals from the pig family. Body length up to 2 m., Height at the withers up to 1.2 m., Weighs up to 300 kg. Upper and lower fangs, especially large ones in males, are bent up and to the sides. The body is covered with coarse bristles, in winter with soft undercoat. The color is brown. Wild boar is common in North Africa, Europe and Asia. It prefers forests and reeds near ponds, mountain forests. Omnivorous. Object of fishing: gives meat, skin, and stubble. A wild boar - the founder of domestic pigs, "having appeared in the lower Oligocene of Europe, wild boars from there settled in Asia and Africa ... Obviously, there were three centers for domesticating wild boar of different subspecies, both European and Asian, and the subsequent mixing of domestic breeds ... In Europe, pigs were domesticated at the end of the New Stone Age." Boar bones were found among the bone remains of the Kostenki on Donsite, dating to the late period of the Valdai glaciation.

Domestic pigs descended from different subspecies of wild boar. Pig domesticated in the Neolithic. The pig of cultivated breeds has preserved the biological characteristics inherent in the genus Sus: poor eyesight, keen hearing, delicate sense of smell, ability to swim well.

Pigs (Suidae), a family of non-ruminant mammals of the artiodactyl order. The sizes are average; the physique is heavy and rough. The muzzle is long with a short movable proboscis ending in a bare flat "patch". The hairline is rare, mainly from bristles. Omnivores. Usually inhabited by forests or coastal thickets. They are found on all continents, excluding Australia and Antarctica. 2 subfamilies: bakers and pigs themselves. Five modern genera are considered to be pigs: real pigs (Sus), found in Europe, Asia and North Africa, in the USSR 1 species - wild boar - the ancestor of domestic pigs; river pigs (Potamochoerus) living in Africa and Madagascar; forest pigs (Hylochoerus), living in tropical Africa; babirussa (1 species - babirussa) - on the islands of Sulawesi and Buru; warthogs - in sub-Saharan Africa.

Deer (Cervidae), a family of artiodactyl mammals. Slender animals, on high legs, with a short tail and long mobile ears. Males usually have branched horns, discarded annually, and in spring they grow again. The hairline consists of rough awn and delicate undercoat. Coloring is often reddish or brown; young spotty coloring. All modern deer belong to 4 subfamilies: muntzhaki, include 2 genera - muntzhaki with 1 species - crested deer; water deer with 1 species - water deer; deer proper (Cervinae), distributed in North Africa, Eurasia, North America; American deer (Neocervinae, Odocoileinae) - in Northern Eurasia, in North and South America. Sometimes deer like the 5th subfamily Moschinae include musk deer in the family. 17 genera, uniting about 40 species; common in Europe, Asia, North Africa, North and South America. In the USSR - 6 species: 3 from the genus of real deer (red deer, sika deer and doe), the rest - from 3 genera, including 1 species (roe deer, elk, reindeer). They live in forests, forest-tundra, tundra, as well as in mountain forests. They feed on foliage and shoots of shrubs and trees, forbs, sometimes moss, lichens, tree bark. All deer are hunting and game animals.

Elk (Alces alces), cloven-hoofed mammal; the largest species of deer family. The body length of the male is up to 3 m., The height at the withers is up to 2.3 m., Weigh up to 570 kg. Legs are long with narrow sharp hooves. The head is long, hunchbacked, with an overhanging fleshy upper lip; ears are long, mobile; a hairy skin outgrowth ("earring") hangs on the throat. The tail is short. Males have spade-shaped horns directed to the sides; females are hornless. The coat is coarse. On the upper side of the neck and withers, long hair forms a kind of mane. Coloring is dark brown in winter, almost black in summer; legs are white. Elk is widespread in the forest zone of Europe (from Poland to the east) and in Asia; enters the forest-tundra, forest-steppe and steppe. It feeds on shoots and bark of willows, aspen, mountain ash, pine and other trees in winter; grassy plants (fireweed, cotton grass, water lilies) also eat in the summer. Long legs make it possible to move in the snow up to 90 cm deep. Horns fall in December, new ones grow by August. The elk is a valuable commercial animal (meat and a strong skin are used); it is used in the taiga as a transport animal.

Deer - moose - antelope - common Indo-European words with an original root - el, ol. It is well known that deer is not a narrowly localized endemic of the southern range. Reindeers live in the tundra, red deer in Central, Western and Eastern Europe. The data on the theriofauna of the Late Valdai confirm the presence of a large-horned and reindeer even on the western coast of Great Britain, only 50 km. away from the edge of the glacier. As for Eastern Europe, here during this period deer are found on a vast territory. So at the Molodov site (on the Dnieper) there are bones of reindeer and red deer, as well as moose. Reindeer and elk also inhabited the Desna, in the Volga basin, in the lower reaches of the Don. In the south of the Volga region (near the village of Perevoloki), during the Late Valdai period, a noble and giant deer, horse, saiga and donkey lived. As for the moose, it "is very widespread, inhabiting the belts of the northern forests of Eurasia and North America." K. K. Flerov believed that among deer, elk should be considered as a form that developed in more northern regions, that this is a "taiga species", and L.M. Baskin believes that: "moose formed as a species adapted to taiga swamp forests and floodplains." Based on this, it is unlikely that the moose was present in ancient Indo-European time (5-4 kb) in the Near East and Asia Minor and Transcaucasia.

Bull-tour-bison. Bulls, large ruminants of the family of low-horned order artiodactyls. They are characterized by a heavy, heavy body with a short neck and short strong legs. Horns are rounded and smooth, both in males and in females (except for hornless breeds). Wild species are found in Europe, Asia and North America; numerous livestock breeds are ubiquitous. Wild bulls live in tropical forests, in the forest-steppe, inhabit open steppe spaces and desert highlands. Herd animals. They feed on a variety of plant foods.

Real bulls (Bos) have no wild representatives. The tour (Bos primigenius), previously widespread in Southeast Asia and Europe, belonged to this genus. The tour was domesticated.

Yaks (Poephagus) are represented by the only wild species (Tibet). In a domesticated state it is found in the mountainous regions of Central and Central Asia (in Kazakhstan, Kyrgyzstan and South Siberia).

Lobed bulls (Bibos) include 3 species from South Asia: gaur (gayal is its domesticated form), banteng (the home form of banteng is Balinese cattle), gray bull (Bibos sauveli), which lives in the forests of Cambodia.

Bison (Bison) include 2 wild species - bison and bison, which have not been domesticated.

Tour (Bos primigenius), tour, extinct wild bull; ancestor of domestic bulls. It was widely distributed in the forest-steppes and steppes of the Eastern Hemisphere. Height at the withers up to 2 m., Weighed up to 800 kg. Skull with a flat, slightly depressed forehead, horns spread out. It was an object of hunting. The tour, as they say, "turned out to be the ancestor of all modern breeds of cattle ... Domestication of the tour took place at the dawn of modern humanity, apparently somewhere between 8000 and 6000 BC ... Regarding the place of domestication of the tour information contradictory. Apparently, this process proceeded independently and not simultaneously in different places: in the Mediterranean, Central Europe, and South Asia. "

The breadth of the range of wild bulls is evidenced by the fact that wild bull bones are often found on the sites of the Upper Paleolithic of Eastern Europe. L. S. Berg pointed to the presence in the loess of Ukraine of the remains of a mammoth, rhino, horse, deer and bull, who lived here in the ice age. In the east of the European part of Russia, in the basin of the Sviyaga River, in the layers of the Late Valdai, researchers found a large number of mammoth, horse, reindeer and bull bones. The bones of the bull are also frequent in the Mesolithic sites of these territories, as they are present in the East Prionegie, in the sites of Pogostishche I and Yagorbskaya (7-6 BC). Thus, it is not possible to speak of a wild bull-tour as a specific endemic of the Near East or Asia Minor.

Bison (Bison bonasus), a European wild forest bull of the bison family of bovids. The body length of males is up to 3.5 m., Weighs 700-1200 kg. The color is brown, various shades. Long hair on the back of the head and lower part of the neck forms a fringe, beard and fringe. The tail is short with a long and magnificent brush. It feeds on bark of willow, aspen, and also shoots and buds of trees and shrubs in winter, and grass and leaves in summer. Herd animals. In historical times, were common in the forests of Central Europe and the European part of the USSR. Back in the 16-17th centuries, bison in our country were distributed in the forest-steppe from the Dniester to the Don. He lived in most of Europe, in the Caucasus lived a special subspecies, characterized by a lighter addition. By the 20th century, they survived only in Russia and were represented by two subspecies - plain, Bialowieza, which inhabited Belovezhskaya Pushcha, and mountain, Caucasian, which lived in the mountain forests of the North-West Caucasus. In these places, respectively, disappeared in 1919 and 1927, only in the zoos of a number of countries 48 bison survived. By 1970, the number had risen to 1000, which is about half the number of livestock in Russia before World War I 1914-18.

Already in the early Paleolithic in the Volga region, the predominance of the bones of the primeval bison was recorded, on the Amvrosievskaya site the remains of the bones belong exclusively to the bisons, in the Kostenkovsky culture on the Don specialized hunting for herds of bisons prevailed, and in the sites of the Donetsk region of the Upper Paleolithic the remains of the bison.

In the Late Valdai in the south of the Russian Plain, a huge number of bison lived, as evidenced by the numerous bone remains of that time. These examples could be continued. But here I would like to again turn to the conclusions of the authors of "Paleogeography of Europe for the last hundred thousand years", which emphasize, speaking about mountain regions located in southern Europe and further in Asia Minor, that: "the animal population of the late Late Pleistocene of these regions in On the whole, it differed little from the modern theriofauna of these regions. The influence of ice cover is practically not felt here. " We do not have information about the presence of bison in the Near East and Asia Minor in the common Indo-European period.

Squirrels (Sciurus), a genus of mammals in the squirrel family of rodents. Distributed in the forests of Europe, Asia and America.

About 50 species. Adapted to a woody lifestyle. Body length up to 28 cm. The fur is usually thick. Coloring varies from bright red to gray and black, many species are colored variegated. There are 3 types in the USSR: common, flying squirrel and Persian. Common squirrel (S.vulgaris) is distributed in the forest and forest-steppe zone to the forest-tundra. Most abundant in dark coniferous and deciduous taiga and in mixed forests. It feeds on coniferous seeds, acorns, nuts, berries, sometimes insects and bird eggs. For the winter makes stocks. Leads a daily lifestyle. One of the main objects of fur trade (taiga zone of the European part, the Urals and Siberia). Flying squirrel (Pteromys volans) inhabits the north of Eurasia from Finland to Chukotka and from Yakutia to Mongolia.

Flying squirrel inhabits old deciduous and mixed forests with an admixture of aspen, birch and alder. In the European part of Russia it is often kept near marshes and rivers with alder stands along the banks. In coniferous forests it is rare, prefers plots mixed with hardwood, especially birch and alder. In the north of the range, it adheres to floodplain thickets. It is also found high in the mountains, within the high mountain forest. The basis of the diet of flying squirrels is made up of buds of various hardwoods, shoot tops, young needles, coniferous seeds (pine, larch), in the summer also mushrooms and berries. Sometimes it gnaws at a thin young bark of willow, aspen, birch, and maple. Its main food is alder and birch catkins. Like an ordinary squirrel, a flying squirrel spends most of its life in trees, but it descends to the earth much less frequently. Between the front and hind legs, she has a skin membrane, which allows you to plan from tree to tree.

Persian squirrel (S.anomalus) is found in forest regions of Transcaucasia; due to its small size and rare coarse fur, it does not have commercial value. In the description of the range of proteins, Asia Minor is absent.

Ferrets (Putorius), a subgenus of predatory mammals of the genus Mustela of the family marten. Body length 51 cm, tail 19 cm. Weigh 1.4 kg. The body is elongated, flexible, legs are short, face is dull, and ears are small. The fur is fluffy, soft.

3 types. Distributed in North America, Europe, North Africa, Asia. There are 2 types in the USSR. Ferret steppe and black is widespread in Eurasia. Moreover, the black

ferret is found throughout Western Europe, including England, on a large territory of the European part of our country, except for North Karelia, the northeast of the Crimea, the Caucasus and the Lower Volga. The steppe ferret is found in the west from Yugoslavia and Czechoslovakia and further east along the forest-steppe, steppes and semi-deserts of the Soviet Union, Central and Central Asia, to the Far East and East China. They are mostly nocturnal. They live in forests, forest-steppes, steppes and semi-deserts. They settle on clearings, burns, in shrubs, in open spaces. They feed exclusively on small animals. Valuable fur species. It, like protein, is not endemic to Asia Minor.

Ermine (Mustela erminea), a marten animal. In summer, the fur is brownish-red, in winter it is snowy white, the tip of the tail is black throughout the year. The body length of the male is about 25 cm; tail length is up to 10 cm. It is widespread in Europe, from the Pyrenees, Alps, and Ireland and further throughout Europe, with the exception of most of Yugoslavia, as well as Albania, Greece, Bulgaria and Turkey (in the Balkans and in Asia Minor there is no ermine). In Asia, ermines live in Afghanistan, Mongolia, in northeastern China, northern Japan, and in the north of the Korean Peninsula. Finally, ermines are found in Greenland and distributed almost to the very south of North America. It occurs almost throughout the USSR - from the coast of the Arctic Ocean to the lower reaches of the Don and Volga and north of the Aral Sea. In Crimea, an ermine is absent, but lives in isolation in the Caucasus, and in the east it is known up to Kamchatka and Sakhalin.

It lives most often in river valleys, near lakes, reed beds, but is also found in forests, copses, mountain placers and fields. The prey is usually mouse-like rodents and small birds. The object of hunting. In West Asia, the ermine does not live and f these areas.

Otter. V.V. Ivanov and T.V. Gamkrelidze note that: "the value of a particular animal" otter "for this token is attested in Kafir, Vaigali - wacak-ok, Avestan - udra, Ossetian - wyrd, Russian - otter, Lithuanian - údra , Prussian - udro. " In ancient Indian - udrá - aquatic animal.

Otter, Poreshnya (Lutra lutra), a predatory mammal of the marten family; valuable fur-bearing animal. It weighs up to 10 kg. The body is flexible, muscular, length over 70 cm.; the tail is long (about 45 cm), thinning towards the end; paws are short, fingers are connected by membranes. Common otter is found in Europe, Asia (except the Arabian Peninsula and the Far North) and North-West Africa; in the USSR it is absent only in the Far North, in the Crimea and in deserts.

In addition, "three more species of otters live in the Old World: the motley otter in Africa, south of the Sahara, the Sumatrin otter in Indochina and the Malay archipelago, the Indian otter in South and Southeast Asia."

The otter swims quickly and dives very well. The fur is not wetted by water and retains air. The main food is fish and frogs; sometimes catches ducklings and water voles. The burrow, the entrance to which sometimes happens, is hidden under water; it suits under the overhanging shores.

In the description of the Olonets province of 1897, it is noted that here: "the most important representatives of the four-legged world: brown bear, wolf, fox, ulcer (badger), wolverine, marten, ermine, weasel, mink, otter, lynx, squirrel, hare, reindeer, moose ... The beaver, which was found in the 15th century, has now completely disappeared".

Beaver (Castor fiber), a rodent mammal. The beaver is well adapted to the semi-aquatic lifestyle. Body length up to 100 cm, tail - up to 30 cm.; weighs up to 30 kg. The tail is flattened from top to bottom, up to 15 cm wide, almost hairless, covered with large horny shields. The fingers on the hind limbs are connected by a wide swimming membrane. It has valuable fur, which consists of shiny coarse outer hair and a very thick silky underfur. Color from light chestnut to dark brown, sometimes black. Beaver was distributed throughout most of Europe, Southern Siberia and parts of Central Asia, as well as almost throughout North America. In the floodplains of the rivers they went north through the taiga zone to the forest-tundra, and to the south through the steppe zone to semi-deserts.

Beaver is a common Indo-European token in {h} ib {h} er, in {h} eb {h} er, in the Vedic - babhrú - red-brown.

As a result of predatory fishing, only certain settlements in Europe and Asia were preserved. In our country (at the beginning of the 20th century), beavers lived only in a few places: in Belarus (on the river Sozh, Berezin, Pripyat), in Ukraine (in the basins of the Pripyat, Teterev) in the regions of Smolensk (on the river Sozhe) and Voronezh (in the basin of the Voronezh river), as well as in the North. Trans-Urals (on the Konda, Sosva, Pelym and others).

74

Outside Russia, beavers remained in France (in the lower Rhone), in Germany (the Elbe basin), in Poland (on the Wisla River), in Norway, as well as in northern and western Mongolia (along the Urung and Bilgen rivers, in the Black basin Irtysh), in Xinjiang province in China.

Thanks to protection and re-acclimatization, the number of livestock is increasing. Beaver is found in most regions of the European part of the USSR and in some regions of Siberia. Lives on quiet forest rivers, with banks covered with willow, aspen, birch, poplar, shoots and bark of which the beaver feeds most of the year. In summer, eating grass. Able to nibble thick trees. It settles in earthen burrows, as well as in "huts" - heaps of branches, silt and earth (up to 2.5 m high and 12 m high at the base) with several internal chambers and underwater entrances. On small rivers, dams are built and channels for alloying branches and stumps of trees felled by them are broken. Appreciated for its beautiful, warm and very durable fur.

"Beavers settle along the banks of slowly flowing forest rivers, elders and lakes, avoiding wide and fast-flowing, as well as freezing water bodies to the bottom. It is important that the reservoir has floodplain tree and shrubbery vegetation from soft hardwoods (willow, poplar, aspen), as well as an abundance of aquatic and coastal herbaceous vegetation that makes up the beaver diet. " Since such landscape characteristics were not characteristic of Anterior Asia and in antiquity, it seems that it was not part of the range of settlement of beaver.

Vyach. Sun Ivanov and T. V. Gamkrelidze consider, speaking of the cult role of the beaver in some Indo-European traditions, that: "These features of the Baltic, Slavic and Avestan traditions, which do not find parallels in other Indo-European traditions, confirm culturally and historically the secondary importance of acquiring special significance by these species of animals, apparently due to changes in the environmental living conditions of the carriers of certain Indo-European dialects."

It is hardly possible to explain this situation in this way. If we follow the hypothesis of the Central Asian Indo-European ancestral home, then for the Balts and Slavs everything is quite logical. Indeed, having left their alleged "Near Asian ancestral homeland" on the territory of Eastern Europe, these peoples could, in the new environmental conditions, make a new animal for themselves - the beaver sacred. But it is absolutely not clear how a beaver could become a sacred animal in the Avestan tradition as well. Indeed, according to the concepts of T.V. Gamkrelidze and V.V. Ivanov, the ancient Iranians of the Avestan period did not move anywhere north of Iran. In the vastness of Eastern Europe, based on this concept, Iranian peoples (Scythians, Sarmatians, etc.) appeared no earlier than 1 BC, when the main ritual and mythological block, the Avesta, has long been formed.

How, then, in the pre-Scythian monument of the ancient Iranians "Avesta", the beaver became the sacred animal of the greatest ancient goddess of the Aryans of Ardvisura - Anahita, symbolizing fertility and the original water element. Moreover, in "Ardvisur Yashta" Anahita describes the blessing of the ancestors of the Aryans Yamu and Paradat, dressed in a fur coat from the skins of 300 beaver females killed only after they brought a certain number of cubs. According to the Avestan tradition, males with the so-called It was categorically forbidden to kill with a "beaver stream" that stimulates the potency of men, since this could lead to the degeneration of the genus Arya.

Avesta claims that; "The man who killed the beaver becomes a criminal and may be subject to male impotence." A natural question arises - where does such an excellent knowledge of animal biology come from in the ancient Indo-Iranian cult monument, worship of which turned out to be an innovation in ritual practice? We again emphasize the fact that it is in the Slavic, Baltic, and Avestan (i.e., 2, etc.) traditions that the beaver plays an important cult role. Many researchers considered and still consider the concept of the ancient Baltic-Slavonic-Indo-Iranian proximity to be very productive. It can be assumed that the Baltic-Indo-Iranian beaver cult could develop only in those territories that have not yet differentiated between the Baltic-Indo-Iranian ethno-linguistic community, where this animal lived from ancient times and in significant numbers, firstly, and where its significance in the life of people from the most ancient times was very large. R. Girshman believes that: "the Avesta's information regarding Anahita refers to the time when the Eastern Iranians were north and even north-west of the Caspian Sea, when they knew the Volga fauna well ... Mention of the Volga, which became something like a mythical tradition, is among the most ancient memoirs of the Indo-Aryans and Iranians, both in the Avesta and in the Rig Veda. "These texts allow us to assume that both came to Iran from Southeastern Europe, or rather, from the territory of the south of modern Russia."

The French explorer connects the beaver area with the Volga region, and Ardvisuru-Anahita with the Avestan river Ra, Mouth or Raha, i.e. Volga. But in the era of Indo-European antiquity, a huge number of beavers also lived in the basin of another great East European river - the Northern Dvina (it is interesting that the term Ar-dvi-sura-anahita literally means "double, powerful, immaculate water").

V. A. Safronov notes that: "the area of beaver in early historical time covered the forest zone of the northern hemisphere. Beavers reached the largest numbers in the zone of broad-leaved forests, penetrating together with floodplain forests far into the zone of semi-desert, steppe and forest-tundra. ".

But we already noted earlier that in the Mesolithic, the zone of broad-leaved forests reaches 60 ° N. and during the climatic optimum of the Holocene, right up to the middle of 1 kb its border is located north of the modern at 550-600 km. V.A.Safronov writes that: "to the south, beavers could descend along the floodplains of forests of large rivers, but we do not know the beaver's bones at the sites of the Neolithic - early bronze -; in Scythian time they are found in the monuments of the steppe zone: Nikolskoye (Dnepropetrovsk region) and Novogeorgievka (Kirovograd region) settlements, as well as the Tyrnavskoye settlement in the Saratov region, the settlement of Bisovskoye (Sumy region) ".

The absence of beaver bones from the sites of the Neolithic - Early Bronze Age of southern Eastern Europe does not naturally indicate either the presence of an ancient and pronounced cult of this animal in these territories, or the significant number of beavers in local forests..

Let us turn to the archaeological materials of the East European North. So S.V. Oshibkina notes that already at the Mesolithic site of the Lower Veretye (Lake Lache basin, Arkhangelsk region), dating back to 7000-5600 BC (i.e. 7-6 BC) the bones of an elk, reindeer, beaver, marten, bear, wolf, dog were discovered. "The beaver is second in importance," she writes. Beaver bones were also found in the Mesolithic sites of Pogostishche I (on the left bank of the Modlona River, not far from the confluence of Lake Vozhe), Yagorbskaya (in the center of Cherepovets, at the confluence of the Yagorba River in the Sheksna River). Of exceptional interest is also the material of the Popovo

Mesolithic burial ground (Lake Lache shore, Kargopol district, Arkhangelsk region), dating back to 7th century AD Here are the remains of trisen (there are a lot of small coals in the filling of the grave pits), a persistent tradition of sprinkling red ocher on the dead and a stable set of accompanying dead sacrificial animals - an elk, a beaver, a dog, a waterfowl.

S. V. Oshibkina notes that in these territories: "Already in the Mesolithic, in the event of a death of a relative, it was customary to arrange something like a funeral feast, for which they killed moose, beavers and dogs."

In the subsequent historical period - the Neolithic era - there are also many beaver bones among faunal remains. D. A. Krainov notes that for the Volosovo settlements of the Upper Volga (3 BC), beaver bones are a common occurrence. Quite often there are bones of beaver and otters in the Volga-Oksky and northwestern settlements of this time. At the Sakhtysh II site, a "sanctuary" was found reflecting a complex sacrificial rite associated with the cult of game animals (elk, reindeer, marten and beaver).

Thus, we can state that, in contrast to the south of Europe in general, and Eastern Europe in particular, in the territories of the Center and the North of the Russian Plain, already in the Mesolithic, a developed cult of the beaver was recorded as a sacrificial animal, which was preserved both in the subsequent Neolithic era, and in the Bronze Age.

Leo (Panthera leo), a predatory feline mammal. The physique is dense, the head is large, and a black brush is at the end of the tail. Height at withers up to 120 cm.; body length up to 210 cm, tail up to 110 cm .; weighs up to 280 kg. It has great strength and agility. The hairline is low, yellowish-sand; belly is light. Part of the head, neck, chest and part of the abdomen in males are covered with long shaggy hair (mane) from light yellow to black. 2 subspecies - African and Asian.

In the Quaternary, the lion was distributed throughout Africa (except for the continuous tropical forests of the western part), in southern Europe, and Western Asia. It is preserved only in the eastern and southern parts of Equatorial Africa and in Asia (Northwest India). Lives in savannas, upland semi-deserts, riverine forests in deserts. The lion hunts at dusk and at night for antelopes, buffaloes, zebras, deer, and livestock; also feeds on birds, reptiles, locusts. There are crosses of a lion with a tiger and a leopard. The voice is a loud roar and a dull growl. A lion differs from large cats in a calm disposition; easily tamed, amenable to training, propagated in captivity.

The presence of lions in the Late Valdai (Ostashkov time, i.e., 23-17 BC) in the Voronezh region (Kostenkovskaya culture) is evidenced by a miniature head of a lioness from the upper layer of Kostenok I. The cave lion is known in the Crimean Mesolith, and in the Eneolithic era (4-3 BC), the population of the Northern Black Sea Region hunted for lions. The fossil remains of cave lions are found in our country in a very large number of places - from Transcaucasia and Crimea to the Urals and Krasnoyarsk. The most recent finds (5-2 century BC) were made in the Crimea and near Chernigov on the Desna River. As the researchers note: "Back in the 8-10th century lions were found even in the south of Europe, in particular in the Caucasus."

Lynx (Lynx), a mammal of the genus of cats. Body length 110 cm, tail 24 cm, usually weighs 19-32 kg. Legs are strong, relatively long, legs are very wide. On the ears are long tassels; there are tanks. Coloring is different: monophonic (fawn, red) or spotty. Distributed in Europe, North, Central and partially Western Asia, North America. It lives in vast dense forests, both on the plains and in the mountains; sometimes it enters the forest-steppe. It feeds mainly on hares, mouse-like rodents and birds; sometimes attacks ungulates. It hunts mainly at night. Climbing trees well.

The Swedish researcher B. Kurten believes that lynx appeared in Europe 500-400 thousand years ago, along with the elephant trogonterium. In the late Pleistocene of the middle strip of Europe, it is a widespread species, along with a wolf, peon, badger, brown bear, leopard, fox, wolverine, otter, cave bear, cave lion, jackal, large-horned deer, elk, hyena, wild cat, wild boar, roe deer, doe, horse, primitive bison, reindeer, European donkey, sulfuric, primitive bull, musk ox, alpine goat, red deer, saiga, hairy rhinoceros and mammoth. During the peak of the Valdai glaciation, the lynx lived in the forests along the banks of the Desna and was widespread in the forest zone of the European part of our country. And now the forests of the European north of Russia are the habitat of this beautiful fur-bearing animal.

Leopard (Pardus), a predatory feline mammal. Body length up to 160 cm. The body is elongated, muscular, legs are relatively short. The fur is thick, fluffy. Coloring is yellow or red with black spots; blacks are sometimes found. Leopard is found in Africa (absent only in the Sahara), in the Near East and South Asia; in the Caucasus, in the mountains of Turkmenistan, Tajikistan and in the Ussuri region. It lives in dense forests and in the mountains. It hunts mainly for ungulates. Sometimes chasing pets, as well as birds and rodents. The number throughout the range is steadily declining.

As noted above, in the late Pleistocene of the middle zone of Europe, one of the characteristic species of mammals in this region was the leopard. On the cult ceramics of the late Tripoli period (3 BC) of right-bank Ukraine, images of large feline predators with long (sometimes "thriving") tails are quite common in which leopards or leopards are easily recognizable. And finally, in the 10th century epic description, the Kiev prince Svyatoslav is compared by a chronicler with a leopard or leopard - a "pardus", swift and light, which indicates a good knowledge of the appearance and habits of this animal. Leopard until the 19th century was found in the North Caucasus.

Horses (Equus), a genus of artiodactyl animals. Large (body length up to 2.5 m., height at the withers up to 1.6 m.), slender animals. The limbs are long. The body is covered with short thick hair; on the upper side of the neck, hair is long (mane). In the wild, they were found in Europe, Asia and Africa. Inhabited the steppes, deserts and semi-deserts. They ate grassy feed. 8 species, grouped into 4 subgenera: real horses, these include Przhevalsky's horse, exterminated tarpan and domestic horse; donkeys represented by wild african donkey and domestic donkey; semi-aids (kulan), zebras. In the USSR, in addition to a domestic horse and a domestic donkey, a kulan is found; until the 19th century, tarpan lived in the steppes.

Domestic horse is common on all continents, except Antarctica, in most countries of the world. It is used as a working animal, as well as a productive animal that gives meat and milk. Domestication began in the 3rd millennium BC. e. Apparently, there were several large independent centers of domestication: between the rivers Don and Dnieper, in southern Siberia, Central Asia.

Among the animals well-known to the Indo-Europeans in their ancient ancestral homeland, T. B. Gamkrelidze and V. V. Ivanov name the horse, suggesting that the Near-Asian area is "one of the possible areas of domestication (or, in any case, the spread of an already domesticated horse) and its use as a draft force" at the end of 3 - beginning of 2 t.d.

But the spread of the draft horse from the Eurasian steppes at the present time is no longer in doubt. The appearance of a domesticated horse here dates back to 4 kb. This point of view of V. I. Bibikova was supported by V. N. Tsalkin, a leading specialist in the problems of ancient cattle breeding. Foreign researchers are in the same position. Thus, one of the leading Western European scientists in the field of the history of ancient horse breeding, G. Potratz, believes that the Ancient East was not the homeland of a domesticated horse, and "the process of taming the horse was carried out on the distant plains of the Eurasian steppe region."

In addition, G. N. Matyushin points out that at the turn of 7-6 kb in the Southern Urals the presence of a domesticated horse is recorded. So, at the Davlekanovo settlement, among the bone remains of domestic animals, horse bones account for 42.3%. A significant amount of bones of a domestic horse was also recorded in the lower layer of the Beryozka settlement, dating from C14 5400 BC. But this date is not calibrated, i.e. the bottom layer of Birches may be 750-800 years older.

The origin of the domestic horse from the wild steppe tarpan is currently being postulated. Tarpan, the European wild horse (Equus caballus gmelini), was previously widespread in the steppes of the European part of the USSR and a number of European countries. They disappeared as a result of crowding out in vivo herds of domestic animals. It was difficult to tame. It was distinguished by small growth (height at the withers 136 cm), dense physique, gray color with a black stripe along the back and black standing mane and tail. "The tarpan lived in the steppes and forest-steppes of the European part of the USSR from the Prut River to the Ural River ... In the forests of Belarus, Lithuania, Poland, and Germany and, possibly, in some other European countries, there was a forest tarpan. The forest tarpan was similar to the steppe and differed from it only in its smaller size and weaker constitution"

Camel (Camelus), a genus of artiodactyl animals of the camelid family (Camelidae). Two species: one-humped or dromedar (C. dromedarius), - height at withers up to 210 cm, reddish-gray color, and two-humped or bactrian (C.bactrianus), dark brown color. Only the two-humped is preserved in the wild, it is found in the deserts of Xinjiang and Mongolia. Distribution is limited to areas of deserts and dry steppes. In the mountains and areas with a humid climate can not exist..

Camels eat desert plants, are content with less water and can drink salt water. Camels are able to lay down on hot (up to 70 ° C) soil. Weight up to 800 kg. In deserts and dry steppes, camels are the most powerful pack and harness animals. The average weight of a pack carried on the back is up to 50% of the mass. Under the rider runs amble about 100 km. per day at a speed of 10-12 km / h. Camels also receive milk, meat, and wool. Milk goes to make koumiss, butter, cheeses. The average annual milk yield of dromedars is 2000-4000 kg. with a milk fat content of 4.5%, in bactrians - 750 kg. with milk fat content of 5.4%. Meat is as nutritious as beef. Wool contains up to 85% of fluff, from which thin woolen fabrics are made. When mixed with sheep's camel hair, it gives the fabric strength. I cut the wool with 5–13 kg of Bactrian and 2–4 kg with Dromedar.

Camels, close to modern, appeared during the habitat of camelids in North America. Ancient camels entered Eurasian territory at the end of the Pliocene and were numerous there until the end of the Pleistocene.

In the Pleistocene on the territory of Eastern Europe, there was a large camel Knobloch (Camelus knoblochi), very close to modern camels. The remains of bactrian camels similar to modern ones were found in the Volga region, on the banks of the Irtysh River and in the Moscow Region. Camels (along with the mammoth, woolly rhinoceros, big-horned deer, etc.) were one of the main representatives of the so-called mammoth fauna that existed in northern Eurasia until the end of the last glaciation.

As V. A. Safronov notes, the elephant and the camel "hide under close names in various ie. Languages and allow you to reconstruct a common archetype of the word. Gamkrelidze and Ivanov consider this word "Middle Eastern migration term, found, in particular, in the Semitic-Hamitic languages." The semantic circle also includes the ancient migration term for ivory. V. A. Safronov writes that: "Syria was the northernmost territory where elephants inhabited in ancient times ... thus, the habitat of elephants reached the Mediterranean coast of Asia Minor, but we do not have data on the habitat of these animals in the more northern territories ". However, L. R. Serebryanny emphasizes that: "One of the important criteria for drawing the lower boundary of the Quaternary is the appearance in Europe of such modern forms of mammals as one-toed horses, primitive bulls, real elephants, camels, etc."

Elephant (Elephantidae), a family of mammals of the proboscis order. Large animals: body height up to 3.5 m. The body is massive, the neck is short, limbs are columnar. The upper lip and nose, fused together, form a long movable trunk, at the end of which there are nostrils. The trunk serves as an organ of smell, touch and grab. Fangs are absent; strongly developed second incisors are found only in the upper jaw, they form tusks that grow throughout life and sometimes reach very large sizes. The skin is thick (up to 3 cm), almost naked, covered with sparse hard hair. Only a mammoth had thick hair. They live 80 years. They feed on plant foods: branches, leaves and bark of trees, juicy rhizomes and fruits, young bamboo, as well as grass. Food is collected by the trunk, but when digging it out of the ground or, if necessary, knocking down a tree, tusks are used. Water is collected in the trunk, and then poured into the mouth. In search of food, they make large transitions, can freely move in thickets or through swamps, easily climb steep mountain slopes, and swim well. To a large extent exterminated by man. Tusks are used for the manufacture of various jewelry, as well as for technical purposes: the meat is edible.

Modern elephants belong to 2 genera: Asian (Elephas) and African (Loxodonta). The genus of Asian elephants is represented by 1 species - the Asian elephant (E. asiaticus). Height up to 3.2 m., Weigh up to 5 tons. Tusks in males are well developed (length up to 2.5 m.). They are found in forest regions of Southeast Asia (India, Pakistan, Burma, Thailand, Vietnam, Sri Lanka and Sumatra islands). It feeds mainly on herbaceous plants. It is well tamed and used for various works, mainly in forest areas; can carry up to 600 kg on the back load or drag trunks of trees weighing up to 500 kg with a trunk.

The genus of African elephants is represented by 2 species: savannah (E. africana) and forest (E. cyclotis). The height of the males of the savannah elephants is up to 3.5 m., The forest elephant is somewhat smaller. Tusks are well developed (length up to 3 m.). They are found in Africa in the steppes, forest-steppes and forests. They feed mainly on tree branches and leaves.

Apparently, Africa was the ancestral home of elephants, where their most ancient fossils were found. In the middle of the Pliocene they penetrated into Eurasia and spread almost throughout the continent. At the beginning of the Pleistocene, elephants came to North America through the Bering land. Their wide distribution and adaptation to existence in various climatic conditions - from tropical forests and steppes to the Arctic tundra - led to the emergence of many species and genera. By the end of the Pleistocene, the elephant's range is rapidly declining; in the Holocene persist only in southern Asia and Africa.

The oldest elephants found in the USSR are known from the Upper Pliocene deposits and belong to the genus Archidiskodon - the Gromov elephant (A. gromovi) and its descendant, the southern elephant (A. meridionalis).

Southern elephant

The ancient forest elephant, along with rhinoceros, bison, tour, elk, red deer, roe deer, doe, beaver, wild boar and bear, lived during the Mikulinsky (Riss-Wurme) interglacial period (130-70 thousand years ago) in Thuringia, on the territory of Poland.

Mammoth (Mammuthus primigenius), an extinct mammal of the elephant family. Inhabited in Europe, North Asia and North America in the 2nd half of the Pleistocene. In size (height 3.5 m.) Did not exceed the living elephants, weighed up to 7 tons. It was covered with thick wool with undercoat, ate grass and shrubs. Chewing teeth with numerous thin dentin-enamel plates were well suited for grinding coarse food. Tusks found in frozen layers are used to make artwork.

Mammoth was a contemporary of Stone Age man, as evidenced by finds in the Paleolithic sites. Drawings and sculptures made by an ancient man were also found. Mammoth remains serve as guiding minerals in determining the geological age of continental anthropogenic deposits.

The mammoth, widespread throughout Europe during the Valdai glaciation, descended from the steppe elephant, developed during the rice glaciation. At the end of the ice age, when forests spread widely and the habitat of mammoths narrowed, their extinction begins. The mammoth found in the Helsinki region dates back to this time (9 thousand years ago). Primitive hunters played a significant role in the extermination of these giant herbivores. And today we do not know what our distant ancestors called them.

Mammoth

There is no exact information about the time of the disappearance of the mammoth. In any case, in Portolan Atlas anonymous Dieppe, 1547, with a realistic depiction of elephants in Africa and other animals, in the north of Russia near the White Sea a dark-colored animal similar to an elephant or rhino is indicated.

Map of South Africa. Portolan Atlas anonymous Dieppe. 1547

Map of Africa. Portolan Atlas anonymous Dieppe. 1547

Map of the North of Europe. Portolan Atlas anonymous Dieppe. 1547

Rhino woolly

Figurine found at the Bor pebble deposit (Sukhona)

91

It makes sense to recall that the legendary unicorn of many Indo-European legends - woolly or hairy rhinoceros - is known in Europe since the almond-rissa. His bones were found in Transnistria, at the Molodov site 5 (27-22 a.e.) and at the Upper Paleolithic Byzovaya site (27-23 a.e.), not far from the Arctic Circle in the Bear Cave on Northern Urals and in cave sites of Dobrudja. During the peak of the Valdai glaciation, woolly rhinos inhabited the Volga basin. And at the same time it was found out that a hairy or woolly rhinoceros died out recently, its corpses were found in many places in Europe and in Siberia. "The remains of his food were found, among which were identified the needles of spruce, fir, larch, leaves of willow, birch, lingonberries and cereals. According to I. G. Pidoplichko, the woolly rhinoceros died out only in the 10th century, as a result of persecution by man."

Thus, the fauna complex indicated Vyach. Sun Ivanov and T. V. Gamkrelizde in the work "Indo-European language and Indo-Europeans", which was known to ancient Indo-Europeans from ancient times, are present only in the forest and forest-steppe strip of Eastern Europe.

S. V. Zharnikova
1989

92

Alexey Artemyev
Why did mammoths go awry?

Mammoths are today. They live in remote places, and people periodically meet with them. The main mystery: why does science not want everyone to know about it? What are they hiding from us? Maybe mammoths died out wrong?

On the question of mammoths, I, like most people, have long been in illusion. He believed in the word that they became extinct in the last ice age. I knew that their remains were found in permafrost, and reflected on the possibilities of cloning this amazing ancient animal. But recently it happened to me to re-read Turgenev's story "Hor and Kalinych" from the series "Notes of the Hunter". There is an interesting phrase there: "... Well, here I am a man, but you see ... With this word, Hor raised his leg and showed a boot tailored, probably made of mammoth skin ...".

In order to write this phrase, Turgenev needed to know several things that were rather strange for the mid-19th century in our current understanding. He should have known that there was such a beast mammoth, and know what kind of skin he had. He should have known about the availability of this skin. Indeed, judging by the text, the fact that a simple man living in the swamp wears mammoth leather boots was not out of the ordinary for Turgenev. However, this thing is still shown as somewhat unusual, not ordinary.

It should be recalled that Turgenev wrote his notes almost as documentary, without fiction. That's why they are notes. He simply conveyed his impressions of meeting interesting people. And it happened in the Oryol province, and not at all in Yakutia, where mammoth cemeteries are found. There is an opinion that Turgenev expressed himself allegorically, referring to the thickness and quality factor of the boot. But why not "ivory"? Elephants in the 19th century were well known.

According to the official version, which we have to debunk, the awareness of them then was negligible. One of the first "academic" mammoth skeletons with preserved soft tissue remains was found by hunter O. Shumakov in the Lena River Delta, on the Bykovsky Peninsula in 1799. And it was a rarity for science. In 1806, the Academy's botanist M.N.Adams organized excavations of the skeleton, and delivered it to the capital. The exhibit was collected and exhibited at the Kunstkamera, and later transferred to the Zoological Museum of the Academy of Sciences. Only these bones could Turgenev see. Before the discovery of the Berezovsky mammoth and the creation of the first scarecrow, another half a century will pass (1900). How did he find out what the mammoth had for the skin, and even determined it offhand? So, whatever one may say, Turgenev's phrase is puzzling. I'm not talking about the fact that the skin is not suitable for furrier at the "ever-frozen" mammoth. She is losing her quality.

But did you know that Turgenev is not the only writer of the 19th century who let slip about the "extinct beast"? Jack London, in his story "The Tertiary Era Shard", narrated the story of a hunter who met a living mammoth in the open spaces of northern Canada. In gratitude for the treats, the narrator presented the author with his mukluks (moccasins), sewn from the skin of an unprecedented trophy. At the end of the story, Jack London writes: "... but I advise all little believers to visit the Smithsonian Institution. If they make recommendations and arrive at school, Professor Dolvidson will no doubt accept them. Mukluks are now kept by him, and he will confirm, if not how they were obtained, then, in any case, what material was sent to them. He authoritatively claims that they are sewn from the skin of a mammoth, and the whole scientific world agrees with him. What else do you need?.. ".

However, the Tobolsk Museum of Local Lore also housed a 19th-century harness made of mammoth leather.

C'mon, why loot the skin when there is enough information about living mammoths. Anatoly Kartashov, candidate of technical sciences, collected a lot of scattered evidence in his work "Siberian mammoths - is there any hope of seeing them alive". He was waiting for a reaction to his texts from the scientific world, but he was ignored. Let's get acquainted with these facts. Let's start from the earliest times: "Probably the first who informed the world about Siberian mammoths was the Chinese historian and geographer Sima Qian (2nd century BC.). In his "Historical Notes", reporting on the north of Siberia, he writes about representatives of the distant ice age as ... living animals! "Of the animals are found ... huge boars, northern elephants in the bristles and the northern rhinos of the genus." Here, in addition to the mammoths, there are also woolly rhinos! The Chinese scientist is not talking about their fossil state at all - it is about living creatures living in Siberia as early as 3-2 centuries BC. "As for the 2nd century BC, it is hardly possible to trust this dating, since Chinese history is artificially lengthened into the past to infinity. However, in our case, this does not change the essence. "Historical notes" by Sim Qian is clearly not 13 thousand years old, that is, it was known after the ice age.

And here is the testimony of the 16th century: "... The ambassador of the Austrian emperor, Croat Sigismund Herberstein, who visited Muscovy in the middle of the 16th century, wrote in 1549 in his Notes on Muscovy: in Siberia" ... there are a great many birds and various animals, what, for example, are sables, martens, beavers, ermines, squirrels, and an animal walrus in the ocean ... In addition, Vöss, just like polar bears, wolves, hares ... ". Please note: along with very real beavers, squirrels and walruses is a certain, if not fabulous, then certainly mysterious and unknown, "Vöss".

However, this "Vöss" could be unknown only to Europeans, and for the locals this, perhaps, rare and endangered species did not represent anything mysterious not only in the 16th century, but also more than three centuries later.

In 1911, the Tobolsk citizen P. Gorodkov wrote the essay "A Trip to the Salym Territory". It was published in the 21st edition of the Yearbook of the Tobolsk Provincial Museum for 1911, and among other interesting things that we will discuss below, there are also such lines: "... the Salym Khanty has a pike-mammoth called" "Vöss" ". "This monster was covered with thick long hair and had large horns, sometimes "Vöss" started such fuss among themselves that the ice on the lakes broke with a terrible roar."

It turns out that mammoths walked with us in the 16th century. Almost everyone knew about them, since even the Austrian ambassador received information. And again the 16th century, this times the legend: "Another legend is also known that in 1581 the soldiers of the famous conqueror of Siberia Ermak saw huge hairy elephants in the dense taiga. Experts are still at a loss: who did the glorious warriors see? Ordinary elephants in those days were already well known: they were found at the governor's courts in zoological gardens and in the royal menagerie. "

And immediately after that, we smoothly proceed to the testimony of the 19th century: The New York Herald newspaper wrote that US President Jefferson (1801-09),

96

being interested in messages from Alaska about mammoths, sent an envoy to the Eskimos. The envoy of President Jefferson, returning, stated absolutely fantastic things: according to the Eskimos, mammoths can still be found in remote areas in the northeast of the peninsula. True, the messenger did not see the living mammoths with his own eyes, but he brought special Eskimo weapons to hunt them. And this is not the only case known to history. There are lines on the Eskimo weapon for hunting mammoths in an article published by a certain traveler in Alaska in San Francisco in 1899. The question arises: why would the Eskimo make and store weapons for hunting animals that had died out at least 10 thousand years ago? Material evidence, however ... True, indirect. "

Of course, for 300 years, mammoths have not gone away. And now the end of the 19th century. They were seen again: "In the magazine McCluers Magazine (October issue of 1899), H. Tukman's short story entitled" The Murder of a Mammoth "states:" The last mammoth was killed in the Yukon in the summer of 1891. " Of course, it's hard now to say that the story is true and that literary fiction, but at that time the story was considered a true story ... ".

Gorodkov writes in his essay "A Trip to the Salym Territory" (1911): "According to the Ostyaks, mammoths live in the Kintusovsky sacred pine forest, as in other pine forests, visit the river and in the river itself ... Often in winter you can to see wide cracks on the ice of the river, and sometimes you can see that the ice is broken and crushed into many small ice floes - all these are visible signs and results of the mammoth's activity: an animal that has played out and diverged with horns and back breaks ice. Recently, about 15-26 years ago, there was such an incident on Lake Bachkul. A mammoth in its liking is a meek and peaceful animal, and affectionate to people; when meeting a man, a mammoth not only does not attack him, but even clings and caresses him. In Siberia, you often have to listen to the stories of local peasants and come across such an opinion that mammoths still exist, but only seeing them is very difficult ..., now there are few mammoths, they, like most large animals, are now becoming rare. "

Kartashov gives a chronicle of human-mammoth contacts in the 20th century: "Albert Moskvin from Krasnodar, who had lived in the Mari ASSR for a long time, talked with people who themselves saw woolly elephants.

Here is a quote from the letter: "Obda (the Mari name for the mammoth), according to eyewitnesses, the Mari, used to meet more often than now, in a herd of 4-5 goals (the Mari call this phenomenon "obda-saunas"- the wedding of mammoths)."

The Mari told him in detail about the lifestyle of mammoths, about their appearance, about relationships with cubs, people, and even about the funeral of a dead animal. According to them, a kind and affectionate food, offended by people, turned corners of barn, baths at night, broke hedges, making a dull trumpet sound. According to the stories of local residents, even before the revolution, mammoths forced residents of the villages of Nizhnye Shapy and Azakovo to move to a new place, which were in the area now called Medvedevsky. The stories contain many interesting and surprising details, but there is a strong belief that there is no fiction or even just a little credibility in them. "

This is not Yakutia and not the north. This is the Volga region, the European part of Russia, the middle lane. And now Siberia: "In 1920, two Russian hunters in the

98

interfluves of the Ob and Yenisei at the edge of the forest discovered traces of a giant beast. It was between the rivers Pur and Taz. The oval-shaped traces were about 70 cm long and about 40 cm wide. The distance between the front and hind legs was about four meters. The enormous size of the beast could also be judged by decent heaps of manure that came across from time to time. Does a normal person miss such a unique opportunity - to catch up and see an animal of unprecedented size? Of course not. So the hunters followed in the footsteps and a few days later caught up with two monsters. From a distance of about three hundred meters, they watched the giants for some time. The animals were covered with a long six dark brown in color and had steeply curved white tusks. They moved slowly and made the general impression of elephants dressed in fur coats. "

"In the thirties, the hunter-hunter Semyon Egorovich Kachalov, as a child, heard loud snoring, noise and splashes of water at night near Lake Syrkovo. Anastasia Petrovna Lukina - the mistress of the house, - reassuring the boy, she said that it was a mammoth noise. Mammoths live nearby in a swamp in the taiga, often come to this lake, and she has seen them more than once. Kachalov told this story to a biologist from Chelyabinsk, Nikolai Pavlovich Avdeev, when he was in the village of Salym during his independent expedition to the Tobolsk region. "

«In September 1962, a Yakut hunter told geologist Vladimir Pushkaryov that before the revolution, hunters had repeatedly seen huge hairy animals with a large nose and fangs, and ten years ago he himself had seen basins the sizes of which were unknown to him."

"It was the summer of 1978," recalls the prospector's foreman S.I. Belyaev, "our artel washed gold on one of the tributaries of the Indigirka River. In the midst of the season, an interesting incident occurred. In the predawn hour, when the sun had not yet risen, a dull thunder suddenly sounded near the parking lot. The prospectors sleep a bit. Jumping to their feet, they stared in surprise at each other with a dumb question: "What is this?" As if in response, a splash of water was heard from the river. We, grabbing the guns, sneaked began to make our way in that direction. When they rounded a rocky ledge, an incredible picture appeared to our eyes. In shallow river water stood about a dozen god news from where the mammoths came from. Huge, shaggy animals slowly drank icy water. About half an hour we looked, fascinated, at these fabulous giants. And those, having quenched their thirst, dutifully one after another deepened into the forest. "

Well, that's all - there are mammoths, and not even very far. The fact is clear. Everyone who only had a chance to meet with a mammoth saw him. These are geologists, hunters, residents of the northern regions. It's time to figure out how it happened that a living and living animal was deeply buried in the ice age. I am far from thinking that all the above evidence remained unknown to the learned world. Paleontologists always begin their research with a review of existing information. But they will rely on the work of reputable predecessors, which neither geologists nor hunters belong to.

Interestingly, I was not able to find a specific scientist who "buried" mammoths at all. As if that goes without saying. It is known that even Tatishchev was interested in them. He wrote in Latin the article "The Legend of the Mammoth Beast". However, the information he received was the most contradictory, often mythical. Most of the evidence described the mammoth as an existing animal. Tatishchev could hardly draw a conclusion about the extinction of this beast. Moreover, the currently prevailing glacial theory of the death of northern elephants could have arisen not earlier than the end of the 19th century. It was then that the scientific community adopted the dogma of the great glaciation. This dogma lies in the foundation of modern paleontology. In this vein, the artificial blindness of the scientific world is understandable.

But if you think about it, then this is not limited to. Everything is much more interesting. A mammoth is an animal that has virtually no enemies in nature. The climate of the middle zone and taiga zone is very suitable for him. The feed base is clearly redundant. There are a lot of untapped spaces. Why should he not enjoy life? Why not fully occupy the existing ecological niche? But he did not take her. Human encounters with this animal are too rare today.

The catastrophe in which millions of mammoths died was clearly there. They died almost simultaneously. This is evidenced by the cemetery of bones covered with loess. Estimates of the number of tusks exported from Russia over the past 200 years show more than a million pairs. Millions of mammoth heads settled an ecological niche in Eurasia at a time. Why isn't it right now?

If the disaster occurred 13 thousand years ago, and some of the northern elephants survived, then they had plenty of time to restore the population. That did not happen. And here there are only two options: either they did not survive at all, or the catastrophe that undermined the mammoth population was relatively recent. Since mammoths do exist, the second is more likely. They just did not have time to recover. In addition, in recent centuries, a person could actually pose a threat to them, hindering the growth of the population.

I think that contesting the terms of a catastrophe is the most painful and unacceptable moment for science. They are ready to do anything to avoid even raising the question itself on this topic, since the accumulated avalanche of pent-up information does not leave them a chance in an open discussion. And this will be followed by a lot of questions that someone really does not want to answer.

Mammoth

South Mammoth

Colombian Mammoth

Steppe Mammoth

Elasmotherium

Tselodont

Southern elephant

Mastodon

Megalozeros

Grigory Maksimovich Bongard-Levin
Edwin Arvidovich Grantovsky

From Scythia to India. Mysterious Beast Sharabha

Among the examples of the ancient ties of the Aryans with the Finno-Ugric tribes are the Indian tales of the fantastic beast Sharabha. He is mentioned more than once in ancient Indian literature, in the works of a very different genre and various religious affiliations. Sharabha is usually described as a wild and powerful beast, able to fight large predators, surpassing even a lion in strength. The ancient Indians believed that the sharabha had eight legs (it was called ashtapada - "eight-legged"), and considered him a "resident" of snowy mountains and forests. True, the ideas about the appearance of the sharabha were different and even contradictory. The ancient Indians could not explain exactly what kind of animal it was: it was even compared with a camel, sometimes with a goat, but most often it was classified as a deer.

The image of sharabha was also popular in Buddhist literature. He is the main character of two Buddhist jatak - instructive tales of the past birth of the Buddha. According to the ideas of Buddhists, Buddha once took on the images of various people, animals and deities. Jatakas are religious works, but they contain popular legends and fables, various folklore plots associated with very ancient mythological representations.

"In a certain remote area, where you can't meet a man and hear a human voice, which served as a shelter for herds of various ancient animals, densely overgrown with bushes and trees ... where neither a wheel of a chariot or a cart passed, nor a leg of a companion ... Buddha lived in the

104

guise of a sharabha, gifted with strength, speed, a large and very strong body ... ". Once the king on horseback, pursuing wild animals, got lost and ended up in that distant forest area. Seeing the sharabha, he was already pointing his bow at him, but the swift beast rushed to run. Sharabha "met a large crevice on the way and, quickly jumping over it like a puddle, ran on." This one, like another jataka, specifically emphasizes the strength of the body, the special power of the sharabha, its resourcefulness, which helps him avoid the deadly arrow even by the most experienced hunter. Somehow, the sharabha, says the jataka, was surrounded by experienced hunters who boasted to quickly kill the beast. But he so skillfully avoided arrows that the hunters could not shoot him, and the sharabha, like a fast wind, managed to slip into the mountains, into the forest.

So, what kind of a fantastic animal of Indian legends is this - a multi-legged forest inhabitant of the Sharabha, possessing great strength and speed, invulnerable even to the deadly arrows of skillful earth hunters? Maybe this is a purely fabulous animal, obliged by its existence in Indian legends exclusively to fiction?

If we trace the development of Indian ideas about sharabha, it turns out that these unearthly features are amplified and acquire a "demonic" character. The specific image of the animal more and more recedes into the background, although its descriptions are preserved as a beast, similar to a deer, but with a larger body, powerful and faster (the tradition of eating sharabha meat for food was also preserved). It can be assumed that the prototype of the sharabha in the Indian tradition was the elk, the most powerful and largest representative of the deer family, living in the northern forest zone, having fast running, the ability to overcome various obstacles, swamps and rivers, entering the fight against a predator ("A good hit of the front leg the moose, - testifies A. Bram, - sometimes the wolf falls down dead"). With an elk - an animal of the northern forests and forest-steppes - the ancestors of the Indians in their ancestral home could well be familiar.

At the beginning of the 20 century the Hungarian scientist B. Munkachi was of the opinion that the ancient Indian word "sharabha" corresponds to the name of the moose among the Ugric peoples of the Trans-Urals - Mansi and Khanty: "shore (e) p"; "Sarp", "sharp", etc.; this point of view was later shared by the specialist in Finno-Ugric languages E. Levy, Sanskritologist T. Barrow and some other scientists. At present, another explanation prevails (the famous Finnish linguist A. Joki, the Hungarian researcher E. Korenchi and others): the mentioned Ugric names of the moose are associated with words from other Finno-Ugriclanguagesused in the meaning "horn" (Finnish "sarvi", Estonian. "Sarv", Mari. "Shur" and others, compare: Iran. "Srva" - "horn"). However, in these Finno-Ugric languages, the moose is designated differently, and its names "sharp", "sorp", similar to the Indo-Iranian "sharabha", are found only in the language of Mansi and Khanty.

Although the etymology of the Indian word "sharabha" remains controversial, noteworthy is the similarity of motives in ancient Indian legends about the multi-legged sharabha and in the Ugrian legends about moose. For example, one of the legends recorded in the Trans-Urals by the Ob Ugrians N.L. Gondatti in the 19th century. At first, the elk lived in the sky, and he had six legs. No one could catch him, running fast. But the moose became proud and began to boast of his strength and speed. The god of the upper world Numi-torum found out about this and sent a celestial hero to punish the moose. The wonderful hero for the elk chased for a long time in the sky, finally overtook him, chopped off two hind legs and threw them to the ground. The moose had four legs, and he became a frequent prey of man. The memory of the six-legged elk, the legend says, remained in the sky in the form of the constellation Ursa Major, and the path along which the celestial hunter chased the moose is nothing but the Milky Way. According to another version of this legend, the god Thunkpoh hunted for a six-legged elk, chasing him for a long time on the skies from the sacred tree. Only when the elk descended to a stone cape, the hunter overtook him and cut off two legs from the beast. Sky elk has become an ordinary animal living in the taiga forests of the North.

A similar story about the hunting of the sacred moose, associated with special cosmological representations, is well known from the ethnographic materials collected from the Evenks. The Soviet ethnographer G.M. Vasilevich wrote down several versions of this legend. Three hunters headed for the moose, but when they saw the beast of the sky, the main shooter, who promised to easily deal with the elk, got scared and ran away; therefore, the hunt for celestial elk is still ongoing: the four stars of Ursa Major are the moose, the three are hunters. According to another version, the hero wanted to kill the moose and shot an arrow at him, injuring the beast; but the master of the upper world stopped the hunter and did not allow him to finish off the sacred animal. The heavenly elk lives in heaven, in the taiga of the upper world; during the day he hides in it more often and is invisible to earthly creatures, and at night he climbs up the mountain peaks and appears in the form of the Big Dipper among other celestials. A change of day and night is associated with him; this taiga beast allegedly runs out of the taiga, climbs to a mountain peak from which the sun can reach. Similar traditions about the sacred moose are recorded in many other peoples of the North, from the Yenisei basin to Finland. Equally widespread is the name of the constellation Ursa Major - "Elk" associated with this legend (it is interesting that it was also called in Russia, apparently influenced by mythological representations of the forest peoples of northern Europe). Based on archaeological materials and rock paintings, Academician A.P. Okladnikov showed that the image of an elk and its connection with the sun is one of the oldest motifs of the common cosmological views of many peoples of the North.

There is, therefore, a certain affinity between the northern legends about the elk and the hunt for it with the ancient Indian traditions about the hunt for sharabha. Some details in the description of this animal also coincide. The Indian story about a multi-legged, fast-moving forest animal living on snowy mountains inaccessible to humans is probably connected with the ideas about moose that existed among the peoples of the forest zone of the North. Moreover, the origin of the Indian tradition of sharabha can be linked with the mythology of the Ugric peoples, it is there that we also find the coincidence of such an unusual detail as multi-legged (six or eight legs). In India, stories about the fantastic beast Sharabha are described in detail in the works of the classical period of the ancient Indian religious and secular literature, when this motif was supplemented by completely different subjects and entered the general folk tradition of the peoples of Hindustan. But there is evidence to suggest that the creators of early media literature and even the Rigveda already knew about sharabha. Sharabha is mentioned in various Vedic texts (Samhita and Brahmanah), in the early Vedic monument - "Atharva Veda" - one of the spells is dedicated to him: "You, oh, exiled sharabha, like a goat, you will be able to overcome hard-to-reach places". The Rigveda speaks of sharabha in a hymn to the great Indra in connection with such an important plot of the mythology of the Vedic Aryans as the abduction of a catfish by a bird; it is also noteworthy that the sharabha appears here as a kind of mythical character associated with the celestial sphere; he is considered to be a divine rishi.

1974

A. A. Tyunyaev
Home moose known from the Mesolithic

The proportion of moose bones in some Mesolithic sites (13–9 thousand years ago) reaches 70% (Stanovoye 4). According to some archaeologists, the elk in the Mesolithic was not domesticated and was a wild animal that the Mesolithic man obtained by hunting. Meanwhile, according to other archaeologists, the version of the domestication of an elk in the Mesolithic has serious evidence. A series of data makes one lean in favor of the latter and look at the problem of the interaction of a man and an elk in favor of closer coexistence in domesticated conditions - for an elk.

Hunting for this animal in the Mesolithic did not differ in seasonality, that is, Mesolithic people hunted moose equally successfully in winter and summer, and had no reason or need to hunt for other animals. As an object of hunting, direct analogs of an elk were completely ignored, which are also much easier to catch, such as deer, roe deer, wild boars, etc. The latter, by the way, are currently more favored and more often hunted objects.

Obviously, moose were more often hunted, not because its meat was more valuable (etc.), but because it was easier to hunt. The only reason this was possible could be because the moose was a domesticated animal that was specially bred for meat and for other purposes.

In support of the domestication of the moose in the Mesolithic era of the Russian Plain, archaeologists know a large amount of relevant artifacts. In particular, sledges and sledges are known. The slide was a transport device on runners, the cross-section of which was almost flat, and the front ends were thin and bent up. The length of the slide reached 4 m. The sleigh had a complex system of parts, consisting of vertical posts, belt cords and a plank platform. The sleigh exceeded 3 m.

According to researchers, the sled with a load could be moved by two or three people. Sleds required a much more voluminous application of pulling force. In Figure 1 shows the postman on vacation (Alaska, 1858), seven dogs pulling his sleigh. It could be assumed that dog pulling force was also used in the Mesolithic of the Russian Plain. However, the fact that the bones of dogs among the detected make up only a fraction of a percent, is against the extensive use of dogs.

On the contrary, the abundance - up to 70 percent - of elk bones suggests a more serious use of this animal. In Eurasia, moose is distributed throughout the following states: Norway, Sweden, Finland, Russia, the Baltic States, Belarus, Ukraine and Poland. Using a moose as a taxable animal does not seem such a fantastic reality. It is enough to look at the photo of a moose in a harness, which testifies to the draft use of Alaska by the Indians in Alaska in 1858 (during the "gold rush").

Alaska

In Sweden, at the beginning of the 17th century, couriers were transported on moose in a toboggan. In the Baltic States, from Peter the Great, a decree was forbidden prohibiting "appearing in cities on moose." In Central Russia, "a hunter drove packs on moose in the taiga. Sheafs were transported on moose in the estate near Smolensk and tried to plow. " "In the sixties of the 19th century, a pair of moose was caught in the Lobinovsky estate (Smolensk province, Vyazemsky district). These moose quickly tamed, bred to a dozen, harnessed themselves to carts and performed many chores perfectly. A similar example was in the seventies of the 19th century in Finland, near Vyborg; one of the local landowners went hunting only in a cart, or a sleigh pulled by a moose. In Yuryev, at the beginning of the 20th century, a splendidly traveled moose appeared on the run, producing enthusiastic enthusiasts among fast-lovers. In Lithuania, Poland, Courland, Livonia and Estonia, in the past, moose were used for riding needs. In the northern Scandinavian peoples, moose were once in the position of domestic animals. In Sweden they were used even for military needs. So under the army of King Charles IX, moose ran in teams and carried couriers, easily running 36 Swedish miles a day. " In Siberia, drawings on the rocks speak of the Mesolithic use of moose as a pet.

Here are a few lines about the successful experience of keeping and breeding moose in Russia in the 19th and early 20th centuries: "The moose calves very quickly get to the point that even those who grew up like a dog run after a person. A calf taken from the uterus weighs 25-40 pounds, this is in the month of May. And in November he reaches 15 pounds! What precocious English pig can compete with such productivity? Take into account that the latter has to be fed with valuable, concentrated feeds: lean milk, flour, grain, root crops. And the food of the reared calf is talnik,

112

alder, etc. the rubbish of our forest vacant lots. Meanwhile, by the named time, he gives you valuable elk, tasty meat, delicacy-jelly, etc. The cost of live moose, according to the same Markgraf, is very impressive. So, S.A. Ellers, fed on the farm, a couple of moose was sold for 750 rubles. Of course, this figure is monstrous and cannot be constant, but figures of 50 - 75 and 100 rubles apiece are not at all uncommon.

In addition to selling live, the products delivered by the elk are quite important and valuable. Skin, meat, milk, lard, wool, horns ... Raw elk skin sometimes weighs up to three pounds and is easily put out on suede (in late autumn or winter, summer skins are bad and full of holes from gadflies). Leather worn with wool, goes mainly to the Doha; True, she is worse than a deer, for it is both heavy and not so greyish. Suede elk is much more solid deer. In the old days, most of our army was dressed in leggings. The wool left over from making suede goes to stuffing high-grade mattresses and art furniture. Males change horns every year, dropping them in January - February - March, depending on the age of the animal. By August, the new moose horns are already in full form and strength. True, the elk is a forest animal, he loves forests very much, but the writer had to see these lines in his native country, in the Vyatka province, how moose lived peacefully in very almost treeless terrain, grazing day and night with peasant herds in the field. Two years ago, a flock of moose lived all summer near the village of Bidegaly, 6 miles from the town of Slobodsky, and the peasants of the indicated village constantly saw them grazing in the field, along with peasant horses and cows. That same summer, a pair of moose became attached to the herd of the local leather breeder M.I. Fofonov and, without hesitation, often went into the barn, together with the cows, where she stood idle until the morning without being afraid of people entering the barn. "

The possibility of the existence of an elk under domestication conditions is perfectly shown by more than half a century of experience in the work of the State Research Institution of the Kostroma Region "Sumarokovo Elk Farm", founded in 1966: "The main result of all work on the domestication of a moose, in my opinion, is the conclusion that the moose It doesn't need domestication, it's a ready-made pet, if it is properly raised and raised. Kids run to the call. And when they grow up, some become cash moose; others turn into huge affectionate bull moose. With proper education, moose are well tamed and pose a danger to others no more than other pets. All animal farms spend their lives outside, with the exception of the following periods: one-year-old moose are kept in pens from the beginning of spring (before the snow cover has melted) until the end of the spring-summer migration activity, moose animals are kept in pens before the snow cover has disappeared and, as a rule, released 2 to 4 days after birth.

Females giving birth to a farm, with rare exceptions, do not leave to graze beyond several kilometers and come to milking twice a day. Males are less attached to the farm, only the single, strongest individual's gain the right to live in the farm area and participate in the rut in the fall. The number of animals is limited by summer feed reserves in adjacent forests, not more than 10 - 15 milking moose at the base of the herd. "

Village moose life

In addition to the draft use of moose, its milk was obviously used in the Mesolithic. As in ancient times, the healing properties of elk milk are now known. The natural diet of an elk includes many plants that are not eaten by other species of ungulates. These are, first of all, tree and shrub species. Perhaps, thanks to them, moose milk has unique healing properties that exceed the properties of milk of other animals.

Moose antlers

Thus, the presence of an abundant number of bones and horns of an elk in the Mesolithic sites of the center of the Russian Plain, finds of sledges and slides, other indirect evidence, together with the possibilities of successful and centuries-old similar use of an elk in the period from the 17th to the 21st centuries, allows us to make a confident conclusion that that in the Mesolithic of the Russian Plain, the elk was mainly a domestic animal, giving meat products, horn (by way of collection) and milk.

Literature:

1. Аляска. Коллекция фотографий «Клондайк: Золотая Лихорадка». 2009.
2. Виргинский В.С., Хотеенков В.Ф. Очерки истории науки и техники с древнейших времен до середины 15 века. М. Просвещение. 1993.
3. Жилин М.Г. Костяная индустрия мезолита лесной зоны Восточной Европы. М. 2001.
4. Жилин, 2002. Жилин М.Г. Северный Археологический Конгресс. Доклады. Ханты-Мансийск 2002.
5. Лихачёв П., О разведении лосей. Охотничий вестник 1917. № 13 - 14.
6. Государственное научно-исследовательское учреждение Костромской области «Сумароковская лосиная ферма». 2009.

The oldest domesticated animals and the image of the goose horse and the deer horse of ancient Aryan mythology

Among the images of ancient Aryan mythology, the image of the goose horse and the deer horse, equally recorded both in the Vedic and in the Avestan tradition, is one of the most interesting and mysterious.

At first glance, everything seems quite simple and natural: the flight of a bird and the rapid running of a horse or a deer, in principle, can be connected into a single image. But, apparently, this apparent simplicity, since following such an explanation of this phenomenon, the following question arises, which is not easy to answer: why the image of a horse in the vast majority of cases in the Vedic tradition is so steadily combined with the image of a goose or swan, not some other bird? And why is the image of a horse so firmly connected not only in the Indo-Iranian, but also in the common Indo-European tradition with the image of a deer? In order to find out the origins of such strange associations, we will try to turn to archaeological, mythological and ethnographic sources, as well as to the data of paleozoology and paleobotany.

E. E. Kuzmina notes that in the Indo-Iranian tradition, horses or birds, or just birds, were usually placed next to a woman or her equivalent tree, but at the same time, "in all Indo-European traditions, equating a horse and a bird is common. So, in to the hymn to the Ashvins - the deities of dawn, it is sung: "... Your magnificent flying horses - reddish birds - may they carry you", and in Mahabharat, the Ashvina riders chant like "first-born, preceding day and night, radiant, boundless, marvelous, beautiful-winged birds", it's the goose that is associated with image of a horse: both the Ashvins and Indra's horses are likened to geese. In the Rig Veda, hañsa is a goose and a horse at the same time.

According to archeological data in Iran, compositions with figures of two horsemen or combined semi-figures of horses with a woman between them belong to the era of the first appearance of the Iranian-speaking population on the Iranian plateau and are dated back to 2 - the beginning of 1 millennium BC, and the images of horses are identical here images of birds.

The answer to the question we posed earlier is why the image of a horse in the Indo-Iranian (Aryan) mythopoetic tradition is so closely connected with the image of a waterfowl - on the one hand, and with the image of a deer - on the other, it probably makes sense to look also in the depths of millennia, in that Mesolithic -neolithic antiquity, when the main sacred zoomorphic complexes were already clearly distinguished. Turning again to the archaeological sites of the north of the European part of Russia, we note that it is here, on the cliffs of the White Sea and Lake Onega, on the border of the Mesolithic and Neolithic, next to the images of waterfowls that are clearly sacred, the images of deer; or rather moose are also constant. Present in scenes of a mythological, ritual nature, the images of a goose-swan and an elk very often outgrow each other. These are rooks ending with a horned elk head on a long goose neck, geese with horns, an elk headed by a line of geese, an image of an elk whose leg is transformed into the body of a goose. It is interesting that in the Vedic tradition "hansa" not only a goose and a horse, but also a "first-class bull", "hansi" is a goose, a duck, but also "hansika" is a mythical cow. Of exceptional interest is the connection between the image of an elk (like a goose) with the anthropomorphic characters of the White Sea and Onega

118

Neolithic petroglyphs. So, returning again to the image of a horned phallic character ("Demonic Traces" on the White Sea), we note that the little finger of his legs is connected to a group of three waterfowl, and the thumb grows into the figure of an elk.

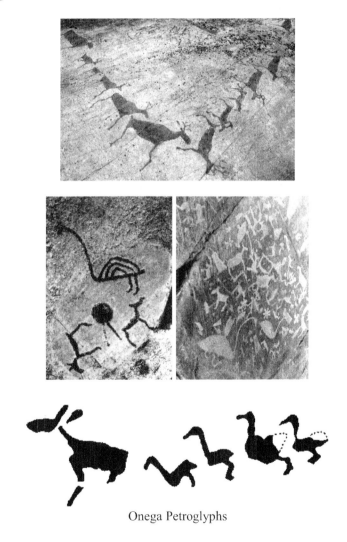

Onega Petroglyphs

119

Petroglyphs. Neolithic

The sacralization of deer and elk, as noted earlier, has its roots in the depths of the Mesolithic, as evidenced by the monuments of that distant time. So on the found, in the settlement of Vis I (last quarter of 7 thousand BC), there were protrusions in the form of elk heads, which served as brakes and stabilizers. A piece of ski with a sculptural image of an elk at the end was found on the Mesolithic settlement of Lower Veretye (Lake Lache, the first third of 7 thousand BC). Carved moose heads completed the headdress of a man buried in 6 thousand BC accompanied by two women on the Deer Island of Lake Onega. The same rods were found on the Deer Island of the Barents Sea, and in the Northern Urals in the Shigirsk peat bog.

120

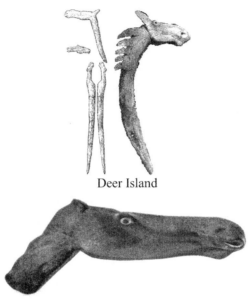

Deer Island

Shigirsky peat bog

We have already noted that B. A. Rybakov, exploring the symbolism of the Oleneostrovsky burial ground, turned to archaic folklore. As an analogy to the ideas of the Mesolithic inhabitants of the coast of Lake Onega, he cites the Evenki legends about the cosmic moose, identified with the constellation Ursa Major, and about two half-women, half-hairy-Mothers of the Universe.

Apparently, the ritual scheme that had developed in the Mesolithic, which was reflected in the burial in the Oleneostrovsky burial ground of a man decorated with elk symbolism and two women accompanying him, was preserved in the Neolithic of northern Eastern Europe. So in the Neolithic petroglyphs of Zalavruga (White Sea), the central composition is a huge figure of an elk and two moose, behind which boats with people are placed. Can we

121

assume that these are boats of the dead, ritual boats? After all, it is known that even in the early Middle Ages in Scandinavia and in Russia noble people were buried in boats. In addition, in Russia in the 15th century the constellation Ursa Major was called "Elk".

But if we turn now to the Vedic tradition, then in it the seven stars of the Ursa Major correlate with the "seven rishi" - the sons of the creator god Brahma, forefathers, ancestors of the Aryans, that is, those on whom the welfare of the living depended, and to whom they aspired descendants after death. Thus, we can assume that in the Neolithic images of the White Sea and Lake Onega, a mythological and ritual tradition has long been established by that time, in which the moose is associated with the seven stars of the Ursa Major and the world of ancestors of fertility and happiness for living, where they go the rooks of the dead, decorated with the heads of elks, like a sacrificial ritual animal.

Onega Petroglyphs

But among the petroglyphs of the north of the European part of the USSR, there is another plot that is very important for us. This is an image of people "skiing" following the elk, something attached to them. That this line connecting man and animal is not a moose tail it is

122

absolutely obvious, as it is quite clearly marked on some images. In addition, in the composition of the southern group of the so-called "Demon Searches" on the neck of the moose below the "earring" something like a collar is shown. It remains to be assumed that the Neolithic artists depicted a moose harness.

Onega Petroglyphs

This option seems quite possible. Even N.Ya.Marr in his work "Means of transportation, self-defense tools and production in prehistory" came to the conclusion that the first mount was not a horse, and "... in the group of animals of movement we cannot deer not take the first place in time". Taking mainly the arguments of N.Ya.Marr, it is difficult to agree that it was the reindeer, since its main parameters, although it makes it possible to use the reindeer in a harness, do not at all indicate its qualities as a riding animal. It seems more likely that this riding and harnessing animal was not a reindeer, but an elk. Moreover, S. B. Pomishin in his work "The Origin of Reindeer Herding and Domestication of Reindeer" concludes that: "All traces of ancient reindeer husbandry were found in the Sayan-Altai region. Modern Sayan reindeer husbandry is considered the remnant of the vast Mongol-South Siberian reindeer herding and the Sayan reindeer herders are the descendants of an ancient culture that has long gone north ... The modern wild deer, presumably, is not a direct ancestor, but a close relative of the domestic deer. Eurasian and North American wild deer are equally unprofitable learn ... The most likely progenitor of domestic deer is the Sayan deer. «He believes that not earlier than 10-11 century A.D. reindeer husbandry began to spread throughout northern Eurasia. S. B. Pomishin emphasizes that in the north and north-west of the European part of Russia, many sites have now been discovered, which represent all eras - from the Late Paleolithic to the Iron Age. "In all these sites various well-preserved crafts made of bones were found ... but no objects involved in the reindeer herding of antiquity were found anywhere." At the same time, it is pointed out that "wild reindeer is less suitable for taming than any of the wild animals."

Wild reindeer

Home reindeer

S. B. Pomishin notes that: "our distant ancestors successfully tamed moose. Rock carvings tell us about how, in various parts of Siberia, people grazed moose many thousands of years ago, rode them on horseback and in a toboggan, kept them in corrals. Moose was also used in Europe."

Solving the question of whom exactly - moose or reindeer are depicted on the petroglyphs of Lake Onega, Yu. A. Savvateev notes that although these animals "vary greatly in appearance, size, lifestyle, but on the rocks they are shown in a similar stylistic manner ", as a result of which" in one group of characters this is an elk, and in another - a reindeer. » However, "most of the images we recognize as moose." He notes an anthropomorphic figure with a moose's head and horns (the western group of the so-called "Demon Nose"), wands with inserts in the form of moose's heads, and concludes that all this reflects the important role of the moose's image and ideological people represented. According to the calculation of Yu. A. Savvateev, the petroglyphs of Lake Onega depict 149 swans, 61 moose, and 17 reindeer. It should be noted that moose themselves differ significantly in the pattern of horns and are therefore divided into deer and horned legs.

Describing the petroglyphs of the island of Yerpin Pudas, this is located in the center of the White Sea petroglyphs, Yu. A. Savvateev states that among the images of animal's moose prevail "dispersed throughout the canvas" and that: "An interesting feature of Yerpin Pudas is the almost complete absence of deer, presented both on Demonic Searches, and on the Zalauruga ". Speaking about the connection of images of animals and people, he notes that, judging by the nature of the scenes; both men and women are represented. "That these are not ordinary hunters in everyday circumstances can be seen from the strange compositional connection with other images."

Yu. A. Savvateev believes: that probably these compositions have a "certain religious and mythological coloring" and "reveal and consolidate the vital connections of nature and man." Since the basic physiological and psychological qualities of a moose, as a biological species, are unlikely to have undergone significant changes over the past 6-8 thousand years, it makes sense to refer to the conclusions made by modern researchers dealing with the problem of its domestication.

The elk, whose image in the White Sea and Onega petroglyphs merges with the image of a waterfowl, is the largest modern deer. On the territory of Russia, the bone remains of this animal are found both in the Upper Paleolithic and in the Neolithic sites; they were found in the forest-steppe and in the forest zone of Eastern Europe, in the Urals and in the Northern Black Sea region.

K. P. Filonov notes that in the era of the Neolithic and Eneolithic in the south of Russia there were not many moose, since they poorly tolerate heat. In addition, the elk's hooves are not adapted to hard steppe soils, and by the type of teeth it refers to animals that do not feed on hard field and steppe grasses.

But in the center and in the north of Eastern Europe, the range of moose is huge and bounded from the north by the south of the Kola Peninsula, the coast of the White Sea and the mouth of the Pechora River. Territories that are part of the moose area, i.e. the center and north of the European part of the USSR were inhabited by people already in the Mesolithic era. So, on the northern coast of Lake Onega, in the region of Medvezhyegorsk, as a result of archaeological excavations that have been going on for about 40 years, more than 140 sites of different times and several burial grounds dating back to the time from the Mesolithic to the early Iron Age (10 thousand BC - 5) were found c. BC). A number of Mesolithic sites have been opened in recent years in the basin of the Sukhona River by S.V. Oshibkina, in the basin of the Northern Dvina and Pechora by G.M. Burov.

And it was the inhabitants of these northern regions who created their ancient pantheon, in which the main roles are assigned to man, waterfowl and moose. K.K. Chapsky writes: "If a person managed to domesticate and breed a comparatively weak reindeer, it seemed quite natural to think about being malleable to the domestication of the mighty forest giant elk. In the conditions of roadless taiga with its thick snow cover, the moose really represents a tempting a mount capable of running off-road in the snow.

He notes that the experiments on growing young animals and taming them to harness were crowned with positive success, as the moose has significant environmental plasticity and is able to withstand to some extent the conditions of captivity. In addition, grazing moose is much simpler than calves, as they themselves follow the shepherd and do not leave him. It was noted that: "the process of taming any wild newborn calf is extremely simple. It begins and ends with the very first feeding of milk from a bottle with a pacifier. The calf is attached to the person feeding him for life."

A. A. Kaletsky reports that the moose, "like little dogs, everywhere followed the man raising them", and "young moose became so attached to their teacher that they were jealous of him to other people." As a meat-producing animal, moose is very beneficial: in the first six months of life, it adds more than 700 grams of weight daily. In addition, as A. A. Kaletsky notes: "With half-free and free keeping of animals during lactation, moose cow gives up to 500 liters of milk (up to 7 liters per day) ... It turned out that in terms of saturation with microelements, content of fat, proteins and amino acids , in bactericidal properties, it significantly exceeds cow ... Special experiments have found that moose milk increases low acidity of the stomach and lowers high to normal, and finally, with four-week treatment of stomach ulcer with moose milk, two-thirds of patients noted the occurrence of an ulcer, and the researchers noted that "the impression is that the sick body like a sponge absorbs the life-giving forces of elk milk." Moose cows quickly get used to milking and transfer their maternal instinct to the milkmaids to whom they are unusually attached. Such behavioral stereotypes, by the way are diametrically opposed to what is characteristic of wild reindeer.

As noted by S. P. Pomishin, "wild deer are untameable at any age. Even their "half-domesticated" crossbreeds ... are difficult or not tamed at all, shy and wild, and, as a rule, are rejected. They are not economically suitable ... taiga-transport reindeer husbandry, where the peaceful and tame animals are highly valued, there is a particularly jealous fence of domestic deer from wild ones." He emphasizes that "the wild reindeer that now lives in Asia is not at all tame in all its ecological groups."

Returning to the elk, we note that, among other things, it has increased fertility, since twins are born more often than loners. The moose is capable of being on the pasture all year round. Tamed moose have a peaceful disposition and lend themselves well to any training. It has been experimentally proved that "after two days of taming to reins, they begin to go in the required direction, and after ten days they already go to harnesses. In the process of training and when harnessing, moose do not show any intentions to injure or bite people working with them, which is far from it's always observed even when a young horse has been run over. In a winter team, moose run at a fast trot, never losing their gallop, and not every horse keeps up with a running young moose. "

E. P. Knorre successfully trained moose to work in harness under a saddle or pack, in a saddle a moose can carry 80-120 kg., and harnessed to a sled up to 400 kg. They are indispensable for taiga off-road, in swampy forests, and also in spring thaw, but in summer moose can be used in a harness only at night, as they suffer from overheating and even die from it. Perhaps that is why people connected with elks in long stripes (reins?) On the Neolithic petroglyphs of the White Sea have always been depicted on skis.

130

131

132

Domestic moose

It is known that in northern Europe, until recently, sledding and harness moose were widely used. N. M. Kulagin writes that: "according to old legends, moose were supposedly used in Sweden to ride, as if riding on them was so fast that the police should have forbidden the use of moose for the purpose that criminals did not hide with the help of quick-legged moose from harassment. " S. B. Pomishin also notes that: "In Scandinavia, these strong animals were widely used for riding in a sleigh. In the 15th

134

century, the moose was used by the Swedish army as a mount."

In the engraving to the "History of the Northern Peoples" by Olav Magnus (1555) you can see: horsemen in cuirasses with clubs in their hands, riding on moose; a team of two moose carrying two archers; a moose carrying a sleigh in which five people sit; and finally a woman milking a moose cow.

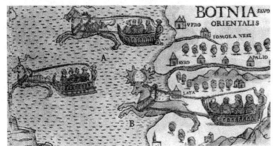

Fragments of the map "History of the Northern Peoples" by Olav Magnus (1555)

N. M. Kulagin points out that moose in captivity on a stall, if they are not ridden and not allowed to run, die after 2 years, and when used under saddle and harness they live up to 35 years. These examples could be continued. So on the engraving of the 17th century, depicting the Dutch ambassador Klenk entering the city of Vologda, you can see the sleigh harnessed by elk, carrying "a noble Russian man."

Въѣздъ Клешка въ Вологду.

1) Посолъ Кленка. —2) Приставъ. —3) Знатные русскіе люди. —4) Голландскіе купцы, за которыми слѣдуютъ литаврщики. — 5) Нѣсколько русскихъ дворянъ. —6) Паны.

Engraving depicting the entry of the Dutch Ambassador Klenk to Vologda

In the 18th century, Swedish couriers rode moose in a toboggan run, and the order of the city hall, which forbade riding around the city, was preserved in Tartu. An engraving by an engraving by DaMan-De Marte of the early 19th century, "View of the Arsenal and the Foundry Palace in St. Petersburg" depicts toboggan carts: one drawn by a pair of horses, and the other two by strange animals very similar to young moose.

In the 50s of the 19th century, in the Vyazemsky district of the Moscow province, 10 young animals were obtained from a pair of domestic moose, which were pairwise harnessed to carts for transporting bread. In Ukraine, in the Volyn province, a forester on tame moose traveled from the town of Olevsk to the town of Ovruch for 120 km. At the end of the 19th century, domestic moose existed in the Vladimir, Ryazan and Pskov provinces. There are indications of tame moose in the early 20th century in Siberia and in the Vyatka province. In the middle of the 19th century in the Shenkur district of the Arkhangelsk lips, there were more domestic moose than horses. Even V. A. Gilyarovsky in 1934 in a letter to A. Zuev recalls riding moose. So he writes: "... I am inspired by the pieces of colorful childhood and the first days of youth rising before me, the paintings that are now in front of you, in your Shenkursk, -

In winter, where they drive without a deafening
On horses with branching horns

Where in the summer gonobobel turns blue
Where doze ate under gray mosses ...

Evidence that moose have been mounts in Eastern Europe since antiquity is more than enough. So even at the beginning of the 16th century, as Sigismund Herberstein notes in his Notes on Muscovy, in Podvinye and Pechora, moose were called "forest horses."

Pliny the Elder (24-79) in the Natural History book 8 writes that: "In the north there are also herds of wild horses, and, in addition, an" alka "(moose), similar to a young bull, but distinguished by standing ears and on the island of Scandinavia there is never seen, similar to "Alka", "Ahlya".

Claudius Ellian (2nd century AD) in his treatise "On Animals" writes: "Horned donkeys live in the Scythian land, their horns withstand Arcadic water (acids), and it breaks all other vessels, even if they were made of gland". And he reports that "wild Scythians ride hand-held deer, like horses."

Ancient Indian legends and myths describe the mighty deer-like beast of Sharabha. The following spell is dedicated to him in the early Vedic monument Atharva Veda: "You, O exiled Sharabha, resembling a goat, can overcome difficult places." G. M. Bongard-Levin and E. A. Grantovsky in their book "From Scythia to India" consider that "the prototype of Sharabha in the Indian folk tradition was the moose, the most powerful and strongest representative of the deer family living in the northern forest zone, possessing fast running, the ability to overcome various obstacles, swamps and rivers, entering the fight against predators ... With the elk - an animal of the northern forests and forest-steppes - the ancestors of the Indians in their ancestral home could well be familiar. " They also note that in the Rig Veda, the sharabha appears "as a certain

139

mythical character associated with the celestial sphere, he is ranked among deified rishis."

Here I would like to turn to Sanskrit. So "sah" in the language of the Rig Veda means - to bear, endure, bearing, enduring, overcoming; "saha" - strong, powerful, overcoming; "sahatâ" - tolerance, endurance, receptivity; "sahana" - overcoming, overpowering, patience, endurance; "sahya" is help. It probably makes sense to recall that in the Russian North the moose is called "sokhaty."

V. I. Abaev believes that the name of the Central Asian Scythians "saka" in the Ossetian language is related to the word "sag", Iranian "saka", Persian - "saha", Russian - "sokhaty". All these words have the same meaning "bull deer (male)."

These examples could be continued, but, returning to the Neolithic petroglyphs, we can assume that with climate change or with an increase in population, some people from the North moved to the more southern, steppe zone; there was no possibility to use moose in their former role of riding and draft animals, since the elk hooves, which allow it to run perfectly through forests and swamps, are completely unsuitable for steppe soils. In addition, it has already been noted that elk refers to animals by the type of teeth, not including in your diet hard field and steppe grasses.

In the new steppe conditions, there was a need for a new riding and draft animal. And he became a horse. Taming and domesticating in 6-5 thousand BC the wild horse, the inhabitants of the steppes and forest-steppes probably used many training methods that had been tested on elk for millennia before, and used a harness that in many ways resembled the one that their ancestors invented for the moose. The horse, replacing the moose in the harness, replaced it in the ritual, taking on all the sacred functions

140

that previously belonged to the moose. He became a chthonic animal, linking descendants and ancestors (as an elk before him), became the main ritual victim (which was an elk before him) and combined with a duck-goose-swan (like an elk before him).

But the memory of the time when not a horse, but an elk was a mount and a sacred animal was preserved among many Indo-European peoples. EE Kuzmina notes that the syncretic image of a deer horse is characteristic of the mythopoetic tradition of ancient Greece, Iran of the end of the 2nd - beginning of the 1st millennium BC; that in Edda, a deer acts as a horse in a world tree. The Scythians had foreheads with the image of deer, "which is identical to the rite of equipping a horse with a deer." Of particular interest in this regard is the ritual mask with powerful, more likely elk than deer, horns found in the horse burial of the Pazyryk barrow.

S.V. Kiselev, in his Ancient History of Southern Siberia, concludes that the ritual masking of a horse in the form of a deer (recall that the elk is the largest modern deer) found in the Pazyryk barrow confirms that "the first mount was deer that the deer in this function only after a lot of time the horse replaced. » He writes further that: "all the evidence suggests that the horse in Altai during the Pazyryk era was a horse, and bulls harnessed to yoke were used to carry heavy loads. Deer under the top at that time, obviously, was no longer used. However, as soon as the matter concerned the centuries-old traditional areas of worship and funeral ritual, the memory of the original role of the deer was revived. And, despite the fact that precious descendants of the "heavenly" and "streamer" horses of Central Asia participated in the funeral procession, the ancient tradition turned them into deer."

Speaking of wooden carved images of horses, carefully wrapped in a fur coat embroidered with gold plaques, found in a piece of ice in the grave pit of the Altai Katandinsky mound, V.V. Kiselev notes that the most remarkable thing about them is the design of the heads of these horses, in which four holes are made for attachment of ears and horns. He compares them with fantastic animals on the gold plates of the Siberian collection, where there are images of animals that resemble the exterior of a horse, but with branched horns. Together with horned horses, a figurine of a fantastic animal, combining a horse, a deer and a bird, was wrapped in a fur coat. With hooves and torso, it resembled a lying horse, which, however, had a heading on the neck, on which were placed extra ears and horns.

Culture of Sayano-Altai

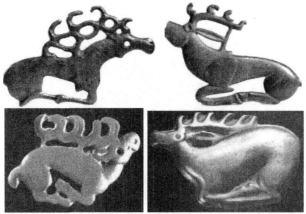

Ordos Culture

144

S. V. Kiselev emphasizes that the modeling of the head of the neck is exceptionally close to that characteristic of vultures adorning Siberian gold plates, vases, scabbards, gorites, and gold plates from such well-known Scythian barrows as Kul-Ob, Chertomlytsk, Alexandropolsk and Solokha.

N. L. Chlenova, speaking of a specific "Scythian" type of image of a deer, notes that in "Scythian deer", as a rule, the characteristic S is a prominent pattern of the processes of horns. But her image of a typical Scythian deer from the Seven-Brothers Barrow (Northern Caucasus) is actually, judging by the characteristic pattern of the head, an image of an elk. And if we compare the numerous Scythian and Saki horse foreheads, psalas with the image of deer, deer on the gold plates of the famous Petrovsky Siberian collection with real elk and reindeer, then there is no doubt - in most cases we see the image of an elk!

It is also interesting that in Scythian plastic the ancient idea of connecting the moose of a goose-swan continued to live. Indeed, noted by N. L. The member characteristic pattern of the horns of the "Scythian deer" is, in essence, a series of S - prominent "geese". And here you can again turn to the petroglyphs of the White Sea and Lake Onega, where geese (swans) depicted in a row, led by a moose, or a silhouette of a moose with a duck on its back are found. Among the bronze products of Koban culture, 1 thousand BC pendants in the form of sculptural figures of horned ducks are not rare. A bronze pin from the middle of 1 millennium BC was found in the Koban cemetery in the form of horns and figures of ducks sitting on them and a bronze plaque in the form of a lying deer with a duck beak.

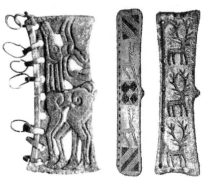
Koban bronze

I.G. Volkov, describing the Scythian slotted pommels from the Kuban region, notes for one of the tops the characteristic humpiness of the deer face and the fact that under the clearly modeled, protruding long ears, "deepened lines mark icons in the form of stylized wings." We add that the very picture of the processes of the horns of this deer is the figures of ducks with wings raised for flight.

The image of a horse-moose (or moose-horse), which arose, probably, still in the Neolithic, was preserved among the tribes of the Yamnaya culture, which in 3 millennium BC. Along with the ritual burial of horses, they performed a ritual burial of deer. The cult veneration of deer (elk) was preserved in the Carpathian era (2 thousand BC). It has already been noted above that the classic horse breeders and Scythian riders constantly combine images of a horse and a deer (moose).

Rigveda "Anthem to the sacrificial horse" (PB, I, 163). This deeply archaic hymn performed during the sacred rite "Aswamedhi" - a ritual sacrifice of white royal silver, his legs are called "antelopes" and his head is "winged", it says that you have a horse "golden horns" and, finally, that "heavenly horses, power playing ... in a series of phrases, close ..."

These oddities can only be explained by the fact that it is not a horse that is described here, but an elk, since a horse (equidrop), unlike an elk, cannot have "hoof hooves," namely moose antlers resembling bird wings can make their heads winged. And, finally, you can't call a goat a relative of a horse, although a moose cannot be denied such a kinship. Interestingly, the composition of the central rock of Zalavruga (White Sea), which shows the huge figures of an elk and two elk described earlier, closes the image of moose walking in a wedge, like flying geese. Is it not these "heavenly horses playing forcefully ..., in a row like geese, close up ..." in the Rigveda hymn?

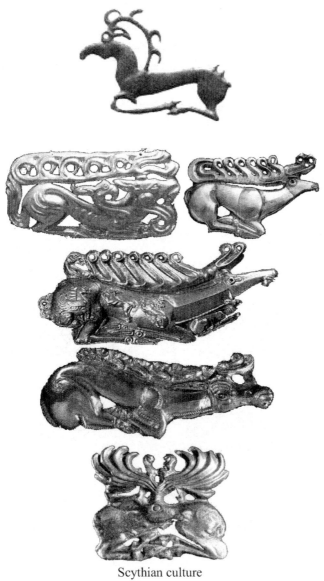

Scythian culture

Returning again to the thought of V.I. Abaev that saka-saha was a totem animal of the Scythian Saks, note that in the Vedic tradition šaka is the name of a white-skinned tribe or race generated by the holy cow of a white-skinned prophet Vasishtha, for the extermination of the army of the black-skinned prophet Viswamitra. In the Baltic languages, in particular in Lithuanian, there is the word šókti, which means "horse" and which corresponds to the above words. And finally, L.G. Herzenberg believes that for the most archaic period of the Indo-European Since the original language coincided with the era of domestication of a wild horse, it is possible to reconstruct the preform not ekûo (equids), but s-ekûo. Thus, the data of linguistics lead us to the probability of the conclusion that at the early stage of the formation of the Indo-European community, including Indo-Iranians, the "moose" and "horse" actually merge into one image, and the historical primacy belongs to the "moose", the image of which in Scythian art of the 1st millennium BC it is gradually partially replaced by the image of a deer, which has become a totem animal of Scythians – Saks, and a horse.

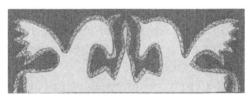

Ossetian ornament

Speaking about the ideological basis of the art of the Scythian-Siberian world, A.I. Martynov notes the uniqueness of the image of a winged deer with a huge shining head on the Tomsk pisanitsa.

Tomsk pisanitsa

He believes that this image "testifies to the tradition of solar symbolism in the steppe Eurasia and its occurrence long before the Scythian era" because "sun deer are known from the Hittites, we can mention the Vedic golden-horned deer pursued by Rama. Myths and legends about the space deer with a shining head are widely known among the Indo-Europeans in images, legends," and only at a later time the sun was combined with the image of a horse." A.I. Martynov notes that at the sculptural head of a deer in the griffin's beak from the Pazyryk barrow in Altai, horns, which are almost seven times the head itself end with miniature bird heads, and that among the materials of the Issyk barrow there is an image where the images of a deer, horse, bird and tree are united.

Thus, the circle of ancient images, probably formed even at the turn of the Mesolithic and Neolithic (and possibly earlier), consisting of a man, a moose and a waterfowl, associated with some archaic complex of mythopoietic representations, was transformed over time and the horse came to replace the moose, which organically fit into the oldest three-part composition.

150

We can find clear evidence of this not only in the monuments of Indo-Iranian mythology and fine art, but also in the Slavic folk tradition, which "is characterized by the preservation of rudiments of archaic phenomena, sometimes not recorded not only in the ancient tradition, but also in the tradition of the Vedic era. So, if in common Indo-European folklore, the horse is likened to a deer or bird, and a pair of ducks symbolizes conjugal love, it is difficult, however, to find somewhere outside the Slavic, or rather Eastern Slavs whose area is such an exact reproduction of precisely the Indo-Iranian pattern, as is the case in Russian, specifically North Russian, folk arts and crafts, and here, as noted earlier, in three-part compositions with a central female character or equivalent tree, and often a woman transforming into a tree, deer-moose, riders, horses, ducks (geese-swans) are depicted, and, very importantly, it is in this tradition that one can meet the image of horses with bird tails, with a swan torso, ducks with horse heads.

The image of a swan horse, a duck horse, a deer horse in Russian art is of the same extreme antiquity as the image of a waterfowl (duck, goose, and swan).

Ustyuzhena district

Kirillov County

Solvychegodsk

Shenkursk

152

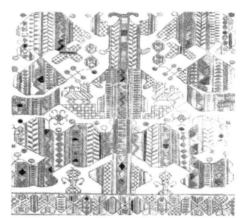

Kargopol

Onega

Arkhangelsk

153

So even in archaeological materials of the 11-12th century, among the pendants found in Staraya Ladoga, figures of skates with a duck head. V. M. Vasilenko believes that "in this image the bird and the horse mysteriously connected." Quite often, on the 11-12th century Smolensk skates, the hind leg of the skate looks like the head of a duck bird. Duck and goose pendants survive in the Slavic tradition until the 12th century and ridge pendants until the 13th century, after which they disappear, but in peasant embroidery the images of horses with horns, duck heads, bird tails, and horse-headed ducks survive to the end of the 19th century 20th century. On Tver's wedding towels, there are images of horses placed among the stars, which on their heads besides a mane are higher spreading horns, and in addition to a flourishing horse tail, there is one more - a bird.

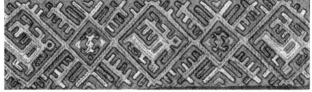

154

155

156

Tver embroidery

It is probably appropriate to recall here again the image of a bird-deer-horse found in the Altai Katandinsky mound at the turn of the 6-5th century AD, the sacred significance of which is clearly indicated by the fact that this figurine was carefully wrapped in a luxurious, embroidered with gold plaque coat, along with figures of horned horses. The fact that birds of the deer and horses of Tver towels belonged to at the end of the 19th and the beginning of the 20th century belong to the sacred sphere (to heaven and space) is evidenced not only by the stars surrounding them,

157

but also by the fact that a number of birds were often placed under the horses' feet. Studying the image of a horse-elk (deer-horse), G. G. Gromov, D.V. Deonik and V.I. Plyushchev, on the material of more than two hundred Arkhangelsk embroideries, came to the conclusion that there is a combination of images of a moose and a horse, and the moose motive prevails.

Kargopol

A similar situation is typical for Vologda embroidery and especially paired weaving. But, the further south, the fewer moose in Russian folk embroidery, and the more horses. In the North Russian folk tradition, even the end of the 19th and beginning of the 20th centuries, the images of duck, horse and moose are interchangeable. So stupid huts of the Russian North can be made both in the form of a

158

"Horse", and in the form - "Ducks", and in the Arkhangelsk region deer or elk horns crowning the roof of the house are not uncommon.

Ohlupnis

Thus, an equal sign is placed between these images at the semantic level, since the horse, the duck, and the moose horns (and therefore the moose), crowning the house, perform the same function. In the traditional decor of the Mezensky spinning wheels, which is extremely archaic both in color scheme and in the figurative system, upper registers are given, as a rule, to alternating rows of geese (swans) and deer (moose), and already below them are a number of horses that differ from deer only the lack of horns. Quite often, salt licks-ducks, buckets, brotins, having the form of a waterfowl, end with handles in the form of horse heads.

Buckets

Spinning Tops

Mezen ornament

The interchangeability of the educated horse, moose, goose-swan (duck) in folk embroidery was mentioned above. It is interesting that back in the 15-16 centuries in Russia, people were quite well aware that they had words from a horse and birds, as evidenced by the lines from "The Words of John Chrysostom about Christianity", where the author cannot say a word about Christian there will be a philosophy and an orator, and everyone will get an answer when his demand is for horses, birds, or something like that.

S. V. Zharnikova
1986

Possible origins of horse-goose and horse-deer images in indo-iranian (Aryan) mythology

The images of horse-goose and horse-deer known both in Vedic and Avestian traditions are most interesting and mysterious among the images of ancient Aryan mythology. At first sight everything appears rather simple and natural: in principle, the flight of a bird and the impetuous run of a horse or a deer can be easily combined in a single image. But the simplicity is deceptive and the above explanation provokes questions difficult to answer. Why does Vedic tradition in the majority of cases combine the image of a horse with the image of a goose or a swan? And why is the image of a horse so steadily connected with the image of a deer not only in Indo-Iranian but also in the general Indo-European tradition"? To elucidate the reasons for such associations, archaeological, mythical, poetical and ethnographical sources should be addressed.

In Indian mythology, theology and natural philosophy a goose is a well-known symbol of the Sun, the Light and the Sky. In Chandogya-Upanishad a goose, the incarnation of the Sun, is akin to fire, the Moon, lighting. **1** According to U.Papoport, the Khoresmian concept of the origin of the Un4erse presents "the initial divinity, comprising parts of the Universe, in the image of an aquatic bird".**2** Zarwan is the name of the d4inity uniting male and female elements, the sky, the earth, fire and water, light and darkness. In Sogdian texts of Buddhistic character Zarwan is just the name given to Brahma - the creator of the Un4erse in Vedic pantheon. Not infrequently in legends a goose is Brahma's embodiment, his usual attendant and "carrier" (vahana),**3** he researcher believes it quite plausible that the image of an aquatic bird reflects the idea of water as the initial element, personified in the Avestian pantheon by the Goddess whose

163

name is regarded to be concealedina triple epithet - Ardvi Sura Anahita".4

It may be recalled that Saraswati, the great Goddess of the Vediepock, was attended by a goose, the incarnation of the all-embracing sky.5 H.Kuzmina also notes that in Indo-Iranian mythology an aquatic bird was the incarnation and the attendant of Mother-Goddess, who was the related with water and usually represented in the form of the World's Tree with birds sitting on its branches, and that a pair of ducks was the symbol of matrimonial love in the folklore of all Indo-European nations. She also points out that according to Indo-Iranian tradition the woman or her substitute - the tree, is represented, as a rule, together with horses and birds, or with birds only, 7 but at the same time, in all Indo-iranian traditions a horse is frequently likened to a bird".8 Thus in Rigveda's hymn Ashwins are likened to eagles. "...Your magnificent flying horses - let these reddish birds carry you...", 9 and in Mahabharata Ashwins are praised as eagles — marvelous birds with wonderful wings. 10 Besides, it is the goose that is connected with the image of the horse; both Ashwins and Indra's horses are often likened to geese.11 According to archaeological data, the Iranian compositions presenting two riders or bound protomae horses with a woman between them date back to the time when the Iranian-speaking inhabitants first appeared on the Iranian Plateau, i.e. the turn of the 1st millennium B.C. 12 The representations of aquatic birds -ducks and geese - were quite significant in Indian and Scythian art as well. According to D.Raievsky these representations as a rule decorated artefacts of cult. In Scythian world the image of an aquatic bird was a fixed religious symbol; in investiture scenes representing the ceremony' of receiving the symbols of power it symbolized monarch's power as given by God.13 It was the image of an

164

aquatic bird that became the symbol of material world in Iranian and Scythian mythology. Why was it so, D.Raievsky's answer is because this creature of Earth's fauna can move in all three spheres - on land, in water and in the air. He writes: "It is noteworthy that in Atharvaveda there is an idea of the triple goose that is most likely connected with the interpretation of an aquatic bird as the symbol of three spheres of, the Universe".[14] This interpretation seems convincing. But still it does not answer the following question: why is the aquatic bird (goose, swan, duck) connected with the image of a horse in Indo-Iranian mythology (e.g. in one and the same Atharvavedas hymn the Sun is named the horse, the eagle and the swan as well)?[15] Another question is this: why is the image of a horse in Indo-Iranian mythology so closely connected with the image of a deer? Paradoxically all these questions can be answered by turning to the archaeological monuments of the European part of the USSR. It was in this region that the representations demonstrating the process of ancient sacralisation of the images of aquatic birds and the deer (or elk) in the mythological, ritual scenes of fertilization, birth and death appeared on the cliffs of Lake Onega and the White Sea at the turn of the Mesolithic and the Neolithic Age. Besides, it was here that the merger of two images (of the goose and the elk) took place. Examples can be found in the boats whose bows are shaped as a horned elk's head on a long goose neck, or a goose with antlers, or an elk leading a single line of geese, or an elk surrounded by geese (fig. 1, 2, 3)".[16] The connection of these images with anthropomorphic characters on the same Neolithic petroglyphes is extremely interesting. Here are some examples: an anthropomorphic figure of a woman in childbirth, whose foot is shaped like a goose; the unique representation of a man, the main character in the

165

composition of the socalled "Besovy sledki" ("Demon' imprints") found on the cliffs near the White Sea, with a horn at the back of his head, whose outsized foot's toe tourches the figure of a young hornless elk, and whose little toe points to a group of three aquatic birds (geese or ducks) (fig. II).

What animals are represented on the cliffs of Lake Onega, elks or reindeer? Solving this problem U.Sawateyev remarks that although these animals "differ greatly in appearance, size and mode of life, they are represented on the cliffs in similar stylistic manner", which results in the fact that "according to some characteristics, they can be identified as elks (the majority of cases)[17] and according to others as reindeer"[18] (italicised by the author.). U.Sawateyev singles out the anthropomorphic figure with the elk's head and antlers (the western group of the so-called "Besov nos" ("Demon's nose"), and staffs with inlaid elk heads. He then concludes that "in human ideology the image of the elk was of great importance".[19] The obvious merger of goose-swan and elk images, most characteristic of the White Sea region, gives rise to the following question: accepting D.Rayevsky's hypothesis of sacralisation of the aquatic bird as a whole, what are then the reasons for the sacralisation of the elk image in the White Sea and Lake Onega regions in the Neolithic times? To give at least a rough answer to this question we must know, first, which animal it is, and secondly, what the Palaeoclimatic situation in the 5th-3d millennium B.C. was like in the North of the European part of the USSR, where the petroglyphes representing geese, elks and deer were made at that time?

The elk, whose image is combined with the image of an aquatic bird (goose-swan-duck), and which is the analogy of the horse in Indo-Iranian tradition, is the largest kind of living deer and an ancient inhabitant of the European part of this country. On the territory of the USSR bone remains of these animals are found in the Upper-Palaeolithic and Neopalaeolithic settlements of ancient man, in the East European partly wooded steppes and forest areas, in the Urals and even in the Northern areas adjoining the Black Sea.20 According to K.Filonov, elks were never numerous in the south of Russia in Neolithic and Aeneolithic times,21 for they can hardly bear heat,22 Unlike southern regions, vast areas in the central and northern part of Eastern Europe is inhabited by elks. The Kola Peninsula, the coastline of the White, Sea and the mouth of the Pechora River are the northern boundary of their habitat.23 The type of the elk's teeth and the structure of its stomack indicate that the elk feeds not oh hard field and steppe grasses, but on leaves, sprouts and roots of trees, bushes and marsh plants. 24 The type of elk's food indicates that the animal is adapted to live in, a definite geographical environment, by no means of the southern type. L.Baskin writes: "The correlation of all the factors (including the paleography of fossil remains, the peculiarities of exterior, the motor system and digestive organs, the contemporary biotonic distribution and the type of feeding)", enables us to conclude that "the elk is a species adapted to taiga marshy forests and water meadows".25 Elks prefer pine (Pinus sylvestris) woods, with aspens (Populus tremula) and birch-trees (Betula), fir-groves (Ricea abies) bordering upon pine woods and small aspen forests, multitiered fir-groves near brooks, and pine forests with juniper undergrowth. 26 If we consider the climate and the landscape of the central and northern area of the USSR is European part in the last phase of the Mesolithic and Neolithic times (5th-3rd millennium B.C.), when Lake Onega and the White Sea petroglyphes were created (ivth-3d millennium B.C.), we shall find an extremely interesting situation. The radio-hydrocar-bonic tests made at the

V.Vernadsky Institute of Geochemistry and Analytic Chemistry of the USSR Academy'of Science, indicate that specimens of peat dating from 7.700 - 3.200 years ago (the middle Holocene), taken from the marshes of the Novgorod, Leningrad, Yaroslavl and Kalinin regions, "contain a high percentage of broad-leaved trees' pollen in the pollen-containing spectra... indicating the peaks in the oak, elm, lime, hazel and alder curves... The mid-Holocen clealy stands out as the Holocen climatic optimum".[27] The spreading of the broad-leaved specimens on these territories had started earlier: about 9780-7790 years ago.[28] Thus, the period between the beginning of the 6th and the end of the 2nd millennium B.C. the territories to the north of those we are interested in (the coastline zone of Lake Onega and the White Sea), were covered with broad-leaved and mixed forests of oak, lime, elm, alder, pine and birch trees. The climate was much warmer than today, the average summer temperatures were 4°C higher.[29] As far as the territories farther north are concerned, during the period of the Holocene optimum, which lasted almost 5.000 years, their climate differed considerably from what it is today. Thus, L.Berg in his work "Climate and Life" points out that in the 5th-ivth millennium B.C. oak-woods with lime, elm and hazel trees extended far into the north of the European part of the USSR. At the same time firtrees started expanding also; and in the 3d millennium B.C. ancient marshes covered up with pine woods and birch groves. L.Berg indicates that truncks and big stubs of pine-trees were found in the peat strata dated from the ivth-3rd millennium B.C. in the Korelian Isthmus and in Sweden, pointing to a warmer and softer climate at that time. L.Berg writes: "... in the northern Urals many travellers found the remains of big trees in the territories now having no forest vegetation. Thus, Kovalsky regestered the remains of a birch grove in the latitude of 66°40'N, which now is the zone of tundra".**30**

The archaeological discoveries of the last decades show that the north of the European part of this country was densely populated in the Mesolithic and Bronze epochs. Consequently, the conviction that existed in science for a long time about these territories being then uninhabited, is not true. Thus, near Medvezhyegorsk on the northern shore of Lake Onega more than 140 settlements and several burials dating from different times were found during iv-year-long archaeological excavations. They date from the Mesolithic up to the early Iron Age (the 10th millennium B.C.-the 5th century B.C.).**31** In resent years a number of Mesolithic settlements were discovered by S. Oshibkina in the basin of the Sukhona River.**32** So, the idea of the uninhabited north of the European part of the USSR in Mesolithic period is absolutely unsound. There were no objective reasons to prevent human beings from living in those areas. Vast forests, good climate, many rivers and lakes, the proximity of the sea, abundant fauna, long summer light day -all these factors should- have attracted people.

At the turn of the Mesolithic and Neolithic periods the inhabitants of the North created their pantheon, recorded in the petroglyphes of the White Sea and Lake Onega. The man, an aquatic bird and the elk or deer played major roles in it. The image of an aquatic bird discussed above was probably included not only because geese, ducks and swans could live in three spheres (land, water, air), but also because their arrival in spring and departure in autumn marked the warm and the cold season of the year. Besides, both geese and swans i bred (and continue to breed) and changed their feathers in the North. A lot of sources tell about numerous aquatic birds coming to the north of Russia

169

even at the close of the 19 century. Thus, the western part of the Novaya Zemlya Island's southern shore (71°-72°N) was known to be called "Goose Land" for abundance of geese. "Numerous aquatic birds-geese, all kinds of ducks and swans-come at the end of June to the Kolguyev Island (in the Barents Sea) from the south-west countries and stay till the middle of September. A group of ten hunters is said to shoot easily 3,5 and even 5 thousand geese and swans during the period of moulting (per month)". Up to 6.400 kg (400 puds) of feathers and down-and 12.000 kg (750 puds) of swan-skins were said to be brought back from the island even at the close of the 19th century.**33** Obviously these birds (during the period of moulting) were the main food for the ancient inhabitants of the shores of the White Sea, Lake Onega and other lakes and rivers of the north of Russia, and that factor played its role in the process of sacralisation of the goose, duck and swan.

It is also believed that the extreme importance of moose (and deer) for human life in this region played an important role in the sacralization of these animals, the second largest zoomorphic Neolithic petroglyphs in the region. The Mesolithic burial of the Oleni Island (the Deer Island) in Lake Onega contained one buried man and two women. His head gear was decorated with wooden rods bearing carved female-elk heads at the ends. Rods of this kind were also found on the Oleni Island in the Barents Sea and in Shighir peat-bog in the Northern Urals.**34** Among the petroglyphes of the White Sea and Lake Onega there are a number of remarkable compositions explaining why the elk was sacred to the ancient inhabitants of the region. Large elks (both males and females) with numerous small figures of human beings and animals around them are represented in the centre of a multifigure composition on the Zalaviruga cliff in the White Sea. The central figure with mighty antlers, resembling a ramified crown of a tree, overlaps long boats with small elk heads at their bows (fig.III).**35** Under one of the boats between the elk's feet there is a figure of a man with three-fingered hands hanging down and a crawling snake. This special composition and large size indicate the sacred image of an elk and a boat with people on board. Perhaps, these are ritual boats with the dead (?). It is no accident that up to the early Middle Ages the high-born people in Russia and in Scandinavia were buried in boats **36**. The Edda called a ship "the deer of the sea" or "the horse of the sea",**37** Moreover, up to the 15th century the Great Bear в constellation was known in Russia under the name of 1 "Elk", and in Polish the "North Star" is still named the "Elk Star"**38**.

Let us turn to the Vedic tradition now. It relates seven stars of the Great Bear constellation to "seven Rishis", the sons of Creator-God Brahma, the forefathers of Aryans, on whom the prosperity of the living people depended and whom their descendants joined after death. Moreover, there is a certain character named Rishya-Shringa in both ethical poems, who was a descendant of Kashyapa, one of the seven Rishis. But he was born by a female-elk, had antlers and was able to bring rain, which according to mythology, was related to the cult of ancestors. **39** All these facts enable us to suppose that the neolithic representations on the shores of the White Sea and Lake Onega point to an ancient mythological and ritual tradition, formed much earlier under which the elk is associated with seven stars of the Great Bear constellation and with the world of ancestors, the givers of fertility and happiness to the living. It is to the world of ancestors that the dead travel in boats decorated with elk heads (possibly representing sacrificial ritual anrmals).

171

But among the petroglyphes found in the north European part of the USSR there is one composition of particular importance for our study. It shows "skiers" following elks and somehow connected with themb **40** hey do not hold the elks by the tail, which is rather clearly seen in some petroglyphes. In the composition of the southern group of the so called "Besovy Sledki" the elk is represented with something like a horse collar on its neck. We are led to suppose that it is an elk harness that- is represented by the neolithic painters. Let us quote the conclusions made by modern investigators of elk's domestication. K.Chapsky writes: "Once humans managed to domesticate and reproduce a comparatively feeble reindeer, it would seem rather natural for them to try and domesticate the elk, this forest giant. In the roadless taiga, covered with thick snow, the elk seems an attractive draught animal able to run across snow without any road". Chapsky remarks that the experiment to breed young elks and treat them as harnessed animals was successful, because the elk is ecologically pliable and can survive reasonable bondage. Besides, young elks are easier to be pastured than calves because they follow a herdsman and do not leave him.**41** It was noted that "the process of domestication of a wild newly born elk was extremely easy. It started and ended with the first feeding on a milk-nipple. A young elk becomes attached for life to the man who feeds him".**42** An elk is a very productive meat-providing animal. In the first six months of its life it puts on weight at the rate of 700gr a day. It is highly fertile, too, for twins are born oftener than singles. Elks can be out at feed all the year round. Does are fast to become good milk is and their milk is good".**43**

Domesticated elks are peaceable animals good at any training. Experiments have .proved that "after two days of getting accustomed to the reins elks can run in the required direction and in ten days they can be harnessed. During the training and when harnessed elks show no intention to hurt or to bite the man training them which a rare case with horses is. In winter harnessed elks run at a speedy trot, never at a gallop, and not every horse can outpace a young elk"**44**.

E.Knorre succeeded in training elks as saddle and pack-animals. A saddle-elk can carry a pack-load weighting 80-120 kg and a sledge elk-up to 400 kg. These animals are irreplaceable in the road less taiga, in marshy forests and during flood season. But in summer elks can be used as saddle animals only at night, for they suffer greatly and can even die from heat.**46** That is why, perhaps, on the White Sea petroglyphes the people connected to elks with long strips (or reins), are "skiers". A question may arise: where did the people of the Neolithic Age first get young elks to make them harnessed animals? As a rule, young elks can be tamed during the first month of their life. Later on they can run as fast as adult animals and are difficult, to catch. As has been already mentioned, a female-elk usually gives birth to twins, and needs only one calf , to satisfy its motherly instinct.**47** Perhaps, it was this "extra baby" that was raised, domesticated and made the first saddle and pack animal in the Neolithic (or Mesolithic) times. It is difficult to say which species was the first to be tamed - the elk or deer.

Sledge and harnessed elks are known to be quite widely used in the north of Europe. Thus, up to the 15th century an elk was a saddle animal in the Swedish army. On the engraving from the 1555 book by O.Magnus, an elk is represented as a sledge animal carrying a sledge with people.**48** N.Kulagin writes that according to old legends elks were used as saddle animals in Sweden, and they ran so fast the police had to ban their use in oder to prevent criminals from escaping with the help of swift elks. The same author indicated that if elks were not ridden, and were not allowed to run, they died in two years. When used under saddle and harness they lived to be 35 years old. **49**

In the 18th century Swedish messengers used sledge elks. In the time of Peter I an edict was passed in the Baltic region banning "to appear in a town riding an elk".**50** In the Vologda province elks were known to be domestic and draught animals up to the middle of the 19th century.**51** In the middle and at the end of the 19th century domestic elks could be found in the Vladimir, Ryazan, Pskov and Moscow provinces. In the Ukranian province of Volyn a forester could cover a distance of 120 km riding a domestic elk. Domestic elks were used (in Siberia and in the Vyatka province at the beginning of the 20th century.**52** More examples of the kind can be given. Turning to the Neolithic petroglyphes we can suppose that with the change of climate and the increase of population in the southern steppe areas elks could not be used as saddle and harnessed animals any more, because the steppe soils and grasses did not suit their hooves and teeth. The steppe demanded a new saddle and harnessed animal. The elk (deer) was replaced by a horse. While taming the wild horse in the 5th-ivth centuries B.C. the people of the steppes and partially-wooded steppes used the methods of training developed in the process of taming the elk thousand of years before, and applied the harness rather like that invented by their ancestors for the elk and the deer.

Having been replaced by the horse as a harnessed animal, the elk was also replaced as a ritual animal. Thus, the horse assumed all the functions formely filled by the elk. The horse became a khtonic animal forming the link between ancestors and descendants. It also became the main sacral offering and was superposed, by the goose-swan. But quite a few Indo-European nations preserved the memory of the times when it was the elk, not the horse that was a

174

draught and sacred animal. N.Kuzmina notes that the syncrethic image of the horse-deer is characteristic of the mythical and poetic tradition of Ancient Greece and Iran at the close of the 2nd-at the beginning of the 1st millennium B.C.; in Edda the deer performs the role of a horse at the World's Tree; and there are Scythian horse chempfrons representing elks, "which means there was the custom to decorate a horse like an elk". S.Kiselev comes to the conclusion that ritual decoration of a horse as a deer corroborates the idea that "the deer was the first animal to be replaced by the horse"; that "all the facts prove that. In the Altai in Pazyric times the horse was a saddle-animal, and harnessed bulls" were used to carry heavy loads... "However, as far as the traditional sphere of the cult and funeral rites was concerned the memory of the original role of the deer surfaced. And despite the fact that the precious descendants of "celestial", "sweet-and-blood" Central Asian horses took part in the funeral procession they used to be turned into deer in accordance with the ancient traditions.55 Concerning the specific "Scythian" type of representing the deer, N.Chlenova points out that "Scythian deer antlers" are S-shaped (fig. Y; 5) 56 gut the representation of a typical Scythian deer from the Semibratny tumulus (in the Northern Caucasus), given by her, is, in fact, the representation of an elk judging by the distinctive outline of its hesd. Numerous Scythian and Sakan horse chempfrons, cheeck pieces and golden plates representing deer in the famous Peter's Siberian collection and other representations (fig. Y; 1, 2, 3, iv), when compared with a real elk or a reindeer, show undoubtly that quite a few cases represent elks. It is also of interest that the ancient idea of relations between the elk and the goose-swan remained alive in Scythian plastic art. The typical outline of the «Scythian deer antlers», marked by n.

Chlenova, indicates, in fact, a series of S-shaped geese heads (fig. Y; 7).

Now we can turn back to the White Sea and Lake Onega petroglyphes, reproduced in V.Ravdonick's works. They represent single lines of geese (swans) led by an elk, or an outline of an elk with a duck on its back.

The image of the horse-elk (or elk-horse) is inherent to the pit-grave culture, where tribes performed ritual burials of both - a horse and an elk. The adherent, of these traditions, Scythians and Savromatians, even in the times of the hut-grave culture (the 2nd century B.C.), continued to honour both animals, the horse and the deer (the elk). Scythians, the classic horse-breeders and riders, who certainly rode neither deer, nor elks, steadily interchanged the images of the horse and ethe deer (the elk).

The memory of the times, when both the horse and the elk were harnessed animals, and when the horse was a saddle-animal and the main animal offering, is preserved in one of the most significant Rigveda's hymns - "Sacrifice Horse Hymn". This truely archaic hymn performed r within the framework of the sacred Ashwamedha rite- the king's ritual white stallion offering-calls the stallion's feet the "elk's feet", and describes it as if flying in the sky like a bird, with his "winged" head and "golden antlers" "widely spread in the deserted space", with the goat, the horse's relative, leading the way. The hymn also describes the "heavenly horses, showing their power, close their ranks and form a single line like geese do...". (It is noteworthy that the composition on the Central Zalavruga cliff (on the White Sea) with two huge elks, female elks and boats is headed by the elks, going in a wedge like flying geese). 59 These strange things can only be explained by the fact that it is a retrospectively depicted elk, and not a horse, for it is the antlers resembling a bird's wings that can form "winged"

176

head. It is difficult to agree with Sayana, B.Kthe mediaeval Rigveda's commentator, who believed the gold antlers to be the horse's flying mane".**60**   In our opinion, they seem to be antlers still.

This set of ancient images comprising the man, the elk and the aquatic bird, all related to a certain archaic complex of mythical and poetic ideas, took shape at the turn of the Mesolithic and Neolithic times, probably earlier. In the course of time it underwent certain transformations whereby the elk was replaced by the horse which easily found its place in the ancient three-unit composition.

The above is proved graphically not only by the monuments of the Indo-Iranian mythology and fine art, but also by the Slav folk tradition which "characteristically preserved rudimentary archaic phenomena fixed neither in the classical Greco-Roman nor Vedic tradition"**61**.   In common Indo-European folklore the horse is sometimes likened to the elk, and a pair of ducks symbolizes matrimonial love. But the exact reproduction of the Indo-Iranian scheme can hardly be found elsewhere but in the Slav, specifically Eastern Slav area, namely in the North-Russian folk applied art. It is here that   the three-unit compositions with the woman or her equivalent, the tree, and not infrequently the woman transforming into the tree in the centre, also represent deer-elks, riders, horses and ducks (or "geese-swans"). And what is particularly important, the representations of horses with bird tails and swan bodies, or ducks with horse heads can also be found in the North-Russian tradition. Even the pre-Slav ornaments frequently represent numerous swans. On the bronze bracelet dating back to the 7th century B.C. of the Radolinek treasure bid found near Poznan they are represented on both sides of the woman with lifted hands **62**. In ancient Greek mythology the swans, Apollo's sacred birds, are associated with the

Northern edge of Oecumena - the place near the shores of distant cold Cronius Ocean, the land of Hyperboreans, where they took Apollo annually. B.Rybakov is probably right to think that "the sunny swans of the pre-Slav world were not a mere borrowing from a classical myth, but the nothern tribes' contribution to the process of joint, perhaps Indo-European, creation of mythology, related to the Sun and the Sun-God". Therefore, the image of a woman with her hands lifted to the sky and the ducks painted on her sides is a very archaic image, though preserved in North-Russian embroidery till the end of the 19th century **63**.

The image of the horse-swan or horse-duck in the art of Eastern Slavs is as profoundly archaic as that of the aquatic bird (duck, goose, and swan). Even among the archaeological finds in Staraya Ladoga dating from the 11th-12th centuries A.D., there are pendants made in the shape of small horses with duck heads. V.Vasilenko believes that "this image unites mysteriously the bird and the horse"**64**. Quite often the small horses on the horse-pendants found in the Smolensk province and dating from the 11th-12th centuries have their hind legs shaped like a duck's head. Pendants in the form of the duck or the goose were preserved in the Slav tradition up to the 12th century. Those shaped like a horse had survived till the 13th century and disappeared later. But in embroidery, especially in North-Russian embroidery, representations of horses with duck heads and bird tails or of ducks with horse heads survived till the turn of this century".**65**

As far as the image of the horse-elk (horse-deer) is concerned, G.Gromov, D.Deonic and V.Plushchev, having examined more than two hundred of the Arkhangelsk embroideries, drew the conclusion that it was the case of the contamination of the images of the elk and the horse with the theme of the elk prevailing **66**. But in the Vologda

178

embroideries the theme of the horse, which is also often contaminated with the theme of the elk, prevails. The farther south we move, the fewer elks we find in Russian folk embroidery, as compared to horses. However, in the North-Russian folk tradition of the end of the 19th century - the beginning of the 20th century the image of the duck, the horse and the elk are interchangeable. Thus, the logs on the top-edges of the North Russian peasant houses' roofs can be made in the shape of a horse head or in the shape of a duck head. In the Arkhangelsk province the roofs of the horses are not infrequently topped with antlers or deer horns. Semantically these images are identical because whether it is the duck, antlers or the elk that are placed at the top of the roofs, they perform one and the same function. The upper tiers of spinning-wheels used in the Mezen province are traditonally decorated with alternate rows of geese (swans) and deer (or elks), which is a very archaic ornament as far as its colours and images are concerned. A row of horses, which differ from elks only by the absens'e of horns, are placed underneath. Rather often salt-cellers made in the shape of a duck and the scroops made in the shape of an aquatic bird, have handles shaped as horse heads. The interchangeability of the images of the horse, the elk and the goose in folk embroidery has already been mentioned. It is of interest that even in the 15th and 16th centuries Russian peasants had a rather clear idea of the sacred meaning of the horse and bird representations, which follows from "John the Golden Mouthed's Words on Christianity". The author of this sermon is indignant with those who are unable to say a word on Christianity, who do not know the number of prophets, but become philosophers and speakers when asked about horses, birds or the like **67**.

The traditon to represent elks and aquatic birds in ritual scenes was born back in the Neolithic Age, as the -

179

petroglyphes of the White Sea and the Onega Lake show. It survived up to the turn of this century in North-Russian peasant embroideries. Some embroidery compositions are extremely difficult to explain without reference to the Indo-Iranian mythology. At the same time the numerous mysteries of Rigveda's and Avesta's hymns can be unravelled if we turn to the rich source of Russian folk art. The image of the horse-goose and horse-deer surviving both in Rigveda's mythical and poetic images and in North Russian folk representative tradition is a case in point.

In conclusion it should be noted that our hypothesis, according to which the elk was the first and the horse was the second to be saddled and made the main animal offering of Indo-Iranian mythology and rituals is corroborated by modern data of comparative Indo-European linguistics **68**.

Notes

1. Чхандогья Упанйщада. М. 1965. 4. p.198.
2. Рапопорт Ю. А. Космогонический сюжет на хорезмийских сосудах. Средняя Азия в древности и средневековье. М. 1977. p.67.
3. Рапопорт Ю. А. Космогонический сюжет на хорезмийских сосудах. p. 68.
4. Рапопорт Ю. А. Космогонический сюжет на хорезмийских сосудах.p.68.
5. Рапопорт Ю. А. Космогонический сюжет на хорезмийских сосудах. p.61. 6.Кузьмина Е.Е. О двух перстнях Амударьинского клада с изображением цариц. Сов.археология. 1979, № 1. p.44.
7. Кузьмина Е. Е. Конь в религии и искусстве саков и скифов. Скифы и.сарматы. Киев. 1977. p.103.
8. Кузьмина Е. Е. Конь в религии и искусстве саков и скифов. p.100.
9. Ригведа. I. 118. Москва. 1972. p.166.
10. Махабхарата. Адипарва. Кн. 1. М-Л., 1950. p.46/

11. Рапопорт Ю. А. Космогонический сюжет на хорезмийских сосудах. p.61. 12.Кузьмина Е.Е. Конь в религии и искусстве саков и скифов. p.103.

13. Раевский Д. С. Очерки идеологии скифо-сакских племен. М. 1977. p.59, 60.

14. Раевский Д. С. Очерки идеологии скифо-сакских племен. p.63.

15. Atharva-Veda Samhita, tr. Whitney W. D. Delhi. 1962. 13. 2.

16. Равдоникас В. И. Наскальные изображения Онежского озера. М-Л. 1936. табл. 6/3. 16/145. 33/13, 15. 34/8, 9, 19, 20. Равдоникас В. И. Наскальные изображения Белого моря. М.Л. 1938. табл. 1, 2, 11, 22.

17. Савватеев Ю. А. Онежские петроглифы и тема зверя в них. Звери в камне. Новосибирск, 1980. p.144.

18. Савватеев Ю. А. Онежские петроглифы и тема зверя в них. p.145.

19. Савватеев Ю. А. Онежские петроглифы и тема зверя в них. p.148.

20. Филонов К. П. Лось. М. 1983. p.23.

21. Филонов К. П. Лось. p.23.

22. Чапский К. К. Преооразование животного мира СССР. М. I . 1957. p.296.

23. Филонов К. П. Лось. p.25.

24. Баскин Л. М. Лось. Животный мир южной тайги. М. 1984. p.49.

25. Баскин Л. М. Лось. p.53.

26. Баскин Л. М. Лось. p.48.

27. Палеогеография и хронология верхнего плейстоцена и голоцена по данным радиоуглеродного метода. К VII конгрессу. М. 1965. p.77.

28. Палеогеография и хронология верхнего плейстоцена и голоцена по данным радиоуглеродного метода. p.130. 29. Палеогеография и хронология верхнего плейстоцена и голоцена по данным радиоуглеродного метода. p.119.

30. Берг Л. С. Климат и жизнь. М.,1947. p. 98, 99.

31. Савватеев Ю. А. Залавруга. Л., 1977. p.299-300.

32. Ошибкина С. В. Мезолит бассейна Сухоны и Восточного Прионежья. М. 1983.

33. Энциклопедический словарь Брокгауза и Ефрона. СПб. 1893. т. IX. p.665, 666, 934, 923.

34. Гурина Н. Н. Оленеостровский могильник. МИД. 1956. № 47.

35. Равдоникас В. И. Наскальные изображения Белого моря. Табл. 2, 11.

36. Ковалевский А. П. Книга Ахмеда ибн Фадлана о его путешествии на Волгу в 921-922 гг. Харьков. 1956. р. 144, 145.

37. Стеблин-Каменский М. И. Древнескандинавская литература. М. 1979. р.39.

38. Рыбаков Б. А. Новые данные о культе небесного оленя. Восточная Европа в эпоху камня и бронзы. М. 1976. р.58.

39. Махабхарата. Удьйогапарва. Л. 1976. р.486. Dowson J. A. Classical Dictionary of Hindu Mythology and Religion. Geography, History and Literature. London. 1967. p.268.

40. Равдоникас В. И. наскальные изображения Белого моря. табл. 5 /16,17. 12 /169, 171. 29/261, 262. 32/61, 62. 33/61,62.

41. Чапский К. К. Преооразование животного мира СССР. р.95.

42. Жизнь животных. v.6. р.477.

43 Жизнь животных. v.6. р.477.

44. Чапский К. К. Преооразование животного мира СССР. р.295-296.

45. Кнорре Е. П. История и итоги проведенных опытов по одомашниванию лося. Одомашнивание лося. М. 1973.

46. Жизнь животных. v.6. р. 477.

47. Баскин Л. М. Лось. р.53.

48. Дмитриев Ю. Д. Человек и животные. М. 1976. р.119, 236.

49. Кулагин Н. М. Лоси СССР. Л. 1932. р.112,129.

50. Дмитриев Ю. Д. Человек и животные. р.119.

51. Описание Архангельской губернии. Статистические труды И. Ф. Штукенберга. СПб. 1857. с.12.

52. Кулагин Н. М. Лоси СССР. р.112,114.

53. Кузьмина Е. Е. Распространение коневодства и культа коня у иноязычных племен Средней Азии и других народов Старого Света. Средняя Азия в древности и средневековье. М. 1977. р.29.

54. Кузьмина Е. Е. Конь в религии и искусстве саков и скифов. р.105. Граков Б. Н. Скифы. М. 1971. табл. XVIII.

55. Киселев С. В. Древняя история Южной Сибири. МИА. М-Л. 1949. р.20.

56. Членова Н. Л. Иранские прототипы "скифских оленей". КСИА. № 78. Памятники железного века. М. 1984. р.4.

57. Кузьмина Е. Е. Конь в религии и искусстве саков и скифов. р.105. Смирнов К. Ф. Савроматы. М. 1964. р.182-188, 236.

58. The Hymns of Rigveda. tr. Griffith R.T.H. Delhi. 1986.

59. Равдоникас Б. И. Наскальные изображения Белого моря. табл. 2 /172-190. 60.The Hymns of Rigveda. p.109.

61. Белецкая Н. Н. Языческая символика славянских архаических ритуалов. М. 1978. p.11.

62. Рыбаков Б. А. Язычество древних славян. М. 1981. p.341-342.

63. Рыбаков Б. А. Язычество древних славян. p.342, 344.

64. Василенко В. М. Русское прикладное искусство. I в. до н.э. - ХШ в. н.э. М. 1977. p.192.

65. Рыбаков Б. А. Язычество древних славян. p.495, 505, 521.

66. Громов Г. Г., Деопик Д. В., Плющев В. И. Применение методов количественного анализа орнаментальных образов русской народной вышивки. Вестник МГУ. 1971. № 4. p.90, 96.

67. Гальковский Н. Борьба христианства с остатками язычества в Древней Руси. v.II. М. 1913. p.252.

68. V. I. Abayev thinks that the word "saka" from the vocabulary of Central Asian Scythians to be related to the word "sag" in the Ossetian language, saka in Iranian; saha in Persian, sokhatyi in Russian. All these words have one and the same meaning - "ma-le-deer" (Абаев В. И. Историко-этимологический словарь осетинского языка. Л. 1978. v.3. p.11-l6), and in-Russian it means "the elk". N. Andreyev in his "The Early European Proto-Language" (Андреев Н. Ранний индоевропейский праязык. Л. 1986) points out that the word "sokti" in the Baltic languages, Lithuanian in particular, means "a horse" and corresponds to the words discussed above. L. Gertzenberg believes that the Indo-European proto-language of the most archaic times, coinciding with the period of domestication of Eucids, contained a pre-form that can be reconstructed not into ekuo, but into s-ekua (Герценберг Л. Г. Гамкрелидзе Т. В., Иванов В. В. Индоевропейские языки и индоевропейцы. "Советская этнография". 1988. № l). On the strength of these linguistic data it may be supposed that at the early stage of the Indo-European community, which included Indo-Iranians "elk" and "horse" merged to form one and the same image. Historically the elk was primary and its representations in Scythian art of the 1st millennium B.C. were gradually replaced with the image of the "deer" which became the totem animal in the Scythian-Sakian tradition (Абаев В. И. Осетинский язык и фольклор. М-Л. 1949. v.1), and with the image of "the horse".

Fig.1.
     1. Petroglyph showing an elk and a ran.
     2. Petroglyph showing an elk and geese.
     3 .   Petroglyph. Elks and geese.

184

Fig.2. "Besovy 'sledki" petroglyphs from the White Sea coast.
The Northern Group.

Fig. 3. Petroglyphs from the White Sea Coast. The central part of the Zalavruga rock.

186

Fig. 4.
    1. Ritual mask from the First Pazyryk mound. Altai.
    2. Representation of an elk. Altai.

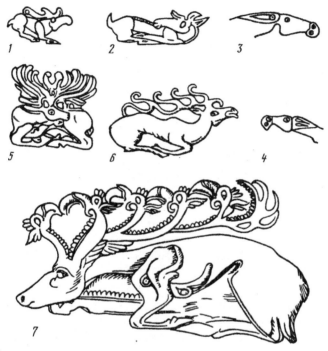

Fig. 5.

　　1-2. Representation of an elk in Scythian-Siberian art.

　　3-4. Representation of horses' heads in the animal style of Eurasia.

　　5. Scythian deer. The Northern Caucasus.

　　6. Elk. Southern Siberia.

　　7. Scythian gold plate of a gorythos. The Ukraine.

S. V. Zharnikova
International Association for the study of the cultures of Central Asia.
1989.

Non-black earth granary of Russia?

At the beginning of this century, the United States General Directorate of Land Management and Agriculture commissioned a team of experts to conduct an unbiased assessment of the world's agricultural land. What was the general surprise when the experts called the wet-weather Northwest of Russia, now called the Non-Chernozem Territory or even a zone of risky farming, the lands of the future!

I first learned about this fact from the lips of a well-known ethnographer, candidate of historical sciences SVETLANA VASILIEVNA ZHARNIKOVA, and was also pretty surprised. Our propaganda represented the North-West (especially the pre-revolutionary) as inferior, defective, impoverished. Let us recall the well-known Leninist assessment: "To the East and north of Vologda there is half-savagery, savagery, and real patriarchalism ...". Then, on the basis of what factors were they called the lands of the future?

- First of all, says Svetlana Vasilievna, this is an abundance of indirect solar radiation. The second is the absence of droughts and the temperature regime sufficient for the growth of grain and vegetables. The third, surprisingly, is the high soil fertility.

- Why are these possibilities still not confirmed practically?

- This is not true. Let's turn to the story. Here is what Academician L. S. Berg wrote in 1947, a scientist whom no one would dispute: "The yield of bread in the taiga subzone (as well as in the mixed forest subzone) is much higher than in the steppes." And then he gives the figures of average grain crops from 1901 to 1910: in the St. Petersburg,

Novgorod, Vyatka, Perm provinces - from one and the Samara, Saratov and Oblast Don Cossacks - from the other side. The excess of average yields of non-chernozemic lands in comparison with chernozems is as follows: oats - 51 percent, barley - 38 percent, spring wheat - 33 percent and winter - 42 percent.

In the middle of the nineteenth century, the famous statistician Ivan Fedorovich Shtukenberg noted that the average rye yield in the Mezen district was fifteen, twenty, in the Kola it was nine, in Kholmogorsky it was at least seven, eight, and the grade " Vase "gave himself eighty!

- If we take into account that today on average two centners of seeds are sown per hectare, then a fantastic harvest is obtained. Three hundred and sixty centners per hectare!

- And this is a recorded historical fact. At the beginning of the century, at the Murmansk Experimental Station, in permafrost conditions, they received grain crops of 26.5 centners per hectare.

And in the Vologda region, in the most remote eastern region - Nikolsky - they cultivated tomatoes, cucumbers, spinach, beans, asparagus in the open ground, and melons and watermelons in greenhouses.

I will refer to one more authority. Report of the professor of the Vologda Dairy Institute D.I. Delarova in 1928 claims that the productivity of northern arable land is the highest in the USSR. "And there is nothing surprising in this," says Delarov, "because the ultraviolet rays in the north at 68 degrees north latitude (this is Naryan-Mar) are twice as many as at 47-54 degrees. In July-August, on the White Sea, each square meter of area receives more sunlight than at the equator in the Indian Ocean. "

In addition, according to Academician Berg, such fertile soils as loess-like loams are almost equivalent to loess soils in Ukraine. And they reach the 64th degree of northern latitude. In the Pechora region, the thickness of these loesslike loams reaches 13 meters. But in our Vologda region, in the region of Gryazovets and Vologda, their thickness is up to 3-4 meters.

- I recall one more legend, which had been stubbornly propagated earlier, that, they say, there was no dairy cattle breeding in the North, and the peasant kept dung cows in order to only maintain the meager fertility of his tithes.

- Of course, this is an artificially created legend. Remember the famous Vologda oil. Indeed, at the beginning of the last century, the Vologda region had no equal in the production of oil, which was sold throughout Europe. Butter cooperation in the Vologda region flourished. It is clear that a dung cow with an annual yield of 900 kilograms could not have ensured this triumph. If you look closely, today's dairy herd of Europe has its roots in our Northwest. The well-known Kholmogorsk breed of cattle was not brought to us, but merchants of pedigree cattle were brought from us to Holland, England.

According to Professor Voeikov, the middle-aged peasant on the Pechora River had 3-4 horses, 15-20 cows, 50-60 sheep at the beginning of this century. He earned from the production and sale of fur from 400 to 2000 rubles for the winter; this is provided that the cow cost 12 rubles.

- Yes, judging by our northern villages, even the ruined ones, we can say that the pre-revolutionary peasant was not in poverty.

- I will refer again to eyewitnesses. Here are the travel notes of Bova, students from St. Petersburg, published in the journal Izvestia of the Arkhangelsk Society for the Study of the Russian North for 1912: "In Kadnikovo (a tiny town forty kilometers from Vologda) there are wooden sidewalks, houses are tall, spacious, inhabited only on the top floor. Below - cellars, stalls, cribs. The stoves in the houses are divorced such that they occupy ¾ rooms, the beds on them are spacious to serve as a refuge for the whole family in winter.

On Trinity and Spirits day, peasant girls and boys, having put on all the festive routine, take a walk in the public city garden, where there are weddings. Girls are in soft blue and pink silk. Chest, ears, hands shone with gold; the guys were also a match: with massive golden chains on vests, in all black and shiny galoshes. "

- So why in our desolation turned out to be our village today!

- This is a topic for another discussion. One can only say one thing: the whole history of our peasantry is a history of failed reforms. I wanted to especially emphasize this trend. In 1992, the USSR national report was written for the International Conference on Environmental Protection, which was held in July 1993 in Rio de Janeiro. There were given materials on climate change in the European North and the north of Siberia. It is supposed to increase the average annual temperature by 2-3 degrees. This trend is stable and suggests the introduction of previously unused lands in the North into agricultural circulation. At the same time, this process will be accompanied by the loss of land, which until recently was considered the basis of agricultural production.

- That is, the lands of the North-West, that is the Non-Black Earth Region, the zone of risky agriculture should become the breadbasket of Russia, and maybe the world breadbasket?

- Yes, the Russian North should and will feed Russia. And this must be understood not only by statesmen, but also by the peasants themselves. Stop talking, stop drinking vodka. You need to seriously engage in business.

Here is what a famous scientist, an expert of the Main Directorate for Land Management and Agriculture in the United States O. Kryshtafovich said at the beginning of the century:

"There are all signs that some of the lands of the future are currently moving into the category of lands of the near future and can be put into circulation tomorrow, the day after tomorrow. The first line, apparently, is the near North - the Arkhangelsk and Vologda provinces. If they are really put into circulation tomorrow, then we have it - only today, to organize this business, and moreover, in the right way. "

And with what words he ends this article: "Ah, if that time and the energy that wasted in Russia for fruitless disputes were dedicated to the matter, how much would have been done!"

Anatoly Ekhalov, Svetlana Zharnikova.
«Русский Север-Пятница». 20.01.1995.

Reconstruction of a possible climate change in the Indo-European ancestral home

Climatologists believe that by reconstructing the conditions of the past, paleoclimatology can pick up analogues to those situations that are likely to occur in the future under new thermal conditions. A directed increase in the global average temperature will lead first to the conditions of the Holocene optimum, then to the optimum of the last (Mikulinsky) interglacial period, and in the not very distant prospect - to the climate that was in the Neogene. Cenozoic (subtropical in the Far North) climates are already included in the range of possible climate scenarios of the 21st century.

Experts believe that the average global temperature will increase by 4.5 degrees. And since at the poles, due to the climate, the temperature always changes more sharply than at the equator, then every degree of global warming will increase the temperature in the Subpolar Region by 4 degrees at once (only 18 degrees). If we assume that warming will continue at the same pace, then the temperature in these latitudes will rise after another 100-200 years by another 6-10 degrees.

According to the forecasts of the Rio de Janeiro 1992 conference, due to global climate warming, wet subtropics can form in Central Asia and Xinjiang by 2025, and dry subtropics can be found throughout the Caucasus and Crimea. Kazakhstan, southern Russia, southern Ukraine and Moldova will be covered by a semi-desert and a desert. Steppes penetrate to Belarus and Vyatka, deciduous forests to the White Sea and Central Siberia, the taiga will reach Taimyr and Tiksi.

In the United States, it was believed that by 2100 a tropical Panamanian climate would arise in the south of the country, subtropics would reach Washington, the steppes would spread to central Canada and the Hudson Bay, broad-leaved forests to the Arctic Ocean, the taiga would remain in Alaska, the Rockies and the polar islands, and the tundra in the south of Greenland and Baffin land. Accordingly, the indicated climatic conditions were earlier.

L. S. Berg noted that during the period of warming (xerotherm), landscape zones were shifted to the north, and the forest-steppe reached the shores of the Gulf of Finland. He emphasizes that dead trees in the mountains above the present border of trees are not uncommon. The good preservation of these residues indicates that climate change has occurred recently, in the historical era. In the Khibiny Mountains, old, long-dead pine trunks, striking in their large size and shape, come across. Many travelers found the remnants of the forest in the north of the Urals, where there is now bare tundra (up to 66 ° N).

Shevelenko A.Ya. pointed out that during the warming in Europe in the 6th century AD-13th century AD groundwater everywhere went deeper into the ground, the level of lakes fell, the area of ponds decreased, swamps dried up, and the space under forests in the North and under meadows in the South increased.

In the 14-16 century, grapes grew in the Harz, Thuringia and Berlin, and then the culture moved south, but in the 20th century, due to warming, stepped to the North. Since 2001, industrial winemaking began in Denmark and southern Sweden.

At the Holocene optimum (4 kb), July temperatures were higher than at present by 4-5 degrees (5 degrees in Central Siberia), but such warming was characteristic only of the northern part of Eurasia, located to the north from 55-

60 N, where the border of the forest shifted north by 300 km. from the present. Memories of this have been preserved in historical monuments. Before the cold snap, the year in the Avesta was in the North - ten months of warm summers and two months of not cold winters.

In xerothermic times, the level of Lake Ilmen was 2-3 meters lower than in the 19th century. The south of Ukraine (Kherson, Odessa) then represented a semi-desert similar to Kalmykia. Note that chernozem can form and exist only in the conditions of a dry climate of the steppes; when wetted; it degrades, turning into loamy soil. Dokuchaev determined the time of the beginning of the formation of black soil in the Russian steppes 4-7 thousand years ago. In the boreal period (7-5 thousand BC) to the north of 60 ° N it was 5 degrees warmer than in the 20th century, colder in the south. Then in the Sahara, precipitation was 400 mm. per year (now 6 mm. per year).

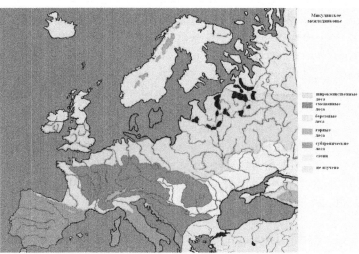

Vegetation of the Mikulin interglacial

During the Mikulinsky interglacial period (130-70 thousand years ago), winter temperatures in the North were higher, 8-13 degrees, and summer temperatures 7-9 degrees relative to the present.

At the end of the Cenozoic, Kazakhstan, Central Asia, southern Russia and Ukraine had a tropical climate. Subtropics extended to the Gulf of Finland, Kostroma, the Urals, Baikal and Primorye. Forests with a plane tree and oak reached Taimyr and Chukotka. And only there was the tundra.

Such warming had a positive effect on vegetation. Suffice it to say that an average warming of 1 degree corresponds to an increase in the growing season by two weeks. Thus, an average warming of 5.4 degrees would lead to an increase in the growing season by almost three months (76 days), by 9 degrees for four months (126 days), by 13 degrees for six months (182 days), by 18 degrees for eight months (252 days). The climate of the Cenozoic is eternal spring and summer.

Academician Pryanishnikov wrote that the disadvantage of the North is the low fertility of the local soils, but this deficiency can be eliminated by the use of fertilizers, yields of 33 centners per tithing are easily achievable and affordable under this condition. Based on this, Academician Pryanishnikov recommended expanding agriculture in the north.

As for soils, then, as you know, loess is the main fertile soil in China, where, with enough heat and moisture, it was able to feed a billion people. But loesses are also common in Russia, not only in Ukraine or the Don. L.S.Berg wrote that integumentary loess-like loams of the

North are connected by completely insensitive transitions with typical South Russian and Ukrainian loess. Loesslike loams are known for many places of the North: Kostroma, Ustyuzhna, Solikamsk territories, for the watershed of Vychegda and Kama. In the Onega basin, they go up to 63 degrees N, the thickness of these loams is up to 15 meters. In the Vologda region, the thickness of loesslike loams is 2-3, rarely 5 meters. They are present in the Gryazovets district. In the Northern Dvina basin, loesslike loams go north to 62 ° N. The thickness of the cover loam and sandy loam in the Bolshezemelskaya tundra is small and ranges from tens of centimeters to 4-5 m. On average, it is 1.5-1.8 m. They were also found in the Pechora basin. L.S. Berg considered them the most fertile in his zone. They could arise only in one of the postglacial dry and relatively warm eras, when steppe plants existed in the North. The presence of such soils probably should have stimulated the development of agriculture in warmer climatic conditions.

Note that in the north under 68 ° N the daily maximum of solar insolation in July and August is greater than in the Indian Ocean fewer than 4 ° N. At the same time, at the latitude of St. Petersburg and Vologda - 60 ° N, the atmosphere is more permeable to ultraviolet radiation than in Davos in Switzerland, despite the lower altitude (experiments 1928). At the beginning of the 20th century, D.V. Fedorov noted that summer in the Far North is characterized by a rather high temperature. On Pechora, it reaches 36 grams in the shade, 53 gr. in the sun during the day and 18 gr. at night, but from May 15 to July 15, there is no night, the sun shines daily for 18-20 hours and therefore not only rye, barley and oats, but also spring wheat and corn ripen here. It should be noted that by 1901 the maximum temperature in July in Vologda was 29 degrees, and by 2001 it had risen to 34 degrees. In the 1980s and 90s, there were 14 warmest years since 1860.

Rye, peas, mustard, beans, vetch, flax, hemp, lupine, poppy, chickpea, oats, wheat, barley, raspberry, lentil, rank, being "plants of long daylight hours", accelerate their development as they move from south to north. During the growing season, they require a large amount of ultraviolet rays, moisture in the soil, the absence of overheating from direct sunlight and a large amount of diffused light, for their earring they need prolonged sunlight (unlike "plants of short daylight hours" - millet, beans, corn, sorghum, cotton). In the spring, long-daylight plants need at least 14-16 hours of illumination for germination, and at least 16-18 hours for growth and development. Based on this, today it is possible to determine the optimal zone for them at latitudes not lower than 52-58 ° N. It is appropriate to recall here that at 7-3 kb the climate of Eastern Europe was much warmer than modern, and spring came 30 to 40 days earlier. With such a shift, the optimal range parameters of these plants were above 58-64 ° N.

Crops increase sharply in the North in warm and dry years; so in a dry 1921 in the Novgorod region, rye productivity increased 2 times (to "SAM" 10). In 1917-22, the Totem district fed bread to the Vologda, Kostroma provinces, partly Moscow and St. Petersburg. In 1922, the harvest in the Vologda province on the lands burned from the bushes was "SAM" 40, 60, 75.

When in 1770-1800, due to climate deterioration in Russia, crops fell by 25%, in the North they fell from "SAM" 10 to "SAM" 3 in 1801. The compensation for the death of northern agriculture was the plowing of the steppes of New Russia. An even greater drop in agriculture was in the 14th century.

At the beginning of the 20th century, L.S. Berg noted that paradoxically at first glance, the yield of bread in the non-chernozem zone is much higher than in the steppes. According to him, the vegetation of the same spring varieties of barley, oats and wheat in Kherson province was 123 days, and in Arkhangelsk 98 (barley, oats) and 88 (wheat).

In the 18th century, the North had the highest yield of rye and oats in Russia. Earlier, in the 17th century, the highest yields of barley and wheat were noted.

Pisarev pointed out that in the taiga of Irkutsk province in the 19th and early 20th centuries, the yield of spring wheat on average exceeded the yield on Akmola chernozems (in Tselinograd) by 72%.

In 1901-10, the average grain yield in the St. Petersburg, Novgorod, Vologda, Vyatka and Perm provinces was higher than in the Samara, Saratov provinces and the Don Army Region: oats by 51%, barley by 69%, spring wheat by 33%, winter wheat by 42%.

According to official statistics, the yields on Pechora were 50% higher than in the rest of Russia (with Poland, Finland, and naturally Ukraine).

In 1913, in the Vologda province, barley harvest was more than Kaluga, Ryazan, Penza, Nizhny Novgorod, Kazan provinces; rye crop more than in Yaroslavl, Smolensk, Vitebsk provinces; oats are higher than Vileno, Nizhny Novgorod, Penza provinces.

According to the findings of D.I. Delarov (1926), the yield of northern arable land and sowing is the highest in the USSR. However, as early as the middle of the 19th century, according to the research of I.F. Stukenberg, the yield in the North was significantly higher than in the central and southern regions.

In the northern regions, the crop to the north is increasing. According to long-term observations (1938-78) in the Kirov region, wheat yield was (centner / ha) in the north - 25.6, in the center - 22.3, in the south of the region - 21.7.

Researchers at the beginning of the 20th century noted that, despite wildly primitive agriculture, the absence of even the traditional Russian three-field, the use of only such tools as a wooden harrow, plow and roe deer, with the conviction of the peasants that sowing grain cleaned from litter is a sin, the crop was harvested on Pechora barley according to "SAM" 12-15, rye "SAM" 18-20.

Many farms in the North did not even have a three-field; barley was sown on the same field for 4-5 years, alternating with rye or black steam. Processing was carried out with wooden plow and harrow, saban and roe deer. The work was carried out without fertilizers and with the hope "at random and no matter how," sowing in May, and the harvest in August. At the same time, the barley crop "SAM" 15-23 (Velsk, Totma, Pechora), rye "SAM" 15-26 (with fertilizer, the yield increased by 50-150%). And this in climatic conditions is incomparably more severe, at average summer temperatures lower by 4-5 degrees compared to the Holocene optimum.

The climate of the Arkhangelsk province in the 19th century was not warm, according to I.F. Stukenberg on Mezen was snowing for 9 months. In 1836 a permanent snow cover was established on Onega on August 6, on Mezen on August 8, on Pechora the ice did not melt at all. Although it should be noted that according to the description of the beginning of the 19th century, peaches ripened in Arkhangelsk.

It is known that in Pechora at the beginning of the 20th century, udorsky rye yielded yields of 60 centner / ha, barley 44 centner / ha. In Ust-Tsilma, in the frosts, they received a total grain harvest of "SAM" 10-12, and in normal years, "SAM" 20-25. On Pechora, in Kozhva, barley produced 37 centner / ha (1893-1903), in Shchelya-Yura 32 centner / ha (1909), in Galov 36 centner / ha (1909), in the Bolshezemelskaya tundra 51 centner / ha (1909), in Kua, rye yields reached 36 centners per hectare (1909), in Ussa 43 centners per hectare (1858), all cereals in the Middle Pechora reached from 61.1 centner / ha (1840) to 114.7 centner / ha (1900).

Rye on Udora

The productivity on Pechora, in Ust-Tsilma in 1860-1934 remained more and less constant, exceeding the Russian average by 4-5 times.

Rye received (centners / ha) 47 in 1900, 23 in 1910, 32 in 1914, 36 in 1930, 32 in 1932, 54 in 1934.

202

Barley received (centners / ha) 68 in 1908, 39 in 1909, 41 in 1910, 35 in 1914, 67 in 1930, 29 in 1932, 44 in 1934.

In 1932, the most barren in 57 years, an average of 18 centners / ha of grain was harvested in these places. But at the same time, in the Veshensky district of the Don, wheat crop of more than 10 centners / ha in 1900-32 was received only in 1909.

On average, in the years 1860-1900, 40 centners / ha were harvested, and in 1900-30 64 centners / ha, which was facilitated by the activities of the agronomic station. At the same time, in 1911, for example, in Pechora, potatoes were obtained at 588 centners / ha.

According to the official data of the Komiselkhozoblupravleniye for 1927, the average yield on Vychegda and Sysol was: rye - 30 centners / ha, barley - 22 centners / ha, potatoes - 19 centners / ha, potatoes - 225 centners / ha, turnip - 750 centners / ha, flax fiber - 9 centners / ha. Higher and lower yields on Pechora, Udor and Vychegda: rye from 18 to 60 centners / ha, barley from 14 to 67 centners / ha, oats 24-25 centners / ha.

In the Mezen district of the Arkhangelsk province, rye yields reached 42 centners / ha (1845), wheat 35 centners / ha (1937), barley 75 centners / ha (1910), oats 35 centners / ha (1937), all grain 75 centners / ha (1857).

In the Murmansk region, in Pyaozero, barley yields were 34 centners / ha (1836), and in the Khibiny, after 100 years, 35 centners / ha (1936).

Sometimes she was in the Far North. The harvest in Kolyma is constituent: in Srednekolymsk "SAM" 2.5, sometimes 30-40 (in 1844-1911 the grains did not ripen once in 1848), in Rodchevo "SAM" 4.4-5, in Verkhnekolymsk "SAM" 9, in the Seymach "SAM" 8, sometimes "SAM" 40-50. Barley, oats, and wheat grew in

Seymach, and barley and winter rye grew in Rodchevo, Verkhnekolymsk, Indigirka, and Alazey.

In the Vologda Oblast, in the Nikolsk Uyezd in the early 20th century, on an open ground were grown: tomatoes, cucumbers, spinach, beans, asparagus, onions, and in hotbeds melons and watermelons. There, in 1915, the Ivan rye crop was obtained in SAM 82. Thus, with the improvement of the climate and warming, the prospects for agriculture in these territories seem extremely favorable. The grain harvest in the dried marshes in Vyatka is 4-5 times higher than average.

P. N. Tretyakov wrote that in the first or third year, in the forests of the North, in the first-third year, the crop reaches "SAM" 150. However, in the Olonets province in 1858, an even larger rye-shrub crop was obtained - "SAM" 599 (1028 centner / ha) (maximum biological productivity of rye - 440 tons / ha).

In Russia until the 19th century, "ovid" was sown, a special type of cereal; in the 20th century it was not available. According to the archives of the Vladimir region, the group of names of field crops united by linguists includes the following: rye, oats, barley (or zhito, zhitarn), wheat, egg (or mowing, rainy rye). The assumption that this spring rye does not correspond to the description of the cereal - it withstood all droughts, had a fine grain, white flour (and not rye) was obtained from it.

In the European north of Russia back in the 19th century, such common wheat varieties as Ladoga and Onega were widespread, the vegetation period of which is extremely short, only 70 days. It was from these varieties that all types of soft wheat of Canada, and more than half of the types of soft wheat of the United States, originated.

204

The most ripening wheat in the world was found on Onega. As early as 1907, early wheat was cultivated on church fields in the Welsh County. According to the analysis of American scientists, made in the early 20th century, Shenkur wheat turned out to be the most precocious, the most drought-tolerant, having the most full-weight grain from all US wheat. In soft wheat of Northern Russia, referred to the Hyperborean group, the grain crumbles and can only be harvested with ears, i.e. Sickle, which indicates the proximity to wild forms.

In general, soft wheat of France is an exact copy of wheat of forest-steppe Ukraine and is very close to northern Russian. Four-row barley from the Russian north is sown in the mountains and arid regions of France.

All types of spelled are similar to the Volga, and in Germany in the 19th century any spelled were considered "Russian". Various European subspecies were called the "Russian powdery spelled", and the Egyptian species (common in Galicia) was called the "Russian spelled". "Russian spelled" arrived in the USA in 1899 from the Yaroslavl province.

Wheat "Turkey" (hard winter red) occupied 99.5% of the area of durum wheat in the USA in 1910, and 1944 - 50% areas. This wheat was introduced by the Mennonites into Kansas in 1873, like Canadian steppe wheat. It was imported to Canada from Russia as Kharkov. Earlier, in the 18th century, she came to Crimea with settlers from the North of Russia, and then Kharkov variety was bred from Crimean wheat.

The Marquis wheat that ranks next in crop area was obtained from Red Fife wheat (wheat from Galicia) and Calcutta hard-grain red wheat. Calcutta wheat was imported from Germany to Scotland, then to Canada, and then to the

United States. At the same time, the possibility of primary import of their material from the North of Russia is noted. Other types of durum wheat in the USA and Canada are obtained from them.

About the import of selection material into the USA from Russia, mainly from the North, American breeders themselves said: "America has taken so much from Russia that it is unlikely to be able to give everything back."

With increasing temperature and the absence of heat shortages, yields can increase significantly, and when temperatures rise to maximum warming, due to the extended growing season (by 70 - 252 days), it is possible, in the presence of early ripening varieties, to harvest two to three crops per year.

According to the records of 1912-26 in the North, cultivated local varieties of cereal crops.

Rye: vaza (shvedskaya), vologodskaya, vyatka, gryazovetskaya, kustovka, marfinskaya, nikol'skaya, pechorskaya, severodvinskaya, sol'vychegodskaya, totemskaya, udorka, ustyuzhskaya, cherepovetskaya, yarenskaya.

Wheat: white-headed, bogoyavlenskaya, vologodskaya, zyryanka, kadnikovskaya, Karelian beechless, red-headed, krokhinskaya, ladozhskaya, mezenskaya, nikol'skaya, onezhskaya, sinegorskaya, sol'vychegodskaya, sysol'skaya, ustyuzhskaya, khludovskaya, cherepovetskaya, shenkurskaya, shenkurskaya, yaranka, yaroslavskaya.

Spelled: vologodskaya, vyatka, mezenskaya, pecherskaya, ustyuzhskaya, yaroslavskaya.

Oats: vel'skiy, gryazovetskiy, kadnikovskiy, nikol'skiy, obdorskiy, orel, totemskiy, ustyuzhenskiy igol'chatyy, ustyuzhskiy, falenskiy.

206

Barley: arkhangel'skiy 4-row, vel'skiy, vologodskiy, vyatskiy, gryazovetskiy, zyryanskiy red, izhemskiy, kemskiy, kostromskoy, krasnoborskiy (mountain), kostromskoy (pillowcase), red kerchemskiy, mezhadorskiy, norvezhskiy, permskiy, pechorskiy, polyarnyy, sol'vychegodskiy 6-row, sol'vychegodskiy, sysol'skiy, totemskiy 6-row, ustyuzhenskiy 4-row, finskiy, cherepovetskiy 2-row, cherepovetskiy multi-row, shenkurskiy, yarenskiy 6-row, yaroslavskiy.

Pyotr Nikolayevich Tretyakov, in his book «The Origin of Agriculture» in 1934, wrote that the birthplace of agriculture is usually seen only in the valleys of Mesopotamia, the Nile and the Indus, but this is not correct. Agriculture in Mesopotamia, Egypt, and China could not have arisen because irrigation is required there. The first farmers in these places were already quite sophisticated specialists who knew what and why to do. Before the invention of plow farming, people were too weak to fight the lush weeds of the South. But in the forests of the North, man had powerful help in the form of fire, capable of deeply burning the soil, destroying weeds, their roots and at the same time fertilizing it with ash. When burning the forest area, the soil warmed up to a temperature above 100°C. In this case, the roots and seeds of plants, insect larvae, microorganisms, spores and rodents died. By burning a plot of forest, it was possible to free the land from the seeds of weed vegetation and at the same time fertilize it with ash. In addition, when burnt, the soil can be treated with "plow". The name and shape of this agricultural tool is directly related to deer horns (elk horns - " wearing plows"), which indicates the emergence of this form of agriculture in the ancient Stone Age.

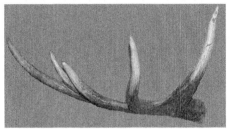
Antlers of a moose ("wearing plows ")

Ralo from the moose horn. Tripolie

On the burned forest lands, for the first three years they receive an unprecedented yield for any other system with an increase of up to 150 times against the sown grain - "SAM" 150. Of course, then the grain yield on the plot fell, but it was used for growing legumes, root crops, vegetables or as a pasture and haymaking. They also burned last year's grass on them, in order to destroy pests, weeds, forest stands, and to fertilize the soil.

In Western Europe, due to too heavy rains, the crop was often wetted out; in Siberia, crops were beaten by late spring and early autumn frosts. Eastern Europe is the most suitable climate for the ancestral home of agriculture, and possessing the only large areas of mixed forests in the Old World - a source of high-quality fuel and ash.

Its north is another center of the emergence of agriculture. The first crops of all the southern ancient countries - Egypt, Mesopotamia, India, and China - barley, spelled, millet, wheat. All these cultures are Northern European in origin.

In Sanskrit, peas - vidala, wheat - bujambu, duma, sumana, javana and rasala. Barley - divya, javanta, kuntala, media, java. Millet - kashku ("kashka - porridge"), flax - atasa, sunlla, uma. Grain - adia ("yeda - food"), avasita ("oves - oats"), ball ("polba - spelled"), bliaca, tsurnaka ("zerno - grain"), zhivanara, kazhkanaka, pala ("polba - spelled"), razhika ("rozh - rye"), rohi ("rozh - rye"). At the same time, there are no proper names for oats, rye and spelled.

Note that in Egypt, the words ruit - grain, Res - upper Egypt, resi - top, grain from Upper Egypt - just rye, and the designations of useful plants: ab – oats ("oves"), ushem – barley ("yachmen"), pura - peas ("pyure"), barbar - type of grain, khetbesha - millet, mak - poppy ("mak"), mehi ("fur - mekha") - flax, kharn - grain, khust - type of cereal, sut - barley ("zhito"), pesh - food ("millet -psheno") is closer to Russian than the corresponding English or Latin words.

For agriculture, it is important not only agriculture, but also livestock farming, which largely depends on the condition of the food supply.

It should be noted that it was in the North (on the Sukhon River and the Vel River) that Timofeevka was first introduced into the culture as a fodder plant (Russian names: lamb, seedling, seedling, stick, spike, orchid, bzhanka, rye, spike), from where it was in the 18th century it was exported to Europe. Timoty Grass brought it to the USA. From the USA it was brought to Britain, Germany. It has been cultivated in Sweden since the mid-18th century, in Norway since the beginning of the 19th century. In 1865-1914, due to the actions of the imperial authorities, grass planting and timothy cultivation in the North reached a complete decline. Nevertheless, according to the records of 1912-26 cultivars of aurora were cultivated: Velskaya, Vologda, Kadnikovskaya, Totemsky, Ustyuzhny.

Before the introduction of grass, the main role was played by natural pastures and hayfields. The following information speaks about the productivity of hayfields (it should be noted that during warming due to the growth of the growing season, the harvest will be much higher, not to mention year-round use of pastures).

Polar meadows on a summer polar night

The area of amenities and meadows in the North was estimated at the beginning of the 20th century to be 53 million hectares, the tundra of 27 million hectares: including Komi - 5763 thousand hectares

(Sysola - 936 thousand hectares, Luza - 432 thousand hectares, Vistula - 33 thousand hectares, Vychegda - 267 thousand hectares, Ussa - 146 thousand hectares, Sinya - 100 thousand hectares, Vishera, Izhma, Vym - 1500 thousand hectares, Sindor - 150 thousand hectares, southern Pechora - 936 thousand hectares, floodplain of the middle Pechora - 205 thousand hectares, floodplain of the lower Pechora - 492 thousand hectares, south of Komi - 511 thousand hectares); Karelia - 174 thousand hectares; Arkhangelsk province - 32622 thousand hectares (Murmansk coast - 171 thousand hectares, Nenets district - 501 thousand hectares, Pechora delta - 260 thousand hectares); Cherepovets province - 567 thousand hectares; North Dvina province - 936 thousand hectares; Vologda province - 2132 thousand hectares.

In addition, the Mologo-Sheksninskaya Lowland, flooded in 1941 - 700 thousand hectares, yielded 35% of grass seeds in the USSR (USSR area -1/6 of the Earth's land).

Note that the tundra in the North was originally called moss swamps, the Arctic meadows were called - the steppe. From the north, the word "steppe" came to Europe and then was assigned to the landscape, now called the steppe. It is not difficult to calculate how many agricultural products could be obtained from this territory, especially when warming.

Livestock productivity, especially milk production in the North, is potentially very high. It should be noted that the highest regional milk yield in the USSR in the 1970-80s, with the exception of metropolitan areas, accounted for the North.

I would like to note that the picture of animal husbandry in the past, when animal husbandry was less dependent on purchased and factory feed and industrial technologies, was variegated and rather ambiguous.

So Academician Lepekhin (1772) wrote: "Livestock breeding at the mouth of the mouth is deliberate, cattle are small, but not skinny and mostly hornless. Cattle breeding is fair, horses are strong, cattle are not thin, but exclusively all hornless ... Peasants in Megra those who live, by the abundance of places, abound in grass, rather keep every kind of cattle. "

Researchers at the beginning of the 20th century reported: "Cattle breeding is developed among peasants, especially the villages of Verkhnyaya and Nizhnyaya Pesha, who own wonderful and vast meadows located near the villages. Most of the meadows do not mow, partly due to the lack of need, partly because there is not enough strength, there's no time, but no hired workers among the population who are completely engaged in their field work, various crafts and work at sawmills. In these villages, middle-income peasants have 15-20 cattle, 5-10 horses and 20-50 sheep per farm, in the remaining villages and settlements, 4-10 heads of cattle, 3-6 horses. "

However, in the neighboring areas of the Arkhangelsk region the situation was the same. According to I. Anufriev (1911), in the Mezen district, on average, there were 3 cows and 2 horses, and 8 cows, 2 horses and 9 sheep in the northern parts of the county.

According to A.E. Chekanovsky (1910), cattle breeding on Pechora was as follows: "There are no special pastures and shepherds. Cattle wander wherever. Anyway, they feed on starvation in winter." They get it just in the winter and information about these milkings and fall into the statistics, which makes the difference with special observations or what was observed with normal owners.

Reindeer husbandry was developed. The poorest reindeer herders had herds of 10–20 animals; the average herd size was 500 animals. But the richest reindeer herder, a peasant Rochev, had a herd of 8,000 animals that he lost from an anthrax epidemic, left a legacy of 200,000 gold rubles received in reindeer husbandry.

This is not surprising, since even with a loss from the case of 20%, the reindeer husbandry's net profit (more precisely, capital productivity, since profit was considered relative to the herd price) was - 100% - he wrote in 1912 about the current Nenets okrug based on the results of a scientific and fishing expedition A. A. Zhuravsky.

It should be noted that in the northeast (and in Scandinavia) horned cattle is common, which Herodotus mentions when describing Scythia. In Scandinavia, impassivity is considered a sign of the northern origin of the species. When horned and hornless are crossed, hornless ones usually appear in the offspring (a sign of impassability is dominant).

In 1946-64, due to the mass import of ordinary Kholmogory cattle in the Komi Republic, local breeds were almost nullified. As a result, there was a sharp deterioration in the quality of milk and a decrease in milk yield. In addition, they tried to improve Kholmogorsk cattle by mixing it with foreign breeds. Although, as indicated in 1919, the import of foreign breeds in the northern region in 1800-1913 did not give positive results. Previously, on the contrary, local breeds were exported to the tribe in Europe. For example, the Kholmogorsk breed was exported as far back as the 16th century to the Netherlands, Germany and England.

In the North, by 1900 there were 17 local breeds of cattle and 28 breeds of hornless. In addition to cattle in the North, there were local sheep breeds: Kola, Pechora, Romanov, Kadnikov, Ustyuzhen, Gray, Northern, Vyatka,

Oparin, and horses: Sukhon, Mezensky, Pinezhsky, Totemsky, Accusatory, Udor, Vyatka, North Dvina, Finnish.

Pinezhsky horses

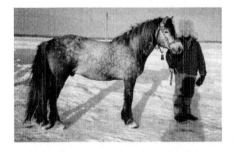

Mezen horses

That is, in the north, with a warmer and drier climate of the Holocene optimum (4 thousand BC) or the boreal period (7-5 thousand BC) or the Mikulinsky interglacial (130-70 thousand years ago) 80-100 million hectares of arable land may enter into circulation (the entire area of arable land in China in 1985 was 100 million hectares).

O. Krshitafovich (agent of the General Directorate for Land Management and Agriculture in the USA) wrote back in 1911: "There are all signs that some of the lands of the future are currently moving into the category of lands of the near future and can be put into circulation tomorrow, the day after tomorrow. At the first the turn, apparently, is the near North - the Arkhangelsk and Vologda provinces, and if they are really put into circulation tomorrow, we only have at our disposal today to organize this business and, moreover, in the right way. "

As the outstanding biologist G.F. Gauze proved back in 1934, each species seeks to occupy the entire available ecological niche at the rate of geometric progression until resources are exhausted, after which population growth stops, and the species stabilizes and then begins to decline in numbers until a new niche appears. Probably, Indo-Europeans went this way in their ancestral home.

Productivity cereal crops "SAM"

Terrain	Productivity	Sam
1	2	3
Olonets province	cereal	80
Olonets County	rye	12
		20
	bush rye	599
	wheat	26
		50

215

	barley	17
Lodeinopolsky district	cereal	10
Petrozavodsk district	cereal	15
Vytegra district	cereal	12
	rye	25
Arkhangelsk province	cereal	60
	rye	12-180
White Sea coast	rye	10
	oats	15
	barley	10
Arkhangelsk County	oats	46
Kemsky County	rye	35
Mezen County	barley	20
Onega County	barley	23
Pinezhsky County	barley	10
Kholmogorsk county	rye	30
		80
		180
	oats	10
	barley	40
Vologda province		
Vologda County	rye	83
		21
	wheat	20
		16
	oats	20
		21
	barley	17
		25

216

Gryazovets district	rye	10
Velsk County	rye	48
		17
	oats	34
	barley	23
Veliky Ustyug County	rye	10
		13
	wheat	14
	oats	13
	barley	15
		11
Kadnikovsky County	rye	18
		15
		12
	wheat	18
	oats	20
	barley	10
Nikolsky County	rye	14
		31
		34
		67
		10
	oats	11
Totem County	rye	17
	barley	23
Solvychegorsk district	cereal	30
Ust-Sysolsky district	rye	90
		12
		20
	forest rye	65

	barley	52
		12
Upper Pechora	cereal	35
	rye	10
		28
	barley	12
		29
Sysola	cereal	16
	rye	19
	barley	10
Izhma	barley	10
Upper Vychegda	rye	28
	barley	29
Yarensky district	rye	90
		12
	barley	26
Udora	rye	38
	barley	29
Pechora County		
Ust-Tsylma	cereal	15
		25
	rye	26
		24
		60
		12
	barley	26
		16
		25
Krasnoborsk	rye	30
	barley	25
Kuya	rye	20
	barley	15
Shchelya-Yur	barley	13
Galov	barley	14

218

Ust-Ussa	rye	24
Big Earth	barley	20
Middle Pechora	cereal	24
		45
Vyatka province	cereal	12
	rye	25
	oats	21
	barley	60
Nizhny Novgorod province	oats	45
	barley	40
Moscow province	spelled	16
Smolensk province	rye	30
Kursk province	wheat	10
	spelled	10
	oats	10
Saratov province	cereal	20
		14
Orenburg province	rye	12
	spelled	12
Don region	rye	20
Stavropol province	wheat	17

Productivity cereal crops in the north

Terrain	cereal crops	Productivity c / ha	Year
Vyatka province	cereal	22	1800
	rye	45	1854
	wheat	23	1909
	barley	28	1909
	peas	21	1909
Vyatka district	rye	47	1968
	wheat	33	1969
	oats	84	1977
	barley	70	1968
		50	1977
	peas	32	1968
Vyatka-Polyansky district	wheat	30	1976
	oats	21	1976
Darovsky district	rye	44	1968
Kirovo-Chepetsk district	rye	38	1950
	wheat	35	1954
	oats	31	1960
Unitsky district	rye	25	1968
Urzhum district	wheat	39	1976
Falensky district	rye	26	1962
	wheat	26	1973-75
	oats	28	1968
Yaran district	wheat	22	1976

Kotelnichesky district	wheat	32	1977
Kukarsky district	rye	56	1975
	wheat	39	1976
Olonets province	cereal	77	1863
	rye	29	1834
	bush rye	1028	1858
	rye	30	1955
		56	1975
	oats	22	1909
		30	1960
	barley	30	1955
	wheat	39	1976
Olonets region	wheat	63	1963
		49	1971
	barley	37	1972
Vytegorsky District	rye	60	1844
		32	1990
	oats	40	1990
	barley	28	1990
Kondopoga district	rye	27	1957
	oats	20	1959
Arkhangelsk province	cereal	58	1878
	rye	24	1909
	oats	22	1909
	barley	25	1909
White Sea coast	oats	45	1910
	barley	36	1910
Arkhangelsk County	rye	33	1925
Kemsky County	rye	58	1843
Mezen County	cereal	75	1857
	barley	75	1910
		40	1937
	oats	35	1937
	wheat	35	1937

	rye	42	1845
Onega County	barley	86	1848
Kholmogorsk county	rye	50	1843
		297	1845
		132	1847
	barley	150	1850
		34	1880-90
	oats	30	1850-60
Pinezhsky County	cereal	25	1910
Shenkur County	cereal	22	1910
Khibiny	oats	29	1936
	barley	35	1936
Piaozersky District	barley	34	1836
Vologda province	rye	22	1909
	wheat	22	1909
	oats	22	1909
	barley	23	1909
	peas	24	1909
Vologda district	cereal	42	1975
		41	1990
	rye	66	1914
		25	1922
	wheat	24	1912
		24	1920
		35	1977
		56	1990
	oats	75	1858
		31	1914
		37	1975
		46	1990
	barley	41	1922
		80	1990

Sokolsky district	cereal	50	1990
Veliky Ustyug County	cereal	31	1990
	rye	25	1667
		25	1990
	wheat	20	1906
	oats	26	1904
	barley	27	1667
		20	1911
		42	1990
Nyuksensky district	rye	20	1970
Gryazovets district	cereal	29	1910
		42	1990
	rye	39	1989
	wheat	26	1989
	oats	64	1986
	barley	59	1986
Mezhdurechensk district	rye	20	1990
	wheat	30	1990
Velsk County	rye	65	1906
	oats	45	1906
	barley	55	1908
Vozhegodsky district	rye	22	1990
	barley	24	1990
Kadnikovsky County	cereal	30	1913
	rye	50	1892
	oats	66	1858
Ust-Kubensky district	rye	28	1990
	wheat	30	1990
	barley	20	1990
Kharovsky district	cereal	32	1970
	rye	20	1990
	oats	38	1990

223

	barley	30	1980-88
Verkhovazhsky District	cereal	30	1989
	oats	22	1990
	barley	22	1990
Syamzhensky District	cereal	26	1990
Totem County	cereal	40	1990
	rye	54	1912
	barley	72	1912
		30	1990
	oats	30	1912
Grandmother's district	barley	23	1990
	oats	28	1986
Tarnogsky District	barley	30	1990
Nikolsky County	rye	42	1911
	wheat	30	1906
	oats	35	1906
	barley	41	1906
Kich-Gorodetsky district	rye	22	1990
	barley	29	1990
Podosinovsky district	rye	22	1916
		44	1975
	barley	32	1916
Novgorod province	rye	32	1928
	wheat	26	1928
	oats	23	1928
	barley	37	1928
Belozersky district	rye	45	1990
	oats	30	1990
Babaevsky District	rye	24	1990
	barley	36	1990

Kirillovsky district	wheat	20	1990
	oats	27	1990
	barley	25	1990
Vashkinsky district	cereal	30	1988
	rye	20	1988
Cherepovets district	cereal	30	1990
	rye	34	1947
Sheksninsky District	cereal	23	1990
Kaduy district	cereal	27	1990
	barley	40	1990
Ustyuzhensky district	cereal	23	1990
	rye	51	1970
		30	1987
Chagodoshchensky district	cereal	50	1990
	rye	51	1970
		113	1990
	oats	40	1990
	barley	61	1990
Yaroslavskaya oblast	rye	58	1975
		37	1990
	wheat	40	1990
	oats	61	1990
	barley	28	1967
Komi region			
Ust-Sysolsky County	rye	197	1858
		44	1910
	barley	86	1906
Upper Vychegda	barley	68	1909
	rye	45	1909
		30	1927
	oats	25	1927
Sysola	forest rye	142	1914
	barley	23	1927

225

Upper Pechora	cereal	65	1910
	rye	45	1927
	oats	25	1927
	barley	32	1909
		68	1927
Yarensky district	rye	144	1858
	barley	69	1908
Udora	rye	60	1884
		60	1927
	oats	25	1927
	barley	68	1927
Pechora County Izhma	cereal	25	1900-30
	barley	27	1930-34
Krasnoborsk	rye	36	1893-1903
		54	1903
	barley	39	1893-1903
		64	1903
		52	1909
Ust-Tsilma	cereal	40	1860-90
		64	1900-30
	rye	47	1900
		36	1930
		54	1934
	barley	68	1908
		67	1930
Kuya	rye	36	1909
	barley	22	1909

226

Kozhva	barley	37	1909
Big land	barley	51	1909
Shchelya-Yur	barley	32	1909
Galov	barley	36	1909
Ussa	rye	43	1858
	barley	22	1858
Middle Pechora	cereal	61	1840
		115	1900

Hay productivity in the North

Terrain	Harvesting hay (centners / ha)
Karelia	40-67
White Sea coast	15
Murmansk Tundra	49
Arkhangelsk County	60
Kholmogorsk county	41
Nenets district	24
Vologda County	60
Gryazovets district	9-26
Totem County	57
Nikolsky County	24-69
Veliky Ustyug County	24-68
Lake Vauge	60-110
Cherepovets district	50
Sheksna River	24-49
Mologa River	10-85
Vyatka River	40-80
Middle Pechora	99-180
Upper Pechora	50
Son River	77
Ussa River	76-114
Sysola	88-95

227

Vychegda	53-96
Yarensky district	35
Wash out	11-65
Udora	28
Arctic	46-91

Maximum milk yield of cattle in the North

Terrain	Milk yield kg / year	Year
Arkhangelsk County	8520	1820-50
Kholmogorsk county	10980	1824
	10955	1926
Murmansk region	6200	1964
Karelia	4000	1957
Nenets district	7081	1953
Komi region	4095	1910
	9150	1964
Vologda province	3276	1909
Vologda County	9000	1900
	7505	1940
Nikolsky County	3944	1928
Veliky Ustyug County	9150	1920
Cherepovets County	10800	1990

Local breeds of cattle in the North

Breed	Milk yield kg / year	% fat	Year
Cattle			
Yaroslavskaya	25040	4.0	1988
	7102	5.0	1926
	5464	5.4	1983
Kholmogorsk	24065	3.5	1988
	5733	4.4	1925
Kostroma	20130	6.2	1988

	4207	5.5	1925
Severodvinsk	9150	4.2	1920
Istobenskaya	8000	4.0	1967
	6192	3.8	1926
Domshinskaya	3781	4.2	1905
Prisheksninskaya	3416	4.2	1929
Vandakur	2460		1929
Vytegorskaya	2400	4.0	1900
Pinezhskaya	1956	3.6	1919
Nizhnedvinskaya	1956		1919
Severodvinsk	1700	4.0	1933
Sumy	1497	4.0	1858
Velikoustyugska ya	1277	4.2	1928
Kadnikovskaya	688	5.0	1902-5
Middle			
Mezenskaya			
Yemetskaya			
Kenozerskaya			
Hornless cattle			
Pechora	2745	6.8	1837
	9150	6.0	1953
Zyryanskaya	6000	6.0	1964
South Finnish	5678	4.4	1929
Karelian	4000	4.3	1957
Lalskaya	3944	5.8	1928
Severofinskaya	3751	5.4	1963
East Finnish	3500	4.2	1964
Ustyuzhenskaya	3355	4.1	1928
Vymskaya	3000	4.7	1920-27
Nizhnevychegod skaya	3000	4.7	1920-27
Nikolskaya	2259	7.5	1929
Ledenga	2200	4.2	1935

229

Vychegodskaya	2015	5.5	1929
Kargopol	2000	4.0	1935
Oparinskaya	1970	4.7	1929
Lenskaya	1555	4.2	1928
Vazhskaya	1060	4.0	1933
Zyryanskaya	1000	4.5	1920-30
Koksheng	1000	4.2	1935
Sukhonskaya	917	4.2	1928
Kinky	600		1927
Permyatskaya		4.7	1947
Kychkarskaya			
Loemskaya			
Mezenskaya			
South Luz			
Kichmeng-South			
Suzemskaya			
Sredneugskaya			

The country	Year	Culture	Productivity centner / ha	SAM
France	1100-1200	cereal		3
	1300-1500	cereal		4,3
	1500-1820	cereal		6,3
	1815	cereal	11	
	1834	cereal	12	
Poland	1350-1550	rye	7,5-13,1	
	1350-1550	spelled	9,3-16,6	
	1350-	oats	6-12	

	1550			
	1565	rye		10
	1595	rye	6	
	1650	rye		5
	1765	rye		3
Württemberg	14th century	rye	7-13	
China Wei	403 BC	cereal	9,7	
	220 BC	wheat	11,6	
	220 BC	rice	21,8	
China	11th century	cereal	6,9	
Si xia	1368	cereal	9,8	
China Ming	1400	cereal	11,2	
	1425	cereal	9,8	
	1850	cereal	15,9	
China Qing	1885	cereal	13,5	
	1915	cereal	15,8	
	1949	cereal	11,3	
PRC	1985	cereal	38,2	
	1350	cereal		12
South india	1800	cereal		30
	1810	rice	32	
Cambodia	1930	rice	12	
	1398	cereal	30,9	
Korea	1444-1500	cereal	12,5	
	1550	rye	7,5-13,1	
	1550	spelled	9,3-16,6	
	1550	oats	6-12	

| | 10th century | barley | 20 |
| Iraq | 10th century | wheat | 19 |

Terrain	Productive phytomass tons / ha	Phytomass whole tons / ha
Polar deserts	1	1.6
Arctic Tundra Wrangel Island	1	2.9
South tundra	2.5-4	20-30
Forest tundra	5-6	40-60
Meadows of Kamchatka and the Kuril Islands	10	100
Taiga Eastern Europe		
Northern spruce	4-6	200
Middle spruce	6-8	270
Southern spruce	8-10	350
Central Yakutia	6-8	120
Wetlands of Yakutia	6-8	170
Swamps of Yakutia	3-7	17
Subtaiga forests		
Scotland	0.4	200-500
Eastern Europe	7-18	200
Western Siberia	12.6	213
Deciduous forests		
Eastern Europe	8-12	340-500
Far East	15-20	300-500
Japan	15-25	500
Meadow steppes	13-17	25
Baraba Steppe	19	36.4
Including reed swamps	63.7	

chopping	9	
Subboreal steppe	10-12	20-25
Northern Black Sea Coast	4-5	10-13
North America Subboreal	11-16	1000-2900
Pacific Forests - Oregon (Pines)		
Subboreal Desert		
Middle Asia	1.5	4.5
Northern Aral Sea	7.7	34
Subtropics wet south of Japan	12-23	240-480
Subtropics European France	6.5-7	315
Subtropical forests of North America (sequoia)	27	1300-4250
Subtropical semi-desert Algeria	0.6-3.7	1.2-4.3
Teak Forest Dean	6-8	
Tropical deserts		
Egypt	0.5-1	0.6-11
Oases of Egypt	38	
Mountains forests of south India	3.8-7.3	
Savannah north africa	4-11	17-40
Savannah forests	17	250
Equatorial forests		
Malaka	30-50	400-600
Katanga Forests	3.3	150
Wet forests		
Including primary	17-34	500
secondary	100-300	
Guinea forests	17	562
Amazonia	7-28	1000

Literature

1. Национальный доклад СССР к Конференции ООН 1992 года по окружающей среде и развитию (проект). М. 1991.

2. Палеогеография Европы за последние сто тысяч лет. М. Наука. 1982.

3. Кооперация Севера. № 3. Вологда. 1923.

4. П. А. Колесников. Северная Русь. В.2. Вологда. ВГПИ. 1979.

5. Труды съезда председателей земских управ, агрономов и специалистов Вологодской губернии по вопросам содействия сельской промышленности 5-16 марта 1914. Вологда. 1914.

6. Труды съезда председателей земских управ, агрономов и специалистов Вологодской губернии по вопросам содействия сельской промышленности 5-16 марта 1914. Вологда. 1914.

7. Деларов Д. И. Северная область и ее место в народном хозяйстве СССР. Север. 1928. № 7-8.

8. Штукенберг И. Ф. Статистические труды. СПБ. 1857-58.

9. Шахов А. Земледелие и кормодобывание Печорского края. М. ВАСХН. 1936. .

10. К вопросу о земледелии в бассейне р.Колымы. Советский Север. № 2. 1932.

11. Природа Кировской области. Киров. ВВКИ. 1967.

12. Происхождение земледелия. М. ИИМК. 1934.

13. С. И. Бараш. История неурожаев и погоды в Европе. Л. Гидрометеоиздат. 1989.

14. Материалы для селекции зерна в США и Западной Европе, полученных с Севера (Швеция,Финляндия,Россия) в XIX веке. Известия Общества изучения Олонецкой губернии. 1913. № 2-3.

15. Шлегубер, Стилуотер. Успехи селекции пшеницы на качественное зерно в Сев.Америке. Оклахома США. 3 международный хлебный конгресс. Гамбург 1955. Изд.Инстр.лит. М. 1958.

16. Кооперация Севера. № 2. Вологда. 1921.

17. Вологодская тимофеевка. Материалы по организации и культуре кормовой площади. Петроград. 1916. Мин.Земледелия. Деп.Земледелия.

18. Труды съезда председателей земских управ, агрономов и специалистов Вологодской губернии по вопросам содействия сельской промышленности 5-16 марта 1914г. Вологда. 1914.

19. Путешествия академика Ивана Лепехина. Часть IV. въ 1772 году. СПб. Императорская АН. 1805.

20. Чекановский А.Е. Скотоводство Печорского уезда. ИАОИРС. 1910. № 2.

21. Труды первого съезда по животноводству Северной области с 15 по 20 января 1919 г. Петроград. 1919.

22. П. А. Колесников. Северная Русь. В 2. Вологда. ВГПИ. 1979.

S.-K. Deekshit
About the primary range of agriculture

The territory of central Russia may claim to be considered the ancestral home of the Indo-Europeans. The people who inhabited these regions were the very people who had mastered the oldest slaughter farming (more advanced arable farming had already arisen in India, Mesopotamia, Egypt), invented the most ancient iron tools, which allowed them to begin their conquests and migrations. In Central Russia, more than two-thirds of the reserves of brown iron ore, from which until the 19th century only received iron; in addition, there are the largest reserves of raw materials for charcoal, on which all metallurgy was based until modern times. In any case, ancient Greek theogeny and epic say that the primary focus of agriculture and the Iron Age is in the Cimmerian countries. According to the Bible, the inventors of agriculture and northern iron are "Gimer" - the plowmen and warriors, that is, the Cimmerians of the north. To achieve a higher degree of well-being and tools of the Iron Age helped them. Therefore, it is natural to assume that their population growth was faster than in other modern societies that still used tools of the Bronze Age, and especially the Stone Age.

1960

236

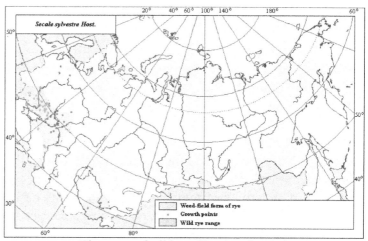

The range of wild rye (Secale sylvestre)

237

Andrey Ignatiev
The Tale of the Pearl Island in Devibhagavata Purana

Let us turn to a fragment of the twelfth book of the
Devibhagavata Purana containing information about the
Pearl Island (Mani-dvipa), which serves as the seat of the
Goddess and her retinue. To begin with, we note that the
mythologies of many peoples have legends about a
wonderful island (or islands) lying somewhere on the edge
of the earth or even in another world. And often, these
legends are associated with the image of a female deity or
some kind of supernatural female being who dominates this
island. Representations of the island among the sea as a
place of serene pleasures, often erotic, are also characteristic
of modern everyday consciousness.

So, the Sumerians believed that the island of Dilmun
was located far in the southern sea. This place is intended
only for the gods, and this country is described as "clean",
"bright", "and immaculate." There are no diseases, no old
age, and no harmful animals. "A raven does not croak at
Dilmun. The bird does not scream yttidu. A lion does not
kill, a wolf lacks a lamb, a wild dog, a goat-eater, he doesn't
live here ... a grain eater, and he does not live here. There
are no widows here ..." On this island, the mother goddess
Ninhursag grows eight wonderful plants. Dilmun Island is
often regarded as the original image of biblical Eden.
Dilmun is often identified with Bahrain. It is interesting to
note that the cities of Indian civilization had extensive trade
ties with Mesopotamia. This is evidenced by the finds of
products from India (mainly seals) on Mesopotamian
fortifications (Ur, Kish, and Tell-Asmar). The islands of the
Persian Gulf could serve as an intermediate link between
India and Mesopotamia. In favor of this is the similarity of
the seals of the Bahrain Islands with the Indian and the finds

of objects made on these islands in cities belonging to the Indus civilization.

And according to the ideas of the ancient Greeks, in the far west are the Blessed Islands (Elysius), where the fallen heroes such as Diomedes, Achilles and Menelaus live a happy and carefree life. There they walk in a beautiful meadow of unfading flowers. The fertile land thrice a year gives them fruits as sweet as honey. According to the traditions of the Orphics, the god Kronos - the father of Zeus, who was the supreme god in the Golden Age, rules these islands. According to another version of the legend, Kronos is "in a dream" in the distant North Sea, which for this reason was called the Kronid Sea. Here we are talking about Tula itself, an island that, according to Strabo (Geography I.4), is six days sailing from Britain, next to the frozen sea. Levka (lit. "White") is mentioned as one of the Blessed Islands, where after death Achilles lives with Elena and where their son Emforion was born; according to other legends, Iphigenia, named Orsilochia, and became the wife of Achilles on Levka.

No less interesting are the islands that Odysseus visits during his long return home. So, he finds himself on the island of Eeya, located in the far west, ruled by the sorceress Kirka (Circe), who lives on this island in a magnificent palace and turns people who have fallen on the island into animals. So she turns the companions of Odyssey into pigs. And only thanks to the help of Hermes Odysseus was able to destroy the evil spell of Kirk, returning his companions to a human face, as well as subjugate the sorceress herself.

Subsequently, the hero finds himself on the island of Ogigia, the owner of which is the nymph Calypso. The nymph lives in a beautiful nature, in a grotto, twined with vines, and is engaged in weaving. She keeps Odysseus in her house, promising to grant him immortality, but cannot make him forget his homeland. At the command of Zeus, transmitted through Hermes, Calypso was forced to release the hero. The name Calypso ("the one that hides") indicates her connection with the world of the dead. Having left this nymph, Odysseus thus conquers death and returns to life.

In the legends of the Celtic peoples, the other world is also located on the islands far in the west. The Gauls believed that the first ancestor of the people and the god of the dead Disputer live in a distant area on the other side of the Ocean, on the island of Predela, where, according to the legend of the Druids, some of the inhabitants of Gaul came. So, in the Irish saga "Bran Swim", it is told about the blessed islands, numbering three times fifty, where time has stopped, and abundance and eternal youth reign. These islands were called by different names: the Great Land, the Land of Life, but incl. and the land of women.

The legendary history of Ireland also speaks of the change of tribes, which in turn conquer and conquer it, coming from these mysterious lands located in the North Atlantic, where they return. In the "Historia Britorum" these lands are called Hyperborea. The first people to populate Ireland were Partolon, who arrived just from these lands. This people fought with the Fomorians - a tribe of ugly and cruel giants. According to legend, the inaccessible tower of Connan, one of the kings of Fomorians, is located on a "glass island in the middle of the ocean." The motif of the glass palace or tower is also present in the traditions of the Welsh, who also placed a "different world" on the islands.

Then, the Neimheidha tribe, or the people of Nemed, replaces the extinct people of Partolon. The people of Nemed were almost completely exterminated in the battle with the Fomorians. Nemeda Fir-Bolg, who replaced the people, was not famous for anything special. The next wave of conquerors was Tuat de Dananne, or tribes of the goddess

Danu. They were the most interesting and significant of the owners of the Green Island. In Irish traditions, representatives of these tribes personified the forces of knowledge and light. The tribes of the goddess Dan managed to inflict a decisive defeat on the Fomorians, and they disappear from the history of Ireland.

Finally, the Sons of Mile arrive in Ireland; they are no longer demigods, but ordinary people. In battle, they crush the power of the tribes of the goddess Danu, but they do not disappear, but as it were, move to another dimension, and since then there are two Ireland: earthly and spiritual. It is interesting to note that in the heroic legends of Ireland, a large role was played by female warriors - Skat, Aif and Medb, reminiscent of the warlike goddesses of the Hindu pantheon.

According to another legend, Tribes of the goddess Danu are removed to their original homeland - the island of Avallon. The word Avallon comes from the Cimrian word afal, that is, an apple, and therefore Avallon is an island of apples. This brings to mind the island of Hesperides "on the other side of the Ocean", and the golden apples that Hercules received by completing one of his twelve feats. The supernatural women of Avallon Island have the ability to "bestow salvation," and in the sir about Tir-nan-og, they argue that on their land there is "neither death nor decay of bodies," and that there the hero Oyzin will be able to acquire a "crown of eternal youth." Here, according to legend, the fairy Morgana was transferred after the Battle of Camlan, the mortally wounded King Arthur. Here he reclines in a wonderful glass palace on top of a mountain, and the spells of women of this land heal him and allow him to fulfill his functions again. But the wounds of King Arthur open again every year. At the same time, there was a belief in the return of King Arthur from Avallon.

But at the same time, Avallon also means "white", "polar", "sunny" island. According to another etymology, Avallon actually is the "island of Apollo," the god to whom the Celts corresponded to Ablun or Belen, and Apollo, as we know, is the god of the Hyperborean regions. Sometimes this island is mixed with the "glass island", which is due to the proximity of their symbolism, since the walls of glass symbolize the invisible protection of sacred places. In later knightly legends, the location of the Grail is closely connected with the same island of Avallon, with the "white island". These legends reproduce the same motifs that appeared before: royal women, a silver tree crowned with the sun, a tree of victory, a spring, a vessel with a drink that never ends.

So, in Danish legends, after his conquest of the East, Ogier of Denmark arrives on the island of Avallon, where he becomes the lover of the fairies Morgana, and sister of King Arthur. There he lives away from the world, enjoying eternal youth. But the Christian world, in terrible danger, again needs its help. Archangel Michael goes to the fairy Morgan and, following the divine will; Ogier reappears in the world and wins.

In traditional Russian culture, ideas about the "blessed islands" are more cheerful. The legend about Buyan Island was widespread, and many Russian conspiracies began with a mention of it. On Buyan is the sacred center of the world - Alatyr stone, as well as angels and saints: "On the sea, on Okiyan, on the island on Buyan, on the white-combustible stone Alatyr, on a brave horse sits Egoriy Pobedonetsets, Mikhail Archangel, Ilya the Prophet, Nikolai the Miracle Worker ". Sometimes the image of a divine virgin is also found: "At the sea, on the Ocean, on the island of Buyan, there is a white-combustible stone Alatyr, on that stone Alatyr there is a red maiden, a seamstress-craftswoman,

242

holds a damask needle, thread a silk thread, yellow ore, sews up bloody wounds. ... " (followed by the wish and closure of the conspiracy with a magic word). Sometimes called the name of the Tsar Maiden - Dawn or Dawn, and she herself is placed in a tall tower. In its sacred functions, it is close to the Goddess Makoshi, weaving fate, or to Athena (Minerva), the patroness of a just war, arts and crafts.

Modern scholars argue about where, in a geographical sense, the prototype of the legendary Buyan Island could be located, in which exactly the "Sea-Ocean". According to one version, it is located in the Black Sea (now the island of Berezan). According to another, more justified - in the Baltic Sea (Varyazhsky, Scythian), where the northern Slavs, the Wends, have long lived. The Baltic Sea itself was sometimes called Alatyr Sea. Buyan's prototype could be Ruyan Island (now Rugen), where the famous Sanctuary of Arkon was located. This name, according to one version, comes from the verb arko - to beg, and according to another - it means "white mountain" (from Indo-European. Ar, arya - white, noble and kon - mountain). The toponym Buyan can be explained through the ancient Russian word "buoy", that is, a hill, a lighthouse, a place high and noticeable from afar.

In the Russian tradition, there are other legends about sacred islands. "In the east of the sun, near the blessed paradise" is, according to Russian "Cosmographies", the Makarii Islands (from the Greek. Makarios - "blessed"), where honey and milk rivers flow with jelly banks and where the birds of paradise Gamayun and Phoenix fly. As we will see, similar motifs are present in the ideas about the Pearl Island.

Now we turn directly to Indian mythology. And then two legendary islands come to mind. Firstly, it is Lanka, the island ruled by the Rakshasa king Ravana, and where Rama went to free his wife Sita, abducted by Ravana. By the way,

243

the widespread identification of the island with modern Sri Lanka or Ceylon described by both epics - Ramayana and Mahabharata remains problematic.

Secondly, it is the White Island (Shveta-Dvipa), which is the "seat of Vishnu, the solar god, the bearer of the Hyperborean cross, the swastika." The twelfth book of Mahabharata contains a story about the journey of Narada to the White Island. This island is located off the northern shores of the Milky Ocean and is inhabited by men with silver-colored skin, who have bridled themselves and are devotees of Vishnu. Having reached the White Island, Narada praises Vishnu, and he appears to him in his universal form (Vishva-Rupa). God instructs the sage on higher reality and tells him about his avatars, such as the Boar and the Fish. After speaking, Vishnu disappears, and Narada returns to his own abode. As we see, a purely "masculine atmosphere" reigns on the White Island, and the highest reality in the instructions of Vishnu is Purusha, the Highest Man above Prakriti, the feminine principle. There is no place for women in the kingdom of God.

Later, the Vaishnavas got the idea that there are two White Islands. One of them is identical to Vaikuntha, the world of Vishnu, and the other, of a lower level, so to speak, is in the milky ocean, which is in each of the brahmands (Airavata dasa).

Another Shaktist version of Narada's trip to the White Island is contained in Devibhagavata Purana (VI.28.1-31.22). This version has a plot similarity with the myth of the journey of the gods of Trimurti to the Pearl Island, which will be discussed below. Common here is the motive for turning a man into a woman. In the version of Devibhagavata Purana, Narada appears on the White Island and sees Vishnu indulging in love affairs with Lakshmi. The sage is surprised, and then Vishnu explains that even the gods, including himself, are not able to curb Maya. Then Narada shows a desire to know what Maya is. In response, Vishnu on Garuda takes him to the ground and, taking him to one pond, offers to swim in it. Entering the waters of the pond, Narada turns to a woman named Saubhagyasundari and loses his memory of his past life.

Soon this woman, Saubhagyasundari, marries King Taladhvaja and, for twelve years indulging in love joys, gives birth to his eight sons. Nothing seems to violate Saubhagyasundari's family happiness. However, her sons fall ill, and then family quarrels begin. Finally, enemies attack the kingdom, and all the sons of Saubhagyasundari perish in battle. When she sees them dead and mourns, an elderly brahmana comes to her, whose appearance is taken by Vishnu himself, and advises to bathe in the sacred place of pilgrimage Pum-tirtha ("male tirtha"). When Narada follows the advice of a brahmana and is washed in the waters of tirtha, his former appearance and memory return to him. So the sage learns what Maya is.

The Pearl Island, which is considered to be located above the White Island of Vishnu, in the Devibhagavata Purana is discussed in two fragments, one of which is contained in the third book and the other in the twelfth.

In the third book, the gods who make up the Trimurti, Brahma, Vishnu and Shiva are ascended to this island by the heavenly chariot, where they see the Goddess (III.3.31–67). There they turn into beautiful young women (III.4.6) and give her praise (III.4.27–5.46). In response, the Goddess talks about herself (III.6.2-29), endows the gods with their Shakti spouses and entrusts them with the fulfillment of their own responsibilities for the creation, maintenance and destruction of the universe (III.6.30–82). After this, Brahma, Vishnu and Shiva leave the island and regain their masculine appearance (III.6.83).

The fragment contained in the twelfth book has no plot, but is an exclusively cosmographic description. First of all, the pearl island is depicted as a world above all other worlds, including Kailashi, Goloka and Vaikuntha (hence its other name Sarvaloka, "[over] all worlds") and surpassing them in splendor (XII.10.1 -4), and, secondly, as an island located in the middle of a vast ocean of nectar (XII.10.6). Enormous walls rise one after another from the coast and towards the center of the island, which divide the island into separate areas. There are twenty-five such walls in total. According to Swami Sivananda, these walls symbolize twenty-five tattvas. In its beauty, each of the following walls is many times superior to the previous (XII.10.18,75). Each of the regions is buried in gardens where evergreen trees grow (XII.10.20-54) or trees made of precious stones (XII.10.17; 11.24; 12.60). The fragrance of these trees is filled with air on the island (XII.10.32, 35-36). Streams of milk and honey flow through the gardens (XII.10.39), cf. with Russian traditions about the Macarean islands. Each of the regions is inhabited by certain deities with their retinues. Among these deities are the Keepers of the World (XII.10.76), sixty-four kala (XII.11.3), thirty-two formidable shakti (XII.11.25), eight envoys of Sri Bhuvaneshvari (XII.11.48-49), eight Mothers (XII.11.56-58), eight counselors of the Goddess (XII.11.76-81), the emerald country is inhabited by Brahma, Vishnu, Shiva, Kubera, Kama and Ganesha with their spouses and incarnations, as well as sixty-four agamas in their embodied state (XII.11.82-99) , deities of the five elements (XII.11.101-102) reside in a coral country (XII.11.101-102), and Mahavidyas and other incarnations of the Devi (XII.11.106) are in the country of Navarata (nine stones). It is emphasized that the Keepers of the world, like other deities that live on the Pearl Island, represent the combined

246

image of those deities from the countless worlds (brahmands) of the Hindu cosmos (XII.10.76; 11.57-58; 11.99). Immediately in memory comes the island of Buyan, on which, according to legend, the angels and saints abide.

In the center of the Pearl Island is a magnificent, dazzlingly shining palace of the Goddess, built from the magic stone of Chintamani (XII.11.108-12.1), cf. Alatyr stone, and glass towers and palaces from Celtic mythology. There are four halls in this palace: love, liberation, knowledge and solitude (XII.12.2-3). First, it is said that the Great Goddess sits on the bed, which is formed by the five great male deities: Brahma, Vishnu, Rudra, Ishvara and Sadashiva (XII.12.11-12). Then it is said that before the creation of the universe she bifurcates, and Maheshvara comes from half of her body (XII.12.13-14), and then the Goddess in the image of Sri Bhuvaneshvari sits on his left knee (XII.12.17). Mahesh or Maheshvara depends entirely on the Goddess (XII.12.39). In accordance with the canonical ideas of female beauty, her appearance is described in detail (XII.12.18-32). From all worlds, worshipers of the Goddess from among various creatures (XII.12.44-45) go to the Chintamani palace and there they reach one of four types of liberation (XII.12.51-52). This palace is a place where eternal celebration and abundance reigns, and where no one knows what old age, illness and negative emotions are (XII.12.46-50). There are deities engaged in the ministry of Devi, representing the aggregate form of deities from all worlds (XII.12.52-53). This section ends with the praise of Pearl Island.

As we see, in the description of the Pearl Island all the same motifs are found that are present in the legends of other peoples about such islands: a land where no one knows old age or disease, with unfading, luxurious nature; often the symbolic color of this land is white (Levka,

247

Avallon, White Island of Vishnu); the achievement of this land is associated with a metamorphosis, whether it be transformation into animals on the island of Kirk, gaining immortality on the blessed islands or achieving liberation on the Pearl Island. The sacred center of the island is either a magic stone (Alatyr), or a tower or tower (glass tower of Fomorians or tower T on the island of Buyan), or a palace from this stone (Chintamani in DBhP). On this island, both gods and other supernatural beings can live, as well as people who are merciful to the gods, and the lady of the island can be a woman of divine or semi-divine nature (Ninhursag on Dilmund, Kirk and Calypso in the tales of Odyssey, the fairy of Morgan on Avallon, the Tsar Maiden on Buyan, Devi on the Pearl island). The traditionalist J. Evola connects the legends of a similar island among different Indo-European peoples with the land that actually existed in the North Atlantic region, on which the Hyperborean civilization was located. Later, due to glaciation or flood, the inhabitants of this land were forced to leave it.

2014

Stanislav Viktorovich Khromov
Nikolshchina

In Russia, there are many places interesting and profitable from a tourist point of view. However, they all have a significant drawback in our time - fame, with the modern development of the media, a person does not receive from travel that charge of energy and unforgettable impressions that he could have received in times not so distant. People understand this and are increasingly staying at home and watching TV.

At the same time, trips to poorly studied and remote areas from large population centers leave a person with completely unexpected, strong and unforgettable impressions. One of such places in the Vologda region is the town of Nikolsk and its environs, located four hundred kilometers from the regional center on the Sharya - Veliky Ustyug section. I will try to briefly and very fragmentarily talk about this unique territory on the banks of the South River.

In December 1871, the famous traveler Grigory Nikolayevich Potanin arrived in Nikolsk, accompanied by a gendarme. He lived here quite a considerable time and had every opportunity to get acquainted with the lifestyle of the local population. In his essay "Nikolsky Uyezd and its inhabitants", published in the collection "Ancient and New Russia" for 1876, he notes: "Fate cast me in the Vologda province, in the city of Nikolsk, on the South River; I spent two years here and had the opportunity to get acquainted with the life of local peasants. "

He was struck here by the dense forests covering the watershed and known by the name of Suzema. "Only eleven roads lead through Suzem within the county. Of these, only two draggers are colonized. " The rest, indicates

249

G.N.Potanin, are "deserted". He is surprised by the diversity of animal and plant life: "There are lakes with fish and shells, a water bird and small animals, and a wolf, only large animals live in the depths of Suzem - bear, elk; in some isolated areas in the wilderness of Suzem there are still herds of reindeer. "

The author of these lines met with people who are engaged in completely different, not historical, research. For example, in the Nikolsky district, several gold-bearing sections of rivers have been discovered, and it turns out that gold mining has been carried out here by local residents since time immemorial. On the Yug River, even the village of Zolotavino was preserved, which from ancient times lived on this craft. Before the revolution, the extraction of golden sand was not the main activity for the local population. So earned money in their free time.

Another fact is also interesting - the presence on the Nikolsk land of evidence of the preglacial period. In one of the distant villages of the Nikolsky district, a former forester named Nikolai lives. We learned about this man by accident. On a visit in one of the villages of the Nikolsky district they saw interesting stones, which upon closer inspection turned out to be petrified remains of "dinosaur eggs," as they say in sensational articles, and very large fragments of shell. Lots of limestone with imprints of shells and mollusks. There were Belemnites among them, or, as they are also popularly called, "bloody fingers." There they told us about the hobby of Nikolai Grigorievich and his findings. We were very surprised that in the Nikolsky district there is such a person, and we decided to visit him for sure.

What was not there: a lot of belemnites of different sizes, stones with holes, which were possibly used in antiquity as primitive weights. Limestone fragments with imprints of various shells and small primitive animals. A

250

small stone - and in it there is an imprint of half the wing of a butterfly, even spots are preserved. Many fruits of some ancient trees, judging by the size of the fruit, the trees should be quite large. Petrified eggs, some preserved along with the remains of the breed where they lay, a petrified fragment of a tortoise shell, with a characteristic hexagonal pattern. It was all so unusual. It is one thing to look at fossils in a museum window, or on a TV screen, and it's quite another to pick up, feel their weight, rough surface, and touch antiquity with your own hands.

An amateur paleontologist transferred part of his findings to the Nikolsky Museum of Local Lore. A large amount of limestone serves as evidence that in the distant past a warm sea splashed here. In addition, fragments of shells came across, sometimes whole, corals of various colors and shapes.

According to Nikolai Grigoryevich, very tall trees grew here before, since the size of the fruits he found is sometimes simply staggering. Who could eat such an "apple" if it was the size of two soccer balls (aren't these apples from the Garden of Eden, which 23 meter Adam and 20 meter Eve were eating?). He did not show us this petrified fruit, because he left it where he found it, it was too heavy. He also found many fragments of stones, which, like a pie, consist of small and broken shells layered with sand, a large number of long-petrified teeth and claws. Nikolai showed a fragment of a claw seven centimeters long. And this is only a small part of it, but it's scary to imagine what its owner looked like.

The villagers, having found some unusual stone, are carrying it. Recently, in this way, when digging a well from a depth of about eight meters, a sink fell into his hands, despite the time that preserved the naturalness of the colors.

And under the roots of an uprooted tree, Nikolai Grigoryevich found a piece of stone about three centimeters thick. It turned out to be a skin fragment, on one side of which blood vessels were imprinted, and the outer side was covered with small scales. I came across Nikolai Grigorievich and petrified pieces of charcoal. On some of them, even annual rings are preserved. There are strange places in the forest. Recently, he found in a forest near the village an ideally flat stretch measuring five by five kilometers, a spring with rusty water that indicates the presence of iron.

Nikolai brought a box from a neighbor, and showed us his findings. Petrified eggs: one - chopped so that the embryo begins to form, the other - with a sintered yolk, a petrified fragment of a tortoise shell, with a characteristic hexagonal pattern.

And, the most unusual, petrified uterus of some unknown mammal. Cleaved as if nature had specially taken care to reveal its secret to us. On the one hand, it's just a stone, dark rough and very heavy, but if you turn it and a miracle will open. All three layers of matter are neatly cut off, revealing the insides, and there the coagulated embryo. You can even see the head, spine, eye, something like paws, and a narrow crest on the back.

Several times Nikolai came to me, told about himself and his hobby. It should be noted that in the Tarnog district of the Vologda region, I saw such stone eggs. A couple of things were taken from an old man in a distant village, he drove them sauerkraut, because with round smooth boulders there, as they say, is stressful. One egg was chopped, inside was a round yolk, which easily separated from the outer shell. The correspondent of the local newspaper used this splinter as an ashtray, it never occurred to him to tell others in his find. All this was perceived as if in the order of things.

Until now, Nikol'schina and all of Suzemye remains a little-known and mysterious region to some extent. And still in Nikolskoye, along with Kerzh, followers of the followers of Vladyka Jerofey, who are popularly called "Erofeyevites," live. This fact is interesting. Several years ago, the regional prosecutor's office received information that an unknown settlement exists in Nikolsky forests, the district prosecutor's office was asked to sort it out. As usual, the prosecutor's office lowered the task to the police department, and those didn't have the right equipment to get to remote remote places. I managed to find people who, in the sixties, accidentally stumbled upon an unknown village in the taiga. They said that people wore homespun clothes there and did not know Soviet money. About we established the area where this settlement is located, but could not go there due to lack of equipment.

It is known that the watershed of the basin of northern and southern rivers passes precisely through the territory of our region. The Unzha River, for example, flows into the Volga, and the South River first flows south as well, and then, as if changing its mind, turns northward, while circling a significant part of our region. In the Nikolsky district, an ecological and local history expedition was conducted over a comprehensive survey of the preserved and lost churches and chapels of the Kemsky Territory.

Sharya is one of the founders of the Aryan peoples, the fourth king of the Solar Dynasty. In the Rigveda a certain

Sharyev hill is called, and the Sharyev hill is near the town of Galich (120 km. North-East of Kostroma). And the name of the city, located 400 km. east of Kostroma, Sharya - talking about something.

Avesta definitely says that already in ancient times a state existed in the territory between the sources of the Kostroma and Kama Rivers. And we are talking about times when there was still a warm climate. Indeed, further Ahura - Mazda says that in revenge for his deed the evil demon Angra - Manyu sent cold winters, snow and frost to these lands.

2004

At the feet of SAH

When we talk about Northeast European highlands that are part of a system of latitudinal uplifts, dividing rivers into currents to the north and currents to the south, which were called **Hyperborean** by Claudius Ptolemy in the 2nd century, we should clearly imagine that these are very numerous geographical objects. Judge for yourself.

On the Kola Peninsula and in Karelia it is:
Pakhty
Khibiny
Kandalaksha Mountains,
Kolvitsky Mountains
Tere Caves,
Caves
Divya,
Murom Mountain
White Mountain
Earth Mountains
Earth belt (Manselkä)

From Karelia to Mezen:
Belomorskie
Summer
Shemokhovskie,
Wind belt
Kia hills
Bow,
Mani Mountains
Permogorye,
Giman Mountain
Dyatlovy Mountains
Zhary
Red Mountain
Pillas Mountains

Culian Mountains
Winter Mountains
Orletsky Mountains
Andom Mountain
Turi Mountains
Holy Mountains
Blue Mountains
Love Mountain
Kaninsky Stone.
And in the east:
Karpovsky Stone,
Osminsky,
Lyalinsky Stone,
Narado-Itvinsky Ridge,
Nero Hoi Range
Harnes
Hara
Harayaga
Chuval Stone,
Ubyshkin Stone,
Tulam Stone,
Shudinsky,
Kogrinsky,
Gold,
Iron Stone
Kvarkush,
Pechora Stone,
Denezhkin Stone,
Cepina Horus
Hyming Stone,
Vyatka Uval
Siberian mountains (Earth stone),
Pai Hoi
Shemakhan Mountains

Beam Mountains
Parma

And this is not the whole list of names.

It was at the latitudes of these heights that Claudius Ptomely placed in the II century A.D. Riphean, Hyperborean or Alaun mountains, similar to the sacred mountains of Meru and Hara of Aryan antiquity. He wrote: **"Alaun Scythians live inside Sarmatia; they make up a branch of strong Sarmatians and are called Alaunians."**

Here it makes sense to refer to the description of the landscapes of the Vologda province, made in 1890 by N. A. Ivanitsky: **"The so-called Ural-Alaun ridge stretches along the southern border of the province, capturing the districts of Ust-Usolsk, Nikolsk, Totem, Vologda and Gryazovets. These are not mountains, but sloping hills or flat elevations that serve as the watershed of the Dvina and Volga systems. "**

It must be assumed that the Vologda peasants, who called these heights (like their fathers, grandfathers and great-grandfathers) Alaun Mountains, for the most part did not read Ptolemy and hardly suspected such an antiquity of this name. The report of N. A. Ivanitsky is also confirmed by the data of 1909 ("Materials for assessing the lands of the Vologda province, Totemsky district), where it is noted that" in the watershed area, 100-120 fathoms reach the heights and are part of the ridge, formerly called the Alauno-Ural or Shemakhinsky." It is also interesting that in the east of the Vologda province in Nikolsky district; all the mountains were generally called Shemakhinsky.

Here, of course, one could assume that this name - the Shemakha or Shemakhan mountains - was brought from the Caucasus, where the Shemakhan principality existed in the first centuries of our era. But archaeological research has long confirmed that it was through the coast of the Caucasus that the militant Indo-European horsemen advanced southward into the Near East and Asia Minor. And the traces of this advancement remained not only in the form of archaeological finds (weapons, ceramics, jewelry), but also in geographical names along the way. So Kh. I. Alishina notes that: **"Onomastics data with a strictly scientific approach are among the important and reliable sources for establishing the ethnic composition of the population in antiquity and for clarifying its movement. Toponyms in many cases are the only linguistic facts that have come down to us, characteristic of the most ancient population of this territory. "**

It is known that in the middle of II millennium BC in the Assinsky Gorge (modern Chechen Republic), people lived who left the burial mounds with bronze ornaments. Ornaments, knocked out by punch on diadems, plaques, bracelets, are completely identical to those that are still woven and embroidered by women in the Russian North. And the origins of these ornaments go back to the depths of millennia, and are already known in the Paleolithic of the Russian Plain.

By the way, the oldest bone remains of a domestic (domesticated) horse were found in the Middle Urals (settlement Davlekanovo) in layers of the turn of 6-5 thousand BC

So, on the territory of the modern Chechen Republic, the population of which calls itself Vainakhs (i.e. Vainaks - warriors), there is a settlement Argun, which is located next to the Argun River, at the point of its branch from the Sunzha River. But on the territory of the Vologda Oblast, or rather the Vologda Province, in Nikolsky Uyezd (where all the mountains were called Shemakhinsky) there is the Argunovka River, on which stands the village of Argunovo.

259

The Argunovka River itself is a tributary of the Sunzha River. A.P. Dulzon believed that **"The preservation of old names on the territory is possible only on condition that the old population, in whole or in large part, remains on this old territory, thereby ensuring continuity in the transmission of toponastics, even if it (the population) itself has undergone a complete ethnographic transformation and including a complete change of language. "**

Note that the village of Argunovo on the Argunovka River, a tributary of the Sunzha River, is located in the region of the Northern Uvali or the Shemakhan Mountains - the Ripey or Hyperborean mountains of antiquity. In addition, there is an Argun ridge in Transbaikalia on the border with Mongolia. The Argun River also flows here and there are settlements of Argun and Argunsk. There is the Argun River, a tributary of the Katun River, in Altai (on the border with China). And finally, in the very south of the Khabarovsk Territory, in the basin of the Ussuri River, between the Kiya and Khor rivers, near Svyatogorye, there is the settlement Argunskoye (border with China).

So marked the advancement to the south and east of the Indo-European horsemen in the Bronze Age, that is, in 3 - 2 millennia BC. By the way, the Chechen Sunzha, Sulak, Ardon have a delta near the Caspian Sea, i.e. in its low coastline. And this is a direct route to Azerbaijan. In addition, in the Vologda province (according to the data of the end of the 19th century), the following rivers were marked on maps:

Unzha
Kunzha
Sunzha
Sulla
Sulak.

Based on all this, we can definitely say that it is the North-East European Shemakha (Shemakhan) mountains that are primary, and the Caucasian "Shemakha" is secondary. A proof of this is also the widespread occurrence of names of this type over the entire length of the North-East European highlands:

From the Shemakha mountains in the Far East to the Shemokhov mountains in the far west,

The Shamoksa rivers (tributary of the Northern Dvina), Shamaksa (tributary of the Northern Dvina), Shamoksha (in the Ladeynopolsky district of the Leningrad region),

And, finally, the villages of Shomoksha near the "Orionov" Kozhozero in the Onega region of the Arkhangelsk region.

Since we have repeatedly convinced ourselves of the full legitimacy of using Sanskrit to explain the geographical names of the Russian North, using it, we obtain:

Sha - in Sanskrit it is eternal peace, paradise, happiness,

Moksha - deliverance, liberation, ultimate salvation of the soul;

Ax - reach, fill, penetrate, eye;

Shama - peace, peace of possession of the senses.

Note that in his "Archeometer" the Marquis of Saint-Yves D Alveider indicated that the term "SheMaX" is a kind of "sign of the beginning, the cornerstone." Possibly, from this meaning the ancient name of the Shamakhy mountains is also derived - the Hyperborean mountains of the ancient Hellenes and Ptolemy, as the main, first, original ones. The outstanding Soviet geomorphologist Yu. A. Meshcheryakov, who in his fundamental work Relief of the USSR pointed out that the higher elevations of Central Russia and Volga **"Arose only in modern times, when the Northern Uvala**

already existed and were the watershed of the basins of the North and South Seas". He considered the sub-latitudinal uplifts of the north of Eastern Europe to be extremely ancient and emphasized that even in the Carboniferous period, when the ancient sea splashed on the site of the future Urals, the Northern Uvals (Shemakhan Mountains - S. Zh.) were already mountains.

In this context, it makes sense to recall that both the ancient Iranian and ancient Indian traditions claimed that when the world was created, the Meru ridges were the very first to be created, stretching across the north of the Earth from west to east, and all the other mountains of the Earth grew from them later (in the Indian tradition), and that the first of all the mountains of the earth were the Hara Berizaiti mountains, also stretching across the north from west to east (in the Iranian tradition). Thus, the Shemakhan (or Shemakha) mountains are truly the "first, original, cornerstone, fundamental" mountains.

And since in Indo-Iranian antiquity it was already claimed that behind these "primordial mountains" there is a "monastery of Light" and a "place of salvation of souls", such names as:

"Shamoksha" from "sha" - "paradise, peace" and "moksha" - "salvation, reconciliation, liberation of the soul";

"Shemox" - "divine heaven and earth, liberating the soul."

262

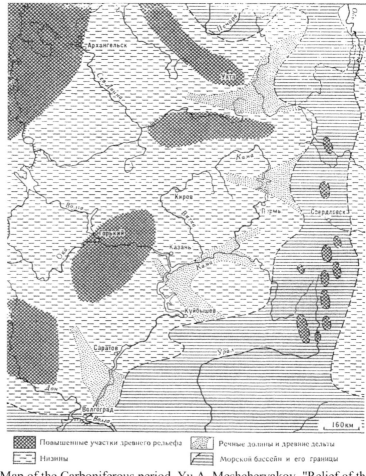

Map of the Carboniferous period. Yu.A. Meshcheryakov. "Relief of the USSR."

S. V. Zharnikova
1999

263

Images of waterfowl in Russian folk tradition

The images of waterfowl - ducks, geese and swans - play an exceptional role in the Russian folk tradition. Often it is a duck, swan or goose that marks the sphere of the sacred in the ritual songs of the calendar cycle. So, "field duck" or "meadow duck" are the characteristic characters of Shrovetide songs - a holiday associated with the cult of ancestors and the fertility spell of the coming agricultural year. In one of the Pancake week songs the Pancake week is called the "white duck", in another Siberian Pancake the Pancake week is watched by flying geese with their cries, in the third - they call it with funny cries when one day is left until the Pancake week. But in reality at this time there are no, and there cannot be geese in these territories - their spring arrival occurs much later, just as there are no geese and swans before Christmas. However, in a song recorded by P.V. Shein in the Pskov province, the following is sung:

Kolyada came before Christmas,
My red-green grape!
Powder attacked a little white snow:
As for this powder
Geese-swans flew - sorcerers, shortcomings.

She echoes grapes from the village of Evseevskaya, Tarnogsky district, Vologda region, recorded by D. M. Balashov, Yu. I. Marchenko and N. I. Kalmykova:

Something about the goose, oh
With grapes and all, yes
Grape, oh
Red-green.

Geologic swans quite often appear in the study songs, which also had ritual significance and were considered a way of magically subordinating to man the forces of nature. So, in

264

one of the songs recorded by P.V. Shane in the Pskov province, there is an exceptionally interesting contrast:

Not geese fly, not swans
Christ has risen to the whole world!

In this connection, it makes sense to recall that both carollers and volostechniki were perceived in the folk tradition as the embodiment of the souls of ancestors who were given ritual alms, and their connection with the geese-swans, apparently, was not accidental. This is evidenced by the ending of the conception above the cited volostological song of Pskov:

Not geese fly, not swans -
Christ has risen to the whole world!
Volupes go on their way,
Parasites-night owls.

Russian folk riddles also testify to the connection of waterfowl with the other world, with death:

On the sea, on the edge
On the island of Buyan
The Oyster Bird is sitting;
She boasts, boasts,
What all saw, just eaten a lot
I saw the king in Moscow
Kings in Lithuania
An old man in a cell, a child in a cradle,
What's what at sea lacking.
(Death)

Sitting duck on a raft
The Cossack boasts:
No one will pass me
Neither the king nor the queen
No red maiden.
(Death)

In such a late spring rite as the "Funeral of Kostroma", also entirely associated with the fertility spell, an appeal to the ancestors - the fertility givers, in the Vladimir province the main character of the rite was addressed as follows:

Kostromushka is mine, Kostromushka.

My white swan.

Does my Kostroma have a lot of gold treasury,

Kostromushka-Kostroma, swan-quinoa!

In the songs of holy divination, foreshadowing the wedding, it is the geese-swans that fly through the grape garden and drop the gold wedding rings. The images of gray geese and white swans are especially widespread in Russian folk wedding songs, where the bride is constantly compared with the "white swan" floating on the "Khvalynsky sea", along the Danube, exclaiming "in quiet backwaters", "lagging behind the herd swan ", with a gray duck or with a pava, which, apparently, was also thought in the Russian folk tradition as a waterfowl (duck or swan). The fact that the pava and the swan in the popular representation are the same thing and that the image of the pava has little in common with the peacocks is evidenced by a song recorded in 1958 in the Arkhangelsk region, i.e. where, as in the Vologda province, the image of pav on wedding towels, sundresses, hem hem was widespread:

What's quiet in silence

Yes on a quiet swan

Yes, there wasn't a pavanka

Yes not pava feathers dropped ...

At the same time, the groom is usually compared to a gray goose. It is interesting that the herd of geese, to which the goose-groom belongs, is connected in one of the songs of

266

the wedding cycle recorded in 1929 in the Arkhangelsk region with the following circle of images:

Because of the mountains, high mountains.
Yes, because of the forest, the forest of the dark.
Yes, because of the green garden.
Because of the green garden.
Yes because of the sea, the sea of blue
Yes, a formidable cloud rose.
Yes with thunder with loud
Yes with molony with palyuchima,
With the scum of molony
Yes, with a large, frequent rain,
With large, frequent rain.
Yes, with a storm - with a pad.
Yes, with a grave little bastard.
Yes, from under that terrible cloud
To from under that impenetrable
A flock of geese flew out
Yes there were geese - gray ducks.
Yes, in black geese - gray ducks.
In the black geese - gray ducks
Yes, a white swan got involved ...

This wedding song has a complete set of sacred symbols of space and natural elements. The spatial characteristics include the mountains, the forest, the green garden, and the blue sea, i.e. all that is connected with the promotion of the wedding train in the songs of the wedding cycle, the transition from one kind to another, the bride changing her social status. The goose herd, of which the groom is a member, is correlated in this song with a whole range of natural phenomena whose sacred nature is obvious. This is both a large frequent rain, and a storm, and "explosive thunder", and "molony scaly" and a snowstorm,

267

which a goose herd in the form of a "formidable cloud" brings with it.

Geese - a cloud, thunder, lightning, and storm - are interconnected. It can be assumed that such a serious attitude to the images of geese-swans in the folk song tradition, which has enough analogues in Russian folk tales, can be explained by the fact that these images took shape in the deepest pagan antiquity. This is evidenced by numerous facts. Even on the Pre-Slavic jewelry there are numerous images of swans. They are located on the sides of the female figure with raised hands on a 7th century bronze bracelet. BC. from a treasure in Radolinek near Poznan. In ancient Slavic ash-houses, places of ritual bonfires, archaeologists find giant figures of swans dug in the ground. Ancient Greek mythology connects swans - the sacred birds of Apollo - with the northern outskirts of Oikumena, where they annually carried God to the shores of the cold Kronian Ocean, to the lands of the Hyperboreans. B. A. Rybakov is probably right in believing that "the solar swans of the pre-Slavic world we should not consider as a mechanical borrowing of an ancient myth, but as an complicity of the northern tribes in some general (maybe Indo-European) myth-making connected with the sun and the sun deity. " He also notes that the image of a woman raising her arms to the sky, with duck birds on the sides, is very archaic, lived in North Russian embroidery until the end of the 19th century. Pendants in the form of a duck, a goose and a swan survive in the Slavic tradition until the 12th century. A. V. Chernetsov notes that "the images of two birds, along with floral decorations (most often on the sides of a tree) are the ideogram of the Garden of Eden traditional in ancient Russian art. This is due to the pre-Christian idea that paradise (irium) is a place where the birds fly away." As for skopje buckets, liqueurs, cups, salt marshes, louder huts, etc.

268

in the form of a swan duck, all this remained in the Russian North until the turn of the 19th and 20th centuries.

It should be noted that in the above wedding song you can find a rather transparent analogy to the ancient Greek myth of the marriage of Zeus and Leda, only there the thunder god, who has already acquired an anthropomorphic appearance, by virtue of his whim becomes a swan, and in the East Slavic (specifically North Russian) tradition we encounter , it seems, with a more archaic mythological layer, when the groom and his family are a flock of geese and a cloud, a storm, thunder, lightning at the same time. Thus, with a flock of geese, and hence with the groom himself, the whole set of those sacred attributes is associated, which will subsequently become the property of only one god of thunder - the deified sky. Since, apparently, the images of geese-swans have common Indo-European sources, it is necessary to turn to the most ancient monuments of Indo-European mythology - the Rigveda and Avesta, which, perhaps, will explain to us the origins of the cult, ritual role of these birds in the Russian tradition.

It is well known that the goose-swan is given great importance in Indian mythology, theology and natural philosophy, where it is a symbol of the sun, the Universe, light and sky, the universal and individual soul, a certain musical harmony - the music of the Universe. Yu. A. Rapoport cites the data "Chandogya - Upanishads" and "Puran", where the goose is the embodiment of a higher being and the Universe. The researcher notes that in the Khorezmian concept of the origin of the Universe there is evidence that "the original deity, which contained parts of the universe, was represented in the form of a waterfowl." The name of this deity, combining male and female principles, heaven and earth, fire and water, light and darkness, is Zarvan. But it's Zarvan in Sogdian texts of a

Buddhist nature that Brahma is called - the creator of the Vedic pantheon Universe, which in legends is often personified by a goose, which is a constant companion of Brahma and its "carrier" - vahana. "It is possible," the researcher believes, "that the image of the waterfowl reflects the idea of the primordial nature of the water element, which was represented in the Avestan pantheon by the goddess whose ancient name is believed to have been hidden behind the triple epithet of Ardvi Surah Anahita." It is also appropriate to recall here that the companion of the great water goddess of the Vedic era of Sarasvati was a goose, which personified an all-encompassing sky. E. E. Kuzmina also notes that in Indo-Iranian mythology, the waterfowl was the personification and companion of the mother goddess associated with water, which was often depicted as a "world tree" with birds sitting on it, and a pair of ducks was in the folklore of all Indo-European peoples symbol of conjugal love.

A very significant role was played by images of waterfowl (ducks, geese, swans) in Scythian art. D. S. Raevsky notes that these images, as a rule, are found on objects of a clearly religious purpose and the image of the waterfowl was a stable religious symbol in the Scythian world, and in the scenes of investiture it was a sign of the God-givenness of the tsarist government.

To the question of why the image of a waterfowl in Iranian and Scythian mythologies became the image of the bodily world, D. S. Raevsky replies that this representative of the terrestrial fauna has the ability to move in all three elements - on land, on water and, finally, on air: "It is significant that the" triple "or" triple "goose is reflected in Akhtarvaved. This is most likely also connected with the interpretation of the waterfowl as a symbol of the three zones of the universe." V.I. Konenkova notes that at the late stage of Koban culture (7th - early 4th centuries BC), numerous pendants on long chains with skates, deer, ducks appear in the North Caucasus, which are considered to be a specific introduction of Scythian sauromats. These examples could be continued, but in order to find the origins of such an ancient civilization, it is probably necessary to turn to the most ancient pictorial monuments, which in one way or another reflected a new attitude towards the goose, duck or swan, as a sacred bird.

Sinking into the millennia, we turn to the archaeological sites of the Neolithic in the North of the European part of Russia. It is here at the turn of the Mesolithic and Neolithic era, during the period of the climatic optimum of the Holocene, when the average summer temperatures were higher than modern ones by an average of 3-4 ° C, and the forest zone came out on the coast of the Polar basin, and the broad-leaved forest strip, which today makes up 200-400 km., was equal to 1200-1300 km., images appear on the rocky shores of Lake Onega and the White Sea, evidence of the ancient sacralization of waterfowl images, constantly present in scenes of mythological ritual character. These are scenes associated with fertilization, birth and death, celestial bodies - the sun, moon and stars.

Of particular interest are compositions in which these birds are associated with anthropomorphic characters. This is an anthropomorphic figure spread out in the position of a woman in labor, whose leg grows into the body of a goose, and a unique image of a huge (main in the composition of the so-called "Weight Tracks" on the White Sea) horned phallic character, the thumb of the huge foot of which is connected with the figure of an elk, and the little finger with a group of three waterfowl (geese or ducks). The image of a

271

waterfowl, along with the image of man and moose, leading in the Neolithic pantheon of the inhabitants of the north of Eastern Europe and recorded in the petroglyphs of Lake Onega and the White Sea coast, probably entered this pantheon not only because duck-geese-swans can exist in three areas, but also because that with their arrival in spring and departure in autumn, the warm season came and went. In addition, ducks, geese, and swans are here, on the rivers and lakes of the North, hatched their offspring, and it is here that these cunning and careful birds, hunting for which is quite difficult during molting they became completely helpless and defenseless.

The huge number of waterfowl flown to the Russian North at the end of the 19th century is evidenced by many sources.

It is known that the western part of the southern coast of Novaya Zemlya Island (between 71-72 ° N), due to the abundance of geese there, was called the "Goose Land".

On Kolguev Island (in the Barents Sea), waterfowl gathered in huge masses - geese, ducks of all kinds, swans, who flew in from the southwest in late June and remained until mid-September. One hunting artel of 10 people could easily get during molting (per month) up to 3.5 and even 5 thousand geese and swans. In the 19th century, 6400 kg were exported annually from the island. Feathers and down and 12,000 kg. Swan skins. It's probably these birds in the most difficult time of the year, in the off-season of spring and summer, were for the ancient inhabitants of the White Sea coast, Onega and other lakes and rivers of the Russian North the main source of meat food, which played an important role in the sacralization of the goose, duck and swan. It is likely that the tradition of keeping Indigir workers - Russian old-timers of the Ust Indigirka - is a tradition in the production of a linear bird ("goose") to keep

272

alive and release the last goose, caught in the network who were asked to bring more of their comrades next year, goes back to the deepest Neolithic-Mesolithic antiquity of Eastern Europe. I would like to note that the geese went to the geese only in the spring, when other supplies ran out. Goosiness was conducted only on a young goose, and never geese with broods were the object of hunting. Maybe because such a fierce hunt was caused by the urgent need for man to save his life and the life of his loved ones (otherwise many would starve to death) people, realizing that, saving themselves, they kill completely defenseless birds, felt guilty before them and therefore in the 19th century in Kargopol it was considered a sin to eat goose meat just like that - on ordinary days.

The worship of the sacred goose swan and duck, established in the deepest Indo-European antiquity, it was reflected in the hymns of the Rigveda and Avesta, associating the goose-swan and the creator god, the goose-swan and the Universe, the goose-swan and the light, the mind, the soul, the goose-swan and a certain musical mood - the rhythm of the Universe. But also for the East Slavic folk tradition, the researchers of which have repeatedly noted that it preserves the rudiments of archaic phenomena, sometimes not reflected even in the Vedas, the same attitude towards the swan geese is characteristic.

And just as the Vedic tradition connects the waterfowl with the supreme creature - the Creator of the world, so the cosmogonic legend about the creation of the earth, recorded in the middle of the 20th century in the Russian Mouth, connects the creator's image with the duck-loon, and this legend is surprisingly close to the Vedic idea of the act creations: "First there was no one, no people, no one.

There was only a spirit in heaven, and from this spirit man was founded, and he lived there, in heaven. When he

273

looked down, he saw the sea, and on the sea a swimming duck-loon." When this spirit-man began to talk with this loon, who was also a saint, he told him: "I became from white foam, from sea flooding, and what did you become of?" - asks.

What gets the answer: "There is a spirit in heaven - I am from that spirit."

The spirit asked the loon where the earth is. Gagara replied that the earth was deep in the sea, and tried to get it, but he lacked the strength. Then the spirit twice added strength to the loon, and he took out the earth on his back. This land was blown up by the spirit of the world, so mountains appeared; dry land and the sea remained. Then the spirit invited the loon to build thrones. The spirit began to build its own, and the loon - its own. But the apostles who appeared with them "to send them to" informed the spirit that the throne of the loon was higher than the throne of the spirit. The Spirit sent two apostles to the loon one after another with a request to build the throne no higher than their own, but the loon did not agree. Then the spirit went to him himself and began to ask the loon about the same, but the loon again refused. "I," says, "set the earth on that."

The spirit argued with the loon and, angry, blew off his throne at sea, and the loon itself turned into Satanail.

We see in this text the ancient, known as the Vedas, the idea of the creation of the divine principle from the sea foam that appeared from the unrest (buttermilk) of the sea, and Christian offerings that turned the holy bird into Satan. And just as the Vedic tradition connects the goose-swan-duck with a musical mood, with sacred musical rhythms in the Russian tradition, geese-swans are closely related to geese (often pterygoid), with a "gusly" carnival, with singing.

This connection is well seen in one of the pre-wedding songs - songs of a bachelorette party recorded in the Arkhangelsk province:

Where were you, geese?
Where have you been?
Where did you sleep, spend the night?
We were with the princess
We visited the newlywed
What does the princess do?
He plays the harp
Gifts equips ...

It is interesting that in the ritual folk dance that has survived to the present day in the Russian North (in particular, in the Nyuksen district of the Vologda region), the main step (frequent, as if drowning along the ground) is called "duck". In such a dance, due to the constant repetitions of rhythm-forming movements, a feeling of a certain space-time is created, outside the context of everyday life. And here again I would like to turn to Vedic analogies, where: hansa - a goose, a swan, a soul who has cognized the highest truth, the highest spirit, the poetic size; such terms are also associated with this term: hansa aksa - the wing of a swan, the name of a particular position of the hand in ganz, and hansa pada - cinnabar. It makes sense to recall that the working part of the weaving mill, creating a fabric pattern, is called "duck" (ducks).

In the Vedic tradition, the concept of the "weft" of the weaving mill is associated with the concept of the universe, where the weft thread, without interruption, is interwoven with the base and forms a fabric pattern in which the base is a substantial-quality (energetic) thread, and the ducks color the basis of nature, implements diversity the pattern of her immense, but uniform fabric. Knowing that in the ancient tradition the musical mood associated with the geese-swans creates the music of Cosmos, that playing the harp is comparable in this mythical and poetic series with the fabric of "world harmony", we can understand why the author of the "Word on Igor's Campaign" connects in a single image the "herd of swans" singing a song of praise to the old heroes and heroes, and the "live strings" of a gusel along which Boyan's fingers move, like the warp threads of ducks, creating the "fabric" of an epic song. Another Indian word prastava, which has an analogy in the North Russian dialect - "prastava", "prestavka" (a band embroidered or filled with a weaving pattern, decorates the unity of the concepts "fabric pattern" and "song pattern", "weave fabric" and "compose a song") shirt, towel, etc.). Sanskrit "prasiava" means "song of praise"!

The fact that the ancient pagan cult of the waterfowl in Russia retained its religious significance for a long time and was well known to the Orthodox clergy is evidenced by the fact that back in the 14-15 century the monks of the Murom monastery on Lake Onega carved a Christian cross not only on the main one in the composition " The Demon Nose "image of the Demon, but also on the image of a swan located at a considerable distance from it.

Ducks, geese and swans of Russian folk embroidery, duck-barked weavers of weaving mills, solonetzes, brackets and brooches in the shape of a duck or a swan, ducks crowning the roofs of houses, wing-shaped geese and geese-swans, ducks of folk ritual songs - all this testifies to the great antiquity and the importance of these archaic pagan images in the folk mythopoetic perception of the world.

S. V. Zharnikova
2009

The battle of Indra and Vritra: a chronology of disaster

Of extreme interest to science is the story widely spread in Vedic literature about the liberation of Indra as a result of the murder of Vrtra, who "constrained" or "stifled" them ("Vrtra" - harbor, abundance, mountain, from the root "Vrti" - shell, cover, obstacle) . Indra gives the earth a firm footing and at the same time frees bound water and releases the fire enclosed in Vritra hill.

It is believed that in the Avesta Varabragna is testified as an independent mythological character.

In the ordinary sense, rituals dedicated to this feat of Indra could probably be perceived in connection with the spring opening of the rivers, the liberation of the waters from the ice and snow that bound them and with spring floods. But if you think about this plot, then at the mythological level such an interpretation is contradicted by the simultaneity and univariance of the phenomenon, repeatedly emphasized in the Rig Veda and Mahabharata, its clear localization, attachment to a specific geographical region, as well as some circumstances that characterize the incident as an extraordinary event.

Considering the main characteristics of the battle of Indra and Vritra, we must note that the time and place of this incident are indicated exactly. According to the Mahabharata, it happened in Crete-yuga:

"The tribes of formidable, ferocious, frantic tribes of Danavas, nicknamed the Kalei, living in Vritra, lived in Crete-yuga ..."

This is also evidenced by the chronology of kings and sages – rishis.

Thus, according to the Puranas and the Mahabharata, immediately after the assassination of Vritra, King Nahush took the place of Indra until he was overthrown and Yayati became his heir. The Yayati era lasted more than 1000 years. The reign of Nahusha also amounted to a significant period. Meanwhile, Yayati was considered "mainly belonging to the Crete-yuga," that is, part of his era went beyond its borders (possibly in its "twilight").

Crete-yuga, according to the total length of 12,000 years adopted by the Mahabharata, began 10,800 years ago and ended 6400 years before the last Kali-yuga began in 3102 BC, i.e. between 13900 BC and 9500 BC If we take into account only Crete-yuga itself without "twilight" (400 years each), then from 13500 BC 9900 BC But the defeat of Vritra was to happen at least 1000 - 1500 years before the end of Crete-yuga, i.e. between 13500 BC and 10,500 - 10,000 BC.

The location of the battle of Indra and Vritra is localized quite definitely.

Firstly, its action took place in the north, since after the destruction of Vritra, Indra hid in the south in the cool "Sea of Manas", which according to the Puranas is located south of Kailasa, that is, in the area south of the modern Pinega River.

Secondly, after the crash of Vritra, Indra "released seven streams for running" and "Manu's waters flowed billowing". It should be recalled that one of the highest peaks of the Polar Urals is called "Manaraga", from which the Manaraga River flows. It is interesting that, according to legend, the forefather of people Manu tied his ship to the spur of one of the highest peaks of Himavat during the flood.

Thirdly, Vritra was considered a Daitya and a Brahmin, but on the whole the east side was Brahmin, while he lay on the great river. The river, which was located in the northeast, is also mentioned in Avesta as the "good Daitiya" adjacent to Ardvi-Sura (Northern Dvina) in Aryan Wedja. This river of daityas could well be called the "waters of Manu" among the Aryans. The only great river flowing in the northeast from the Urals near the Northern Dvina is Pechora, a tributary of which is the same river Manaraga.

But 11000 BC - This is the end time of the continuous glaciation of the Far North of Eastern Europe. At the same time, as noted by the paleogeographers: "It was established that the degradation of the last ice sheet of the Pechora lowland, as well as of the entire north-east of the European territory of the USSR, occurred in an unusual way, fundamentally different from the degradation of the Scandinavian ice sheet ... the destruction of the ice sheet was accompanied, and possibly was caused by a process of seismic nature, i.e. earthquakes."

The question is, what force should an earthquake be in order to destroy the Pechora glacier, with a capacity of up to 700 meters, and what caused him paleogeographers leave open but note that: "About 13,500 years ago, Pechora Valley Lake was lowered and along the zone of loss of continuity formed channels of permanent drains (Pechora and other rivers), the Barents Sea ice sheet collapsed part of which was the Pechora Glacier. "The findings of the researchers are extremely interesting, that "according to the calculations that a powerful glacier similar to the Antarctic would arise from a small glacier, 14180 years are required at temperatures characteristic of the Valdai maximumIn the presence of a warm climate of Middle Valdai or marine climate 16-17 thousand years. The following lines of the Mahabharata say that Vritra "for the sake of strengthening power, sixteen thousand years committed the killing of the flesh."

We need to ask a question: could the destruction of this North-East European glacier and the myth of Indra's victory over Vritra be connected?

This is how Vritra is described in the Mahabharata:

"Vrita, which covered itself with heaven and earth, was guarded from all sides by giants - Kalaneys; when they waved their arms, it seemed: the mountains soar their peaks."

"Vritra said: Having appropriated the smells and tastes of various creatures of the slain, I thrived in three worlds. Framed with a radiant crown, I ruled in the heavens, invincible to all creatures, I never experienced fear."

The following fragment of Mokshadharma, which tells about the meeting of the gods and Vritra, seems especially striking:

"Once upon a time surrounded by a somn of gods, Indra rode in a chariot and saw in front of him a standing mountain-like Vritra. "He went up five hundred yojanas, a destroyer of enemies, and over three hundred yojanas he was in girth."

The horns of Vritra are also spoken of in the hymns of the Rig Veda:

"You, O Indra, this mountain, great, wide,
A club of thunder, oh thunderer, split into pieces
You released the bound waters for running.
In the secret of being secretly hidden in the waters
Secretly living, witching serpent,
Overlapping the water and the sky
You killed, oh hero! "

Singing Indra, the hymns say that he "split the mountain with force, throwing the vajra" (ie the club), they

280

constantly compare Vritra with the serpent "resting on the mountain", emphasize that he is "legless, armless, faceless." These descriptions are not very suitable for spring snow or ice on rivers, but to a large extent correspond to the Barents Sea ice sheet.

So the size of Vritra - mountains of 300 yojanas in a circle (4800 km.) - Corresponds to 1528 km. in length and width, which is equal to the established size of the Barents Sea ice sheet.

The Barents Sea glacier occupied the entire shelf of the Barents Sea, the Kara Sea, the Bolshezemelskaya and Malozemelskaya tundra, adjoined the Scandinavian and Kara shields and had an area of 2.1 million km and an ice thickness of up to 3.5 km. (an average of 1,870 km.) and an ice volume of 4 million cubic km.

An altitude of 500 yojanas (8,000 km.) May mean that something happened at that altitude. In this regard, a fragment of Indra's anthem (PB, 4.17), which speaks of his birth, is very interesting:

"The sky shook from the flash at your birth,
The earth shook with fear of your fury.
Strong mountains swayed
Deserts parted, water flows ...
When you are born, you are first of all
He terrified all these peoples, O Indra.
Snake damming stock
You cut the vajra, oh generous. "

The same hymn says that Indra "set in motion the wheel of the sun", he stopped the sage Etasha running through the sky and threw him, furious, "to the bottom of the hide, dark space, into its bosom," that is, into the depths of the earth.

The further description of the battle after the meeting at an altitude of 500 yojanas is extremely interesting: "From the skies of Vritra a shower of stones was showered with a hail of stones, and the angry crowds of the gods began to throw arrows, stone rain from everywhere, beating, brought down by Vritra in battle."

When the battle of the gods and dans, the defenders of Vritra began to boil, then: "It was visible ... how the heads fell from the heavens, like fruits ripped from cuttings ... Armed with clubs with iron spikes, gold armor, they were approaching the gods, as if covered the flame of a mountain forest fire. "

But Vritra did not help "neither lightning, nor thunder, nor the fog that he spread, nor hail" - the gods moved south to the Sarasvati River, and then returned, armed with a heavenly thundering mace - vajra, and: "When Indra and the serpent fought for (all) future times the generous defeated."

Already as Indra returned and the host of gods with a blazing vajra to continue the battle with Vritra, the last one had "fever" and completely enveloped him: "He was terribly pale, his mouth was inflamed, a strong trembling gripped his body, his breathing was very frequent, his body hair rose "He was breathing quickly and hard ... In a fire, a blazing flame burst from his sides ..." "Vritra erupted in terrible screams. The sides of the world, the firmament, the heavens, the earth and the mountains trembled from his roar "and when" the inhuman cry of that great asura was heard: he opened his throat, (he shouted), gripped by a heavy fever ... the perun thrust Shakra into its open mouth; the brilliance of that perun was very bright, it looks like a kind of flame. Instantly, the huge body of the Vitya daitya fell. ”

So, Indra's celestial mace "with force chopped the head of Vritra, who oppressed both worlds”, as a result of which Vritra sank to the "bottom of space”, and "the earth

282

increased ten times" and the peoples were able to "spread it".

Thus, the great battle of Indra and Vritra, at the same time going both in heaven and on earth, ended with the fact that: this mountain, great, wide, with a club of thunder (Indra) ... split into pieces; let go of bound water for running; drilled water (channels) ... cut through the bowels of the mountains ... like mowing cows, heading straight for the sea, waters run away ... (he) released seven streams for running ... Through a lifeless reed lying like a shredded reed (Vritra), flowing billowing water Manu. "

Vritra himself, "faceless from the breach ... was crushed lying scattered in different places."

It is characteristic that the nature of the terrain of the battlefield has also changed: "The land was stretched exactly, even the mountain, which was trying to escape, stopped. The mountain sat down without dodging. "

Interestingly, about 12,000 years ago (that is, at the turn of 11-10 millennia BC) there was no geomagnetic field of the Earth.

It can be assumed that the myth of the battle of Indra and Vritra describes the interaction of the glacier with a certain cosmic body. Moving at an altitude of 500 yojanas (that is, 8,000 kilometers), for some reason it drastically braked and approached the Earth. At that time, probably, the breakaway parts fell and as a result of the impact of a sharp tidal wave and the rise of the earth's crust, an earthquake occurred and strong volcanic activity began. Deviating to the southwest, this space object pushed a small cosmic body from its orbit over the Central Russian Upland (or a piece broke off from it).

The following lines of the Mahabharata testify to the rotation of such a body in near-earth orbit: "Indra killed

Visvaruna and cut off his head with the unbreakable, indispensable perun, arising from the bramins of the Brahmin, penetrated by Vishnu. Immediately after this son of Tvashtar, who emerged from the fragmented body of Vishvaruna, Indra killed the enemy. "

But this "directly", judging by the fact that Vritra existed for at least 16,000 years, lasted quite a long time. All this time, the vajra revolved in low Earth orbit. As the space object returned to its orbit and the vajra approached the glacier, tectonic oscillations, volcanism, and glacier bombardment by meteorites intensified. Because of them, cracks went through the massif, intensive melting began, fog from the vapors rose above the glacier, and fire fell on its foot. At the same time, the roar of volcanoes was blocked by a whistle from the falling vajra ("noisy club of thunder"). With thunder and thunder, returning, it crashed from the southwest into the body of the glacier, finally breaking a single mass of ice. The debris from it, bouncing off the surface, scattered in different directions, subjecting the glacier to additional bombardment, as the vajra "scattered into hundreds of pieces on the head of Vritra."

As a result of tectonic changes, part of the surface in the Barents Sea was lowered and the existing mountain ranges were destroyed. Paleogeographers note a number of features of this region. A characteristic feature of the history of the Barents Sea cover was the very rapid rate of decay, which began, however, relatively late, in the form of destruction and fragmentation of the glacier.

As noted above, detailed studies have shown that "the degradation of the last ice sheet of the Pechora lowland, as well as the entire North-East of the European territory of the USSR, occurred in an unusual way, fundamentally different from the degradation of the Scandinavian ice sheet. Its

284

destruction was accompanied and possibly caused by a process of seismic nature, i.e. earthquakes."

But the power of these earthquakes should have reached at least 12 points in a vast area from Pechora to Svalbard; otherwise they simply would not have been able to destroy a glacier with an area of 2 million square kilometers with 4 million cubic kilometers ice.

In modern science, the question remains open, what could have caused such catastrophic earthquakes in this tectonically calm region, moreover, then balanced by three kilometers of ice, which quenched the oscillations of the lithosphere crust (glacioisostatic deflection reached at least 150-170 meters). In the marginal part of the glacier, the ice thickness was also significant - at least 450-700 meters.

The answer proposed by the Mahabharata and the Rig Veda in the form of a double effect of tidal disturbance from a space object and the fall of fireballs explains this.

The question of the time for the final destruction of the Barents Sea glacier is somewhat more complicated.

So a number of researchers believe that the final melting of the glacier on Pechora occurred after 8000 BC. This is connected with the descent of the valley lake, which existed at the mouth of the Pechora River in 7400 - 7200 BC and carrying out runoff through Sulu and Indiga to the sea.

But if there was a drain in the Barents Sea, it means that there was no continuous ice on the sea. The river could be blocked both by a residual mountain glacier and as a result of a local tectonic uplift.

Other researchers believe that evidence of the existence of a glacier at the turn of the 7-8 millennium BC there are traces of moraines, as well as carbon dating C14 of buried vegetation in the layers of the moraine Marchid 7000 - 6700 BC.

Firstly, under them lies the woody vegetation of 8000 BC. That is, at least at that time a forest was growing at the mouth of Pechora.

Secondly, as indicated in the "Paleogeography of Europe over the last hundred thousand years", moraine formations from "dead" ice, covered with sediment, in the blades of glaciers reaching 250 meters in height, could exist even covered with vegetation, not less than 3500 years. Also noted that in the postglacial period catastrophic mudflows were widespread even in the valleys and most 15 km long moraine formations and 1 km wide relate to them.

Thirdly, C14 dating for this time (i.e. 8000 BC) is rejuvenated by 1-1.5 thousand years compared to the present age.

According to the latest data, the destruction of the Pechora glacier occurred 12,500 years ago, i.e. in 10-11 millennia BC then the glacier in Western Siberia, which was part of the same ice sheet with Pechorsky, disappeared.

The fact that the Mahabharata after the destruction of Vritra, after a long period of time, the Northwest Ocean was drained to get rid of the Danavas, and this condition lasted at least 3 millennia, also testifies to the correspondence of the described events. Meanwhile: "at the turn of the Upper Dryas, the Baltic glacial lake itself is formed. Initially, it had a limited connection with the ocean, but after a catastrophic descent north of Mount Billingen, the reservoir level dropped by 25-30 meters and the ocean waters penetrated into the Baltic. This event occurred after the formation of the second ridge of Salpausselkä; according to varvametric and radiocarbon data, it dates back to 8300 BC. The invasion of the ocean led to the creation of a brackish basin, known as the Yoldian Sea. It occupied only the central part of the Baltic Basin, southwestern and southern regions were subaerial (at the same time water slept in the reservoirs between the Baltic and the White Sea, connecting these seas). Low sea levels persisted until the litorin transgression in 5200 - 4700 BC, when the warm Litorin Sea arose. "

The findings of the researchers are extremely interesting, according to which a glacier similar to Pechora and Barents Sea he could not melt. Reaching a maximum a glacier in modern climate would melt at least 50 thousand years (that is, we would still have the opportunity to observe cover glaciation throughout the north). At temperatures 2 ° C higher than modern (i.e. Holocene optimum), it would melt for 10 thousand years, however, such temperatures should have been maintained above the glacier itself during the ice age. With the temperature increase that actually existed at the end of the Ice Age, by 5 - 6 ° C from the Valdai maximum, the glacier would remain stable since a further increase in temperature would not be allowed by a thick ice sheet, and melting would compensate for the increase in mass due to increased precipitation. Thus, the Pechora and Barents Sea glaciers could not melt by themselves. The only possibility of melting was that the system was supposed to remove external influence from stability, and quite long (which is not observed), or quite powerful (which is observed both according to sources and according to paleogeography).

Should be glad that the asteroid (satellite) fell so well that destroyed the glacier because he's not in a plastic ice mass, able to absorb impact energy, and into the ocean or land, the consequences for humanity could be extremely adverse. After all, a piece of a comet with a diameter of 5 km. was able to cause disaster even on Jupiter (the power of the blow reached 1 trillion Hiroshima), what can we say about the Earth.

They may object that no traces of his blow were found. However, the ice sheet in the Northern Hemisphere has melted quickly, according to information obtained by drilling ice in Greenland, for a period of less than a year, possibly for months or days. Of course, the streams of water formed as a result of this flood, rushing to the south (along the valleys of the Volga, Don, Dnieper, Mississippi) on their way caused great damage to the ecosystem, but, nevertheless, they created a modern world. The starting point of this is described in the Rig Veda and Mahabharata. And in reality their data is not to be doubted.

S. V. Zharnikova, A. G. Vinogradov
1989

Senkovsky Joseph-Julian
Scientist trip to Bear Island

According to the theory of Baron Cuvier

On April 14 (1828) we set off from Irkutsk on a further journey towards the northeast, and in early June arrived at the Berendinskaya station, riding over a thousand miles …

As we approached the coast of the Lena, the view of the country became more and more entertaining. Anyone who has not been to this part of Siberia will hardly comprehend the magnificence and variety of paintings, which here, at every step, attract the traveler's eyes, exciting in his soul his most unexpected and most pleasant sensations. Everything that the Universe, for its various destinies, contains in itself the beautiful, rich, captivating, terrible, wild, picturesque: shrunken mountain ranges, funny velvet meadows, gloomy abysses, magnificent valleys, formidable cliffs, lakes with a sparkling surface dotted with beautiful islands, forests, hills, groves, fields, streams, majestic rivers and noisy waterfalls - everything is collected here in incredible abundance, tastefully laid out or set with incomprehensible art …

But Spurzmann, as a personal friend of nature, receiving money from the King of Hanover ... affirming positively that she was forced to that external force, one of the great and sudden upheavals that transformed the former warm lands, where palm trees and bananas grew, where mammoths, elephants lived, mastodons to cold countries littered with eternal ice and snow, in which polar bears now crawl and barely vegetate pine and birch. As evidence of the fact that the northern part of Siberia was once a hot strip, he brought bones and whole skeletons of animals belonging to southern climates, scattered in many on its surface or buried in the upper layers of its fat soil together with trees and fruits of warm countries of the world. The doctor was purposely sent by the University of Gottingen to collect these bones and enthusiastically pointed to an ivory tooth or wine berry, turned into stone, which he sold him one Yakut off the coast of Aldan ...

The banks of this beautiful, noble river, one of the largest and safest in the world, are furnished with magnificent cliffs and cleaned by an unbroken chain of rich and beautiful views. In many places, the cliffs rise steeply and present to their eyes the deceptive likeness of ruined towers, castles, temples, palaces ... Indulging in a comforting dream, I saw in Lena the ancient Siberian Nile and in the temple-shaped cliffs the ruins of antediluvian luxury and the education of the peoples inhabiting its shores ... But by the way about the Nile. I traveled around Egypt for a long time and, when I was in Paris, I had the honor of being one of the most ardent students of Champollion the Younger, who became famous for discovering the key to hieroglyphs ... It is true that Mr. Ghulianov disputed the thoroughness of our system and suggested another way for them to read the hieroglyphs, which makes sense this text comes out completely contrary to the one obtained by reading it according to Champollion; ... the hieroglyphic alphabet invented by Mr. Gulianov is so uncomplicated that if it has ever been in use anywhere, then is it really with the Egyptian clerks and eponymous, with whom we don't want to deal...

Finally, we saw before us vast meadows spread on the right bank of the Lena, on which Yakutsk was built. On June 10th we arrived in this small but very beautiful city, with the elegant taste of many wooden buildings reminiscent of Tsarskoye Selo streets...

290

Ivan Antonovich the Strabinsky went to the mouth of the Lena, having an order from his superiors to survey him in the relations of mineralogical and mining... and volunteered to accompany him to the 70th degree of northern latitude, where he still hoped to find a means to penetrate further, to Fadeevsky Island and even to the Bony Strait ... happiness to visit beyond 70 degrees of latitude, in New Siberia and the Bone Strait, where we will find the abyss of beautiful bones of various antediluvian animals ...

The time was clear and hot. Lena and its shores have not ceased to delight us with their beauty for a long time: this is a real panorama, tastefully composed of the most excellent views of the universe. As you move away from Yakutsk, the trees become smaller and smaller; but for this imperfection, the eyes are rewarded in abundance with the gradually increasing grandeur of a lifeless nature. Under the 68th degree of latitude, the river is already likened to an infinitely long lake, and the adjacent mountains take on a formidable alpine appearance.

Finally we entered the deserted kingdom of the North. Greenery is almost invisible. Granite, water and sky occupy the whole space. Nature seems ruined, blown up, plundered by its recently retreating enemy. This is the battlefield between the planet and its atmosphere, in the eternal struggle of which summer is only an instant truce. In the opaque, dim air above the pole, dissolved winter and storms hang, waiting only for the removal of the sun, so that in the darkness, with a new bitterness, rush to the planet; and the planet, having thrown off its beautiful plant dress, draws barefoot to meet the frantic elements, the ferocity of which, as if it wants to frighten with the sight of sharp, black, gigantic members and its iron ribs.

On July 2, we anchored in a small bay, at the very mouth of Lena, the width of which extends several miles.

So, we were at the mouth of this mighty river, under the 70th degree of latitude; but our expectations were somewhat deceived: instead of a magnificent, unusual appearance, we did not see anything here. The river and the sea, in their combination, presented us with one flat, blue, boundless expanse of water, in which the splendor of the shores completely disappeared.

The doctor stopped my attention on the special structure of this mouth, which seems to be truncated. The banks here are not lower than those that we saw for a hundred and two hundred miles up the river; from both corners of the mouth comes a long alley of rocky islands, the end of which is lost sight of in the distant waters of the ocean. There can be no doubt that this is the continuation of the banks of the Lena, which in ancient times was supposed to stretch incomparably further to the north; but one of those great upheavals in nature that the doctor and I constantly talked about, apparently, reduced its course, transferring a significant part of its channel into the possession of the sea...

After a three-day voyage, we saw a low island to the right, called maly; high cliffs to the left, forming the southern edge of Fadeevsky Island. Soon the inaccessible shores of New Siberia, loaded with ice mountains, also appeared, around the southwestern corner of which the ship's clerk pointed us a high pyramidal mass of stone with many ledges. It was Bear Island.

We arrived there on July 8, around noon, and immediately went ashore. Bear Island consists of one, almost round; granite mountain surrounded by water, and is separated from New Siberia only by a small strait. Its peak dominates all the heights of the nearby islands, towering 2260 feet above the surface of the sea...

This is only new evidence that the so-called Egyptian hieroglyphs are not Egyptian, but were handed over to the priests of that region by a very ancient people, no doubt people who survived the last flood. So, the hieroglyphs are, obviously, pre-flood letters, literae antediluvianae, the primitive letter of the human race, and were in common use among the peoples who lived in a warm and beautiful country, now partly transformed into Northern Siberia, partly absorbed by the Arctic Sea, as is sufficiently proved and the very device of the mouth of Lena. That is why we find the Egyptian inscription on Bear Island...

"...None of them will see any of the homelands, the greatness, or the splendor of their ill-fated ancestors. Our beautiful homelands, our palaces, monuments and legends rest at the bottom of the sea, or under the cover of new huge mountains. Here, where this stormy sea covered with ice floes now stretches, until recently a strong and rich state flourished, bright roofs of countless cities shone, noisy crowds of people moved among the greenery of palm groves and bamboo plantations and herds grazed under a bright and beneficial sky. This air, streaked with ugly flakes of snow, mixed with gloomy and heavy fog, was recently saturated with the fragrance of flowers and sounded by the singing of lovely birds, instead of which you can hear only the dull croaking of a raven and the piercing cry of cormorants. In the place where today, on the raging waves, this distant, high ice mountain rushes, constantly growing with new blocks of snow and petrified water - in the same place, a few crossings from here, five weeks ago, our magnificent Khuhurun, the capital of the mighty The barracks and beauty of the universe, vastness, luxury and splendor surpassing all cities, like a mammoth surpasses all animals. And all this disappeared, like a dream, like a ghost! ...

On the 10th day of the second moon, 11 789, a small comet appeared on the northeastern side of the sky...

Barabia was then in a war with two powerful powers: to the southwest (near Spitsbergen and Novaya Zemlya) we waged a bloody war with Murzujan, the ruler of a vast state inhabited by blacks, and in the inland sea (now the Kyrgyz Step), our fleet fought with glory against the combined forces of Psharmahia and Garra. Our king, Marhusahab, personally led the troops against the black ruler, and the messenger who arrived the day before brought the joyful news of our unforgettable victory ... the real goal of our campaign against the blacks Shah-shuh (Novaya Zemlya)...

The comet ... since then has unusually increased in volume. Her head was no longer inferior to the size of the moon, and the tail of pale yellow, divided into two strips, covered a huge part of the heavenly vault ... I made observations of the tail of the comet ... Do you know its size? ...

It extends over 45 million miles: it is more than twice the distance of the Earth from the Sun... This comet completely changed its appearance. Before, it seemed small, pale blue; now, as it approaches the Sun, from day to day it appears to be more significant and has become yellow with dark spots. I measured its core and atmosphere: the first, apparently quite dense, is only 189 miles across; but its atmosphere stretches for 7,000 miles and forms from it a body three times the size of the Earth. She moves very fast, flying over 50,000 miles per hour. Judging by this and its direction, in three weeks it will be only 200,000 miles from Earth.

...claims that this comet, although it will come quite close to the Earth, will not do any harm to it; that, having entered into the circle of her attractive force, if she is well asked, she can become her companion, and we will have two moons instead of one: otherwise she will fly by and disappear again; that, finally, there is no reason to fear its

294

collision with the globe, nor that it would smash it to smithereens, like an old pot, because it is liquid, like jelly, consists of dirt and vapors, and so on and so forth ... there was time when comets fell to the ground, like rotten apples from an apple tree?

... And the proof that comets more than once fell to the ground, you have in these high mountain ranges, menacingly sticking out onto the globe of our planet and cluttering its surface. All of these are comets that have fallen, bodies that adhere to the Earth, crumpled and broken in their fall. It is enough to look at the structure of the stone mountains, at the disorder of their layers, to be convinced of this truth.

Our eyes fixed on the comet... but that night she terrified us too. From last night its size almost tripled; her appearance contained something ominous, involuntarily making her tremble. We saw a huge, opaque ball compressed on both sides, dark silver in color, likened to a round lake in the middle of the vault of heaven. This egg-shaped ball was, as it were, the nucleus of a comet and in many places was covered with large black and gray spots. Its edges, outlined very weakly, disappeared into a foggy, dirty shell, clearing as it moved away from the dense mass of the ball and finally merging with the clean, transparent atmosphere of the comet, illuminated by beautiful crimson light and extending around the nucleus for a very considerable distance: through it, even the flickering of stars was visible.

But even in this transparent atmosphere, apparently composed of an airy liquid, dark spots flickered in different places, similar to clouds and, probably, resulting from the condensation of gases. The tail of the luminary looked even more formidable: he was no longer, as before, on his side, facing east, but, obviously, was directed to the Earth, and we seemed to look at the comet at the end of its tail, like a tube; for the core and the crimson atmosphere were placed in its center, and its rays, like the sun, overshadowed them from all sides. For all that, it was possible to notice that it still hangs indirectly to the Earth: its eastern rays were much longer than the western ones.

This part of the tail, as more facing the recently setting sun, also glowed with a crimson color, similar to the color of blood, which gradually turned pale in the northern and southern parts of the horizon, and in the eastern part it turned yellow, green and white stripes appeared. Thus, a comet with its circular tail occupied a large half of the sky and, so to speak, with all its mass gravitated to the air of our planet. The luminous matter that forms the tail seemed even thinner and more transparent than the comet's atmosphere itself: thousands of stars, obscured by this multi-colored, round fan, shining through its walls, not only did not lose their luster, but still burned stronger and brighter; even our pale moon, entering into the circle of its rays, was suddenly illuminated by a new, beautiful light, quite similar to the radiance of a mirror lamp.

Despite the fear and anxiety that involuntarily took hold of us, we could not help but admire the majestic spectacle of a huge celestial body hanging almost above our heads and set by an even huge wheel of crimson, pink, yellow and green rays, spread around it in the form of a magnificent peacock tail, to which countless stars flickered, like lamps, decorated with multi-colored glasses.

... She is now only 160,000 miles from Earth, which is already floating in her tail. Tomorrow at seven in the morning we will follow from her a total eclipse of the sun... Now you yourself deign to see how its core is dark, opaque, heavy: it is obviously made of a huge mass of granite and is only immersed in a light transparent atmosphere formed around it in fumes and gases, like our air...

The circle of her devastation will be limited. The nucleus of this comet... for the most part it extends only 189 miles. So, with its ruins, it can barely fill three or four regions - let's say three or four kingdoms...

... The comet was likened to a large round cloud and occupied the entire eastern country of the sky: she lost her rich, bright shell and was a brown color, which every minute darkened more and more. The sun, which has recently arisen from behind the horizon, has already hidden its western shore beyond the edge of this gigantic globe...

After a quarter of an hour, the sun completely disappeared behind the nucleus of the comet, which appeared to our eyes as pitch black and so close to the ground that pits, elevations and other irregularities could be seen on it. Almost night darkness spread through the air, and we felt a noticeable cold.

The eclipse continued until the second hour of the afternoon. Around that time, the sky brightened somewhat, and the narrow edge of the sun flickered due to the edge of the comet facing to the west ... Soon the sun shone with its full brilliance; but in his absence, the circle of the comet surprisingly expanded. On the one hand, a significant part of its dirty and rough disk plunged beyond the eastern horizon, while the opposite bank rested against the top of the vault of heaven. Such an increase in its appearance, with a visible distance from our eyes to the east, clearly proved that it flies to the Earth indirectly. At five in the afternoon she completely rolled up...

The sun was already setting... The underground thunder with a deafening crash and howl continuously rolled under the very soil, which with incomprehensible elasticity either swelled or rose up, then suddenly fell, forming terrible depressions, like ocean waves. At the same time, its surface swayed from north to south, and after that the line of movement changed, and there was a cross swing from east to west or back. Then it seemed as though the soil was spinning beneath us: we camels and horses fell to the ground like intoxicated; only mammoths and mastodons, spreading their thick legs and twisting their trunks to maintain balance, kept themselves from falling.

It was night already. The earthquake did not decrease... Despite the internal torment of the planet, which at any impact should seem to break into small pieces, night reigned over its surface, as beautiful, bright and quiet as yesterday's... The sky was blazing with stars; but, to my surprise, no comet was visible ... underground strikes became much weaker and less frequent. The thunder that was raging in the bowels of the globe turned into a dull rumble, which sometimes ceased completely...

Finally the day has come. We almost did not recognize yesterday's ruins ... the city looked like an extensive mound of debris. The majestic Lena... left her channel and, turning to the west, paved herself a new path through the overturned towers, along the walls of former palaces and temples spread out on the ground... The earthquake was hardly noticeable, but did not stop, and from time to time a more or less powerful blow threatened, it seemed, the resumption of yesterday's horrors.

We have already left the city; we have already climbed to heights... The soil we passed through was cracked into strange patterns, and wide cracks often came across on the way, through which we should jump. The hills were destroyed: some crumbled and erased; others lay broken into several parts. In other places, a spreading planet spewed from its bosom heaps of huge cliffs. The old lakes dried up, and others appeared instead. But the most remarkable sign of devastation was the trees: forests were ripped up; in the grove and on the field there were no two trees left in the perpendicular position to the ground: everyone stood at random, at different angles of inclination, and everything in their direction. Many oaks, teaks, sycamore and plane trees were twisted like linden branches, and some were split so that a person could comfortably pass through them through a stump, like at a door... Not only Lena changed her direction: all the rivers and streams in general left their beds and, having encountered obstacles on the newly chosen path, began to flood the plains. Water ... constantly absorbed more and more space. Some claimed that it flows out of the ground, and here for the first time a terrible word was uttered between us - the flood! Everyone was of the opinion that it was necessary to go to the Sasakhaar Mountains...

Finally we reached the mountains, riding a mammoth at six hours ninety geographical miles. We were on the border of our beautiful fatherland, which separated it from two large states, Khabar and Casco. Stopping, we noticed that the earth is still moving beneath us. In some places, the stone ridge seemed still warmed by the underground fire, shortly before flying with thunder in its inside. The destruction of nature was presented here in the most majestic and terrible form: the granite walls were covered with cracks, of which many looked like abysses; the gorges were littered with collapsed peaks, thick layers of stone were blown up and blown up, the cliffs, along with the forests growing on them, were overturned, crumpled, and pulled apart. After yesterday's earthquake, the Sasahaar Mountains were likened to the beds of two young lovers, which they had just left in the morning in a picturesque mess: the ruins of passionate passions, still breathing the volcanic warmth of their hearts, among the already cold traces of the first explosion of their love...

Their opposite slope was littered with stones of various colors and types, among which many surprised us with their beauty, transparency and fiery brilliance, and others with their similarities to thunder arrows. But from one cloudless peak, fugitives from those environs showed us an even more curious sight on the northeastern side of the horizon - the long range of mountains, shrunken by extremely tall and sharp masses that had never been there before. It was only the tip of the ruins of a comet that erupted on the Earth yesterday, which spread out across it with an immense line with countless lateral branches; which shocked her at the very base and, having cluttered with her core a huge strip of our globe, on the sides of the gigantic masses of granite matter he piled with it, filled the whole space of adjacent lands and covered it with rain from mud and sand and a strong stone hail that went for several hours during and after her fall. Traces of this city, which touched the very bottom of the Sasakhaar Mountains, we saw in those unfamiliar colored stones and shiny naked, and the fugitives presented us with samples of red and yellow sand, which, apparently, formed the soil of the comet and they picked up on the plain adjacent to the mountains. The yellow sand, beautifully glossy with its appearance, especially charmed our eyes and hearts...

According to their stories, its fall was preceded by a terrible hum with a bang in the high countries of the atmosphere and soon perfect darkness cut through by bright lights, as if squeezed out of the air, crushed by its onslaught, increased the horror of the fateful minute. At that time, five hundred thousand soldiers of Khabar and Casco stood on the battlefield, defending the blood and life of the ambition of their leaders, the vanity of their fellow citizens and the inviolability of a small piece of land, useless to their leaders, fellow citizens and themselves. The military leaders inflamed their courage, interpreting terrible celestial phenomena in the sense of a good foreshadowing for them and reminding them of imperishable glory, which should soon crown their great, immortal exploits; cities, villages, villages, roofs of houses and hills were in full swing with people waiting in anxiety for the consequences of the fiery struggle of the elements and the bloody struggle of their neighbors; the fields and meadows were full of innumerable herds, which, dumbfounded with fear, forgetting about feed, in their common foreboding of death, combined their sad mooing with the roar of lions, tigers and tapirs, trembling in forests and nativity sites; the air rattled with a mixed cry of an incomprehensible multitude of birds flying in dense swarms in ever-increasing darkness - when a heavy mass of air stone poured with lightning speed all over the country! .. Humanity and the animal kingdom spewed out one sudden, hoarse moan, and together with this moan they were smashed by mountains that flashed from the sky, which they flattened in a moment, crushed and buried forever, hopes, pride, glory and anger of countless millions of creatures. On the boundless grave of fifty proud peoples and five hundred depraved cities, a huge, impregnable, thundering death echo and hiding its domes behind clouds of death monument suddenly appeared on which the fate of the universe scribbled in granite letters in a mysterious inscription: "Half of the organic life of this dull, green planet of the third category rests here."

We stood on a cliff and in despondent silence looked for a long time at the pale, ugly corpse of a comet lying in the corner of our horizon, yesterday still so bright, brilliant, and beautiful, yesterday moving its own power in the depths of space and as if purposely flown from distant worlds from others suns and other stars...

Meanwhile, another phenomenon that took place above our heads penetrated us with new fear. Even before that, we noticed that the sun did not go down too long: many claimed that it stood motionless; it seemed to others as if it was moving around the same point; others... argued that it had obviously gone astray... the sun was moving and, like a flying star, quickly running the rest of the way, plunged into the sky. In one blink of an eye, the sight changed: the light went out, the sky brightened with stars, we found ourselves in deep darkness, and a cry of despair rang out around us in the mountains... We spent several hours in this position; but while some of us were already considering ways to build up the rest of our lives in gloomy imprisonment on our unfortunate planet, waves of bright light inadvertently flooded our eyes with a dazzling brilliance... of the sun, which inexplicably rose from the side where it had happened shortly before sudden sunset. Having reached a certain height, it suddenly rolled south; then, turning back, took the direction to the northeast. Before reaching the ground, it hesitated and began to slide parallel to the horizon, until again it fell over it near the southern point. Thus, within fifteen hours it ascended four times, each time in a different place; and each time, having scribbled him with crooked lines of his tangled path, he went at another point and plunged into night darkness... it was impossible not to guess that it wasn't that the sun wandering so strangely over us, but that the globe, burdened by the exorbitant weight of the comet, lost its balance, strayed from the former center of gravity and staggered on its axis, looking in its huge mass, enlarged by an alien body, a new center for itself and a new axis for its daily circulation. In fact, we saw that with each appearance of the sun the point of its ascent more and more approached to the north, although the sunset did not always correspond to the new east and fell alternately on the right and left side of the South Pole. Finally, for the fifth time, the sun shone already at the very point of the north, and, having zigzagged through the vault of heaven at seven o'clock in time, it set almost right in the south. Then the long night came, and after eleven o'clock in the dark, the day began to squeamish again in the north. The sun has risen, still preceded by a beautiful dawn... after the loss of the former east and former west.

Suddenly the weather changed. The air began to be overshadowed by some kind of transparent, like hot steam, fog, and the strong smell of sulfur struck our sense of smell... Soon the sun became dull, bloody, huge, like during a winter sunset, and in the upper atmosphere a flame of blue and red began to flicker, resembling the dust of lighted alcohol. After half an hour, the flame intensified so much that we were as if covered with a moving arch of fire...

The validity of this remark was not in doubt: the air was set on fire!.. The atmosphere fire took on terrible tension. Instead of the former small and frequent pieces of flame, fire burned in the sky in huge masses, with a deafening crack; and although there were no clouds at all, the rain poured in large drops on us. But the flame was held at a certain height, not at all dropping to the ground... Within hours, a large half of the people saved in the mountains became her victim...

...we still felt in our mouths a scorching, sour taste, obviously coming from the air, for, despite all the means used, we could not get rid of it. But the air itself represented a much more amazing phenomenon... it was cleansed of misty steam and of the flame burning in it, but completely changed its color and seemed blue, whereas before the natural color of the sky in light weather was light green... in addition to the dense, stony mass of the nucleus, the comet brought with it to Earth its atmosphere, composed of vapors and gases, most of which are alien to our air: including, probably, there was one gas of a special kind, gifted with an acidic and scorching principle; and he made this fire in the air, which was burned from displacement with it, oxide and even transformed its appearance... the old, sweet, soft, beneficent, healing air no longer exists; that the rush of new volatile liquids completely spoiled him, turning him into a tasteless, smelly, drunk, caustic, destructive... We could hardly breathe it into our breasts and, breathing in, disgusted immediately with disgust. We felt him burning, gnawing, and eating our insides. One day we all grew old for twenty years... in this air, human life should be significantly reduced and that people should not live in it for five hundred years or more. But this thought could not upset us for long: in two days we were so used to the new air that we did not notice the difference in it with the former...

...There was a rumor in the mountains that the Inner Sea (where now the Kyrgyz and Mongolian Steppes) emerged from its bed and poured into another land; that it has already flooded the entire space between its former shore and our mountains. The natives who occupied the lower strip of the ridge ... brought us the sad news that its sole was already surrounded by a sea pushed out of its abyss by forcibly swaying the globe, and that we are completely separated by water from the whole world...

A fierce wind with heavy rain and a blizzard swept through the air and abyss our fragile shelters and our selves... Meanwhile, the water did not stop rising, the waves intruded with noise into all the cavities and gorges, and we climbed the steep walls of the ridge every day higher and higher. The tops of the cliffs, ledges and platforms of the mountains were littered with people, huddled together in

304

dense piles, like swarms of bees hanging with tassels on tree branches... Robberies, killings, violence, vengeance every hour by the whole thousands reduced the number of mountain population, not yet exterminated by the poison of rampant diseases and the fury of the elements...

The comet, when it was destroyed, piled a layer of yellow shiny sand on this place, which I mentioned above, unknown on the earth before it fell; and these madmen, inflamed with greed for the precious gift brought to them from other worlds, maybe, to perdition the whole human race, rushed at him in droves... they plucked it from one another, irrigated it with their blood, slipped in blood, fell to the ground and, standing up, wounded and half-crushed, still enthusiastically raised up the handfuls of metal sand mixed with their blood, which they managed to capture under the feet of other seekers... At night, the water rose so high that the chain of the Sasahaar Mountains was finally completely dissolved: their entire huge building was drowned in stormy abysses; waves were rolling freely along the ridges of medium heights, and only the tops of the higher mountains were not yet swallowed by the ocean wandering into foreign lands: in the middle of it they formed many rocky islands, representing the appearance of a vast archipelago...

The mountain... was the highest and most impregnable in the entire Sasahara Range... it turned into an island...

Rains with a strong new southerly wind continued unceasingly, and the water still rose, swallowing several mountain peaks every day, so that on the sixth morning there were no more than five islands from the archipelago, significantly reduced in volume. On the seventh day the wind changed and blew from the new north, our former west. A few hours later, the whole sea was covered with countless strange objects that were worried on the surface of the water, dark, oblong, round, from a distance resembling short logs of ebony...

15th. Of the sixth moon. Water has fallen significantly. Several mountain peaks again appeared from the sea in the form of islands...

19th. The sea, with a new north-north wind, yesterday was covered with frequent ice floes …

28th. Ice mountains form around...

30th. The cold intensifies …

With these words, the long hieroglyphic inscription of the famous cave, called the Written Room, ends, and this is the end of our translation.

... A comet that fell to the earth with its core and atmosphere in 11879, on the 17th day of the fifth moon, at the fifth hour of the afternoon... This is called the Baraba Steppe in Siberia.

– How did you translate these hieroglyphs?

– I translated them in Champollion: every hieroglyph is either a letter, or a metaphorical figure, or neither a figure, nor a letter, but a simple decoration of handwriting.

If the meaning does not spell, then...

1833 Fantastic travels of Baron Brambeus.

It should be noted that the genre of writing political or scientific texts on behalf of literary characters or under a pseudonym was widespread not only in Russia of the 19th century, but also in Europe, due to censorship and possible repression.

The author of the description of the catastrophe is Senkovsky Joseph-Julian (wrote as Baron Brambeus) (1800-58), orientalist, state adviser, professor, corresponding member of the Imperial Academy of Sciences.

He came from a noble Polish, Lutheran family. At Vilnius University he graduated from the Faculty of Physics and Mathematics, Philology, and the Moral and Political Faculty. He traveled to Turkey, Syria and Egypt (1819-21). In addition to the main European languages, he knew Turkish, Arabic, Persian, Chinese, Mongolian and Tibetan.

Member of the St. Petersburg Free Society of Lovers of Literature;

Full member of the Society of Science Lovers in Warsaw;

Honorary Doctor of Philosophy, University of Cracow;

Member of the Academic Society at the University of Cracow;

Member of the Asian Society in London;

Corresponding Member of the Imperial Academy of Sciences;

Member of the Society of Northern Antiquaries in Copenhagen;

Professor Emeritus.

His first experience in historical research was "An Appendix to the General History of the Huns, Turks and Mongols" (1824, in French). His first experience in Russian literature was the cycle of Oriental Tales, which were half translations from Eastern languages. In 1833, in the almanac of the largest St. Petersburg book publisher and bookseller A.F.Smirdin, "Housewarming" was published under the signature of Baron Brambeus "Fantastic Travels of Baron Brambeus", which was a resounding success.

In 1834-47, the editor of the monthly "magazine of literature, sciences, arts, industry, news and fashion, composed of literary and scientific works..." "A library for reading", in which he published his numerous articles on a variety of topics, mainly stories and literature, also preachy entertaining novels and short stories. Oriental, secular, everyday, satirical novels published under the pseudonym Baron Brambeus made him especially popular. This was the first encyclopedic magazine in Russia, covering all aspects of the life of a more or less educated Russian person.

Since 1821 he served as a translator at the Foreign College. In 1822-47 he was a professor at St. Petersburg University in the department of Arabic and Turkish literature. He became the de facto founder of the school of Russian Oriental Studies. Senkovsky argued that until the 12th century, "there were no Georgians at all." In 1828-33 he served as censor, was the de facto author of the "liberal" Censorship Charter of 1828. In addition to Oriental studies, he studied Scandinavian sagas and Russian history, acoustics, theory and history of music, inventions of musical instruments, wrote many articles on ethnography, physics, mathematics, geology, medicine.

Speech 12.01.2011 at the International Club of Scientists

There is such a phrase: "In the beginning was the Word, and the Word was God, and the word was with God." What happened then with the religious system, with its deformations and profanations, is not worth talking about, but this phrase, which has been used at all times, has all the most ancient times. It is no coincidence that even at the turn of the 12th-13th centuries, teachings against paganism said that Russian pagans on the first day of the week, on Sunday, worship the Light, claiming that it was not the Sun, because the Sun is a thing of Light, i.e. material embodiment of Light. They worshiped the Light - the White Light. And for this they were abused by the churchmen of that time.

We also know that all the oldest Vedic texts are of northern origin, I will not waste time on the evidence base, and it is quite extensive. Let us turn to the most important of the Vedas - the Mahabharata, about which the Indians say that if you put the four Vedas on one scale and the Mahabharata, which is the epic, on the other, then the Mahabharata will outweigh them all. Various characteristics: geographical, physical-geographical, astronomical, toponymic and others indicate that the oldest texts of the Mahabharata were born near the pole, in the Subpolar region. And, as suggested, were created in the interglacial period, i.e., about 70 thousand BC.

(Modern anthropologists believe: human groups went to the coast of the future Arctic Ocean no later than 70 thousand years ago, so all arguments about Neanderthals and Cro-Magnons are groundless).

Reign, Reveal and Nav

In our Slavic, or rather, Russian tradition, there is a concept of trinity, such as Prav, Jav and Nav. Rule is a cosmic law that creates everything in the universe.

Reality is the manifested world. Nav is new, fresh, and young, i.e. the world into which the soul goes for purification and return or not returns, depending on how she lived her life.

The Mahabharata's Forest Book says that the Most High Vishnu, in which everything is embodied, as claimed by Abureyhan Biruni, who translated Indian texts, is called the "Creator of Light, which dispels darkness. To those who are, was and will be." The visible eternal god, he is an immutable law.

It is by his thought and word, i.e. spoken thoughts, and therefore voiced, a huge egg appeared. In it, the true light was Brahmo, the unimaginable, omnipresent. One who is a hidden and elusive cause of the real and the unreal. The one who created the space and produced the basis of the personality is essentially heavenly. Brahmo is called ether.

"The ether is the highest of the elements, it has only one property, and it is called sound." The sound wave begins the process of creation. The air generates seven sounds and a chord. Then the waves of ether or the heavenly ocean give rise to motion or wind, which already has two properties: sound and touch, and touch is its own property of motion, i.e. inertia.

Then the Light itself is born, which already has three properties: sound, touch and image. The image is the seven colors of the Spectrum or visible Light.

Born from sound and movement, it is light, visible light, that is located on the borderline, referring as Light to the divine world - Rule and as an Image to the manifested world -

Reveal and having a visible image in the universe. It transforms into various forms, being one in essence. The Upanishads say of him: "... that which is one, devoid of color, through diverse power creates different colors according to its hidden purpose, and in which the Universe is concentrated at the end and the beginning. He is God, may he endow us with the power of clear comprehension. One fire, penetrating the world, is likened to every image, remaining outside of them. This whole world shines it with light. "

By the way, in the Frisian chronicle of Ur Linda, which was called a fake of the mid-19th century, the same thing is said: "Vralda is the oldest of all, beyond all antiquity, because it created all things. Vralda is everything in everything, for it is eternal and infinite. Vralda is present everywhere, but it is nowhere to be seen, therefore this entity is called the Spirit. All that we can see in it is the essence of creation, thanks to it coming and going. Vralda is a single omnipotent being, and any other power comes from it and returns to it, and nothing was created without it. Eternal laws have been put into Vralda's creation, along with the great Yul; everything created will change; only Good wills remain eternal. Vralda is not subject to change. Since it is immutable, it is the only being for which everything else is an appearance, an illusion. And there is nothing that would not be in him. From the life of Vralda and thanks to the life of Vralda, time and all things arose. His life spans time and all things in general. Our spirit is not the spirit of Vralda, but it is the radiance of the spirit of Vralda. "

A simple replacement of the term "Vralda" with "Brahmo" allows us to state the identity of the text. It is unlikely that in the 19th century the Frisian peasants studied the Mahabharata, the vast number of Upanishads and

Rigveda hymns and, bringing it all together, created knowledge. Therefore, in the text itself there are words: "Take care of this knowledge, it is sacred to us. The current priests will try to destroy knowledge, for, having lost this knowledge, you turn into slaves, possessing it, you are free people, for you know what is what and that everything is nothing. "

The sun is materialized light

Russian peasants claimed that there is only one, another, higher Light, and the Sun is just "a thing of Light". (Schoolchildren usually wonder why, in ancient Egypt, Pharaoh Akhenaten was rejected, renounced. And he replaced the Light as such with the material embodiment of light. Amon Ra is the law, and Aton, which Akhenaten put down, is just a solar disk).

It is no accident that in our tradition the sun is called red. In the developed range, the first color is red.

Any star is the first material embodiment of Light, and it is naturally called red. Beautiful as red is the first form of embodiment. It is no accident that the term itself - Svarg means - materialized Light, which moves in harmony (and Svarog is the sovereign of heaven). Any star is a materialized light moving in harmony. Or a harmonious movement leading to the birth of the embodied Light. B. A. Rybakov wrote: "This Light, which has no visible source, is not tangible and inscrutable as the emanation of a deity creating the world, was an object of worship of Russian pagans and an object of denunciation of churchmen." Having this knowledge, it had to be a) fixed and b) preserved. In order to preserve it, all conceivable and inconceivable methods were used. If we talk about the people, then he never stores anything unnecessary to him. If

312

something has been preserved for centuries, then it is true. For thousands of years there has been a selection of useful and harmful information. What is needed for the biological survival of the community and what is not needed.

Time and space. Fabric of life

In ancient texts there is the concept of "Kha Point", and, only the day of this point was 864 times 10 by the 24th power of the years. Point Kha has another name - Purusha. The Universe is created from Purusha. In the hymn of Purusha it is very clearly said: "the Moon appears from the crown of Purusha, and the Sun appears from the eyes of Purusha."

We have an apocrypha - the Pigeon or the Deep Book, in which "the Moon appears from the crown of God, and the Sun appears from the eyes of God."

Our consciousness reflects, because we look at all reality, but perceive, see only the one that has passed through our consciousness.

Thought is the moon, and eyes are the sun. That's how everything is structured.

The Kha or Purusha point has the following description: "unmanifest above the great Atman, Purush above unmanifest. There is nothing higher than Purusha. This Purusha is awake in the sleeping, gives rise to one desired image after another. He is pure, he is Brahma, he is called immortal. All worlds are approved in it, no one goes beyond it. Truly this is One. The whole world is filled with this Purusha. "

One of Mahabharata's tales of "Indignation" reads: "Every form is formed by threads that freely weave it and also freely come out of it."

The energetic threads are stretched in the Universe as the warp threads of a weaving mill or a string of a musical instrument. In Narayana, the Purusha is called "the subtlest, three eternal sounds involved in the foundation."

It is appropriate to note here that on the Russian gusli, the game on which was considered at one time by the Orthodox Christian Church a terrible sin, and which were burnt during the reign of Alexei Mikhailovich Romanov, there were exactly three strings. On the three strings of a musical instrument, which are at the same time the basis of the weaving mill, as the ancient hymn of Atharva Veda says, "Two young men scurry the base, two scavengers on six pegs, stretch the yarn one by one, and do not tear it, do not interrupt. These are the pegs, they are the foundation of the sky, the voices (or voices) for weaving shuttles have become." And another interesting thing, Purusha says: "I am less than small and like great, I am this whole diverse world." In the Upanishads we find texts about the realization of Purusha through sound that leads to no sound.

Trinity - Sacred Knowledge

The three eternal sounds involved in the foundation of the Universe are not the whole spectrum of sounds, they are just sounds, or before sounds. In the petroglyphs of the White Sea and Lake Onega, and this sixth is the fifth millennium BC - the trident marks the sphere of the sacred. It is constantly found in northern embroidery: three-fingered hands of goddesses, tridents on the heads of horses and birds, a trident crowning the tree of life, and other sacred things.

In medieval Russian iconography until the 17th century, the trident sign was a constant attribute of Nikolai Ugodnik, it was placed on the forehead of a saint, whom the

314

Russian people called Nicolo. (Like Kupalo and Yarilo, i.e. in the male version of the name. This is called: you drove us out of the door, and we climbed into the window to you. If there is an introduction of a foreign system of religious consciousness, confessional pressure that reduces previous knowledge, people still preserve it. Well, you give us Kolo, we will give you Nicolo. Kolo is the Sun. Nicolo is not the Sun, but the Divine Light. It is no accident that foreigners in the 17th century claimed that the Russians revere Nicola as God. Only on the icons of Paraskeva Friday and Nikolai Ugodnik we can meet a red background).

In Russian, ancient Egyptian, Hebrew script, the sign "Ш" means the sound "Ш". In words like **шелест, шорох, шёпот, шум**, a certain intermediate state between the sound and not the sound is manifested. Even profanity **«ша!»** means - silent, silent, although in Sanskrit - **ша** - paradise, eternal peace, happiness. This is the first whistling letter of the Sanskrit alphabet. All whistling sounds are the embodiment of Prajapati, i.e. Purushi or Kha points.

Fabulous time ciphers

On the strings of the universe plays the matter of the universe. But in order for this to persist, various storage modules are needed. It can be embroidery, it can be weaving, songs, and there can be icons.

Look carefully at the icon "Savior in power." I'll just give you a fairy tale. Adults become stupid over time, not everyone is wise, unfortunately, otherwise they would not have arranged a war, did not sort things out, did not beat each other's faces.

But children always remain children, and at three, and at five, and at ten, they also fight, but they have a different perception, they tell each other tales. A fairy tale is one of the most serious and powerful forms of preserving information. If this fairy tale is oriented toward the positive, and not negative, then the children will remember and pass it on from generation to generation.

I would like to introduce you to a fairy tale that you all know well, but I think you don't know. What did the ancestors want to convey to us in it? What is an important text that must be carried through centuries and millennia?

So, we are left with knowledge, from which no secret is made, a fairy tale is told, for example, "The Frog Princess".

The plot of the tale: three brothers shoot from a bow, each gets his wife. At the beginning of the tale, a sacred meaning is manifested. In Prakritian hunting songs, archery is a manifestation of a man's sexual strength. Why Hercules forces his sons to shoot from a bow, why Penelope forced her grooms to pull her husband's bow ... Only someone who has the right to procreate can pull a bow, he must be physically very strong.

So, in our fairy tale, one brother received a hawthorn, the second - a merchant, i.e. the upper layer of society is removed, and the third goes to the frog. In the old version of the tales recorded by Afanasyev, Ivan says: "The frog is no match for me, how will I marry her?"

He does not have a question that she is a frog, but status is important. Then there are claims that it would be necessary to bake a cake, weave a carpet overnight. It was inconceivable for a normal person to bake the pie that the frog baked, to weave a carpet on which the whole kingdom-state is also, but Ivan Tsarevich had no questions. He, apparently, was handsome, strong, but extremely stupid.

The fact that she came to the feast in the guise of Vasilisa the Wise, that is, the Queen of Wisdom, says a lot.

And she demonstrates there the act of creating the Real World.

The swan on the waters in the hymns of the Upanishads is the Light, the one who weaves the material world. Vasilisa and showed how materiality is built on the waves of light.

And Ivan Tsarevich, instead of thinking who his wife is, goes home and burns her frog skin. And since the frog is an intermediate state between the earthly incarnation of a woman and the highest heavenly female principle (the toad in Russia was called the women of the first years of marriage. Pearl embroideries with gold thread on the headdresses of young women often portrayed Rozhanitsa in the image of the Frog and connected the earthly woman with the divine woman the highest principle), the possibility of being embodied in the female form of Ivan Tsarevich Vasilisa the Wise deprived. And she is a white swan, i.e. with light, returns to the Eternal World, saying, you will find me at Koshchei.

Please note that she does not ask to kill Koshchei, she just says that she needs to be sought there. The old man who meets Ivan says: "Ah, Ivan Tsarevich, why did you burn the frog skin. You weren't given it to you, not you to wear it. After all, Vasilisa the Wise turned out to be wiser, wiser than her father. This is Koschey and turned it into a frog for three years. "

Yes, she returns to Koshchei the Immortal, her father, and not to that sharply negative beginning, which we used to take under the name Koschey the Immortal.

In the usual interpretation of Koschey, the Immortal is an absolute evil. But this is not so, since he is the father of the Queen of Wisdom - Vasilisa the Wise.

His immortality is also relative. It is at the end of the needle, the needle is in the egg, the egg is in the duck, the duck is in the hare, the hare is in the casket, and the casket is on the oak, which Koschey takes care of like an eye.

We understand much in this tale now exactly the opposite. In Vedic mythology, Prajapati (Father of Yarn - Creator) created all living things, embodied in the cosmic turtle Kashyap. All living beings are descendants of Kashyapa. The son of Kashyapa Vivasvat - radiant - the ancestor of people. The Hindus called him Surya, i.e. the sun is the son of Kashyapa.

Being the father of gods and asuras (Asur-as-i: Ur-light), Kasyapa stands at the very beginning of manifestation, at the source of the movement of space and time.

At the very tip of the needle, unfolding a great universal action. A needle is a point that unfolds into a cone.

Kashchyapa is immortal, but he is immortal only in the process of unfolding, the manifestation of this universe. If the process of movement stops, then it dies, because Kashyap is this process itself.

Ivan Tsarevich, looking for his wife, begins to destroy this world. Firstly, the oak tree on which the universe rests is torn out. "Two birds joined together cling to the same tree. One - eats a sweet berry, and the other looks without eating. On this tree, a man immersed in the sorrows of the world, blinded, mourns for his powerlessness. " The casket, of which the Upanishad speaks, was broken: "the casket, the inside of which is airspace and the bottom is the earth, is not being exhausted, for the cardinal directions are its corners, the sky is its upper opening, the casket contains wealth, all that exists is resting in it."

The hare is torn, and the hare in the Slavic and Old Indian traditions is a sacred phallic symbol and a symbol of the reincarnation of souls who have gone to another world,

318

into new human beings, newborn children. A symbol of the way information codes go in order to return back in the image of people. In addition, in Slavic and Old Indian mythology, the hare is a month, the one who takes the souls of the departed, cleans them in his reflected light and returns to the earth with water, dew or snow.

Duck killed - Mother of all images, weaving on the energy threads of the Universe the fabric of manifest matter. The goose, swan, duck in the hymns of the Rigveda are associated with the Creator God, the Universe, the Mind, defined by Lada, the original music of the universe.

An Egg is broken in which the eternal Brahmo was the true light. It is he in the image of Kashyap who begins to expand the universe.

The end of the needle is broken, the Universe is gone. We cannot know where Ivan Tsarevich will be and whether he will be happy.

A clear lesson was taught in this tale. Like Pushkin: "A fairy tale is a lie, but a hint in it, a lesson for good fellows."

In a fabulous form, it is reported about how our distant ancestors represented the structure of the universe and the place of man in it. In this context, it becomes clear why, in the 15-17th century, priests in confession asked: "Didn't he tell tales?" Because it was considered a mortal sin in the Orthodox Christian tradition. Listeners of fairy tales are asked questions of morality, moral freedom, freedom of choice, responsibility for their actions, and the legitimacy of happiness due to unhappiness and even death of other people. After all, stupidity, vanity, endless egoism can destroy not only our fragile earthly home, but the whole universe. Everyone should give answers to questions for himself, depending on the purity realized by the freedom and responsibility of the soul. Before you is an ordinary fairy tale. And we have a lot of such tales.

S. V. Zharnikova
2011

Archaic roots of the traditional culture of the Russian North

Introduction

One of the most important tasks set by time for cultural workers is the task of restoring national self-awareness, self-respect of the people. The solution to this problem is impossible without studying, restoring and promoting popular culture, that system of value orientations that has developed in the people over the millennia of its historical existence. In this regard, the problem of revealing the deep roots of the North Russian folk culture is extremely acute today. One of the main issues is temporary stratigraphy in connection with the latest data from paleoclimatology, paleoanthropology, linguistics, and archeology. So, at present, thanks to the discoveries of paleoclimatologists, the time frames of the period of the initial development by the human collectives of the territories of the Center and the North of the European part of Russia are being reviewed. It is assumed that already in the Mikulinsky interglacial epoch (130-70 thousand years ago), when the average winter temperatures were 8-12 degrees higher than at present, and the climate in a significant part of the Russian Plain right up to the northern regions was identical to the modern climate of the Atlantic areas of Western Europe, human groups went to the coast of the White and Barents Seas. During the period of the glacial Valdai (70-24 thousand years ago), people with a fairly developed level of cultural traditions continue to live in the Center and the North of Eastern Europe, as evidenced by the burial of Sungir in the Vladimir region and the Mezinskaya Upper Paleolithic site in Chernihiv (25-23 thousand to A.E.). During the Valdai glacial (20-18 thousand years ago), as it is now clear, not all the territories of the Russian Plain (in particular, the Russian North) were covered with glacier, because its extreme eastern border passed along the Molo-Sheksninsky line. Thus, to the east of this border (right up to the Urals) mixed spruce-birch and birch-pine forests and meadow-grass steppes grow, i.e. territories suitable for human life. In the Mesolithic era (10-5 thousand BC) in the vast expanses of the European North, a period of warming begins, and by the 7th millennium BC. e. here average summer temperatures are set at 4-5 degrees higher than modern, and almost 550 km. a zone of mixed broad-leaved forests is moving north of the modern border of its distribution. On the territory of the Vologda Oblast, studies by S.V. Erroneous revealed a large number of Mesolithic monuments. Anthropologically, people buried in burial grounds of this time are classical Caucasians without the slightest admixture of Mongoloidity. The population movements for this period from the territory of the Urals and Trans-Urals (the zone of formation of the Finno-Ugric tribes) were not identified. Similar conclusions were made by D. A. Krainov from the Neolithic era.

Such shifts are also unlikely in the Bronze Age, when the population advance to the north of Eastern Europe is recorded, as a rule, from the lands of the Dnieper, Middle Volga and Volga-Oka interfluve. Analyzing today the numerous finds of the Mesolithic, Neolithic and Bronze eras in the territories of the Center and the North of the European part of Russia, we can confidently assume that up to the end of the Bronze Age (i.e., the end of the 2nd millennium BC) here lived the tribes of Caucasians belonging to the Indo-European linguistic community. Already in the Mesolithic, Neolithic and Bronze eras in the Russian North, a whole complex of ritual and mythological structures was formed, which in various transformed, and often extremely archaic forms remained in the context of folk culture right up to the turn of the 19th and 20th centuries and even to the present. These are ritual texts, a drawing of ritual dances, an ornament-amulet, etc. It is not by chance that the researchers believe that in Russian folk culture the elements were preserved archaic not only of the ancient Greek, but also recorded in the Vedas.

Thus, the previously adopted paradigm of the historical development of the European North of Russia, which claimed that these territories starting from the post-glacial period were inhabited by Finno-Ugric tribes who came from the Urals (as a result of pressure from an excess of the population), which until the Slavs came here at the turn of 1-2 thousand n e. had a hunting-gathering and fishing type of economy, is currently being revised.

The new paradigm seems to be the following: according to modern data from paleoclimatology, anthropology, linguistics, ethnography, and other adjacent sciences, in the territories of the European North of Russia at the time of the arrival of the Slavs, mainly descendants of the ancient Indo-European population, which preserved the most archaic Indo-European cultural traditions, the archaic type of vocabulary and archaic anthropoedean, lived a type. Their contact and mutual influence with Slavic groups advancing on these territories was facilitated by the proximity of language, anthropological type and many cultural traditions inherited by both from their common Indo-European ancestors.

Summary

Eastern Europe as the ancestral home of the Indo-Europeans

The old Indian epos «Makhabharata», the oldest known written artifact of history, science, culture of all Indo-European peoples, narrates the war between two relative clans - of Pandavs and of Kauravs.

That war was finished with the battle in the place of Kurukshetra (Kurskoye Pole) in 3102 BC. The events narrated in the epos took place in the country called Bharata. But Bharata bears no relation to present India, as at that distant time there were no Indo-Europeans either in India and Iran or especially in Western Europe. In those remote days the ancestors of all succeeding Indo-European nations lived in their ancient native place - in Eastern Europe. This fact is proved by the legends of «Rigveda», «Makhabharata» and «Avesta», as well as by some geographical names brought down to the present.

For instance, on the one hand, it is well-known that the Rah (or Ranha), a sacred river of Old Iranian «Avesta», is the today's Volga. On the other hand, the Ranha of «Avesta» and the Ganga of «Makhabharata» are considered to be the same river. One of eighteen «Makhahharata»'s hooks entitled «Forest» enumerates more than 200 sacred rivers of an Aryan origin. Among them are the rivers, which flowed between the rivers of Ganga and Yamuna. Assuming the Ganga is the Volga and in view of the described geographical position, the Yamuna should be the present Oka River. Moreover, the old Aryan texts give us the name of Kala as another name of the Yamuna. And we find that today the estuary of the Oka is also called the Kala. In its middle flow the Yamuna was called the Vaka, the name, which is given today to the Oka's part that passes across Ryasan Region.

The table given by the author demonstrates 30 names of the today's rivers flowing between the Volga and the Oka, at present these rivers bear the names given them 5 thousand years ago. The names and geographical positions of the sacred water reservoirs mentioned in old Indian «Makhabharata» coincide with those of the Nowaday Rivers in the Middle Russia. Besides the rivers' names, there are other ancient geographical names preserved today. For example, one of seven sacred cities, an ancient Aryan educational center of Varanasi (or Varanash), on the one hand, and the southern Russian city of Voronezh, on the other, seem to be the same place. A village of Kostyonki in Don Region, famous for its ancient archaeological artifacts (the most ancient dates back to the 30th millennium B. C.), on the one hand, and the city of Khastin that after the battle in Kurukshetra became the Aryan capital, on the other, are considered to coincide also. These suppositions are confirmed by the names of the rivers, which are mentioned in «Makhabharata» and which today flow beside the city of Voronezh and the village of Kostyonki.

About the location of the sacred mountains Meru and Khara described in Indo-Iranian (Aryan) mythology

For two centuries the researchers from different countries have been trying to determine the location of Aryans' native land described in old Indian «Rigveda», «Makhabharata» and old Indo-Iranian «Avesta».

The main geographical landmarks of that land were the sacred northern mountains, described as stretching from west to east and curving southwards like a bended bow. In the old Indian tradition these mountains were called the

325

Meru with the highest peak being Mandara, while the Old Iranian tradition called them the Khara Bersaiti the highest peak being Khukarya. These mountains were considered to be the main watershed of the Aryan land as they divided all the rivers into two groups: flowing northwest into the Molochnoye (Milky) Sea and flowing southwest into the Southern Sea. These mountains were mentioned in Scythian legends. They were written about by ancient Greek and Roman authors and by medieval Arab travelers. For a long time the mountains were supposed to be unreal and mythical.

But the author of the article managed to determine the location of these sacred northern mountains and to prove their real existence in the north of Eastern Europe. In her opinion, these eminences stretching from west to east include the present mountains of the Kolsky peninsula, of Finland and Karelia, the eminences called Avmga and Kharovskaya Gryada, the Northern Uvaly, and the mountain of the Polar Ural. Moreover, the Northern Uvaly, which in the Aryan antiquity (5-iv thousand years B. C.) were 300-iv00 meters higher, have always been the main watershed of the southern rivers (the Caspian Sea basin) and of the northern rivers (the White Sea basin). Here even today the geographical names of an ancient origin can be found. Here up to the 20th century the weaving and the embroidery of northern peasants had been embellished with intricate geometrical ornaments rooted in the old Aryan culture.

Archaic motifs in the North Russian folk emboroidery and their parallels in ancient ornaments of the Eurasian steep population

The article analyses the geometrical motifs preserved in the North Russian territory (Vologda and Arkhangelsk

Regions) up to the early 20th century. The ornaments embroidered and woven by female peasants in Northern Russia comprised rhombs, meanders, saltire crosses, z-formed and swastika figures of different designs and configurations. It is well-known that for the first time in the history of mankind the meander and swastika depiction appeared on the territory of Eastern Europe in the old Stone Age (the 23rd millennium B. C.). These figures are depicted on the things made of fossil ivory found near the city of Chernigov (Mezin site). During the following millennia these ornaments became more complicated, they were transformed, modified and in the course of time became a carpet-design decor. Such ornaments were mostly characteristic of the so-called Andronovo pottery from the 2nd millennium B. C., which is referred by researchers to ancient Aryans. The recovered ornamented pottery helps to trace the migration of Aryan groups in different directions: east and south-east (the Caucasus, the Trans-Caucasus, Iran, Afghanistan, India and China), south-west (Greece, Italy, and the Balkans), west and north-west (Germany, Scandinavia), etc.

Today the researchers suppose such ornaments to be a sort of a totem, a symbol of clan and ethnic affiliation for the person whose possessions were thus decorated. These ornaments acted as talismans, which preserved their owners from harm during all their life and even after it. Pieces of ceramics with intricate ornamental designs are usually found m graves, so this kind of decor was of a ritual character.

It is interesting that these intricate old Aryan ornaments in their variety had been reproduced by the women of Northern Russia on towels, shirts, aprons, waist-bands, tahle-clothes, bed valances up to the 1920-1930s. Some of these ritual things repeat the ornamental compositions of the 23rd millennium B. C. in detail.

The author assumes that similar simple ornamental elements could be reproduced by different, even not related, nations. But it seems incredible that the peoples divided by vast territories and long millennia (in case they are not ethno genetically linked) could invent the intricate ornamental compositions, which are identical down to the smallest detail and which discharged the same ritual function of a talisman and a totem.

About several motifs in folk embroider on Solvychegodsk kokoshniki - headdresses of Northern Dyna type
(Using materials of the Vologda regional museum-reserve)

Of the numerous motifs in the Russian folk embroidery, the archaic one depicting a woman in childbirth is considered to him the least studied today. The most interesting motifs are depicted on the North Russian female headdresses called «kokoshniki». Several of them are kept in the archives of the Vologda museum-reserve. These headdresses made of red, crimson or cherry-colored hard silk or velvet are embroidered with a gold silver thread and decorated with pearls, cut nacre, natural semi-precious stones and strasses. The upper part of kokoshniki depicts either a zoo-anthropomorphic creature combining the features of a human and an animal, or a stylizing golden tree, which outline resembles a woman in childbirth.

These central personages are connected hy a thin band - a «naval-string» - with other figures, creatures or trees, smaller in dimensions. Usually zoo-anthropomorphic heings have the horns on their heads.

A headdress in the North Russian costume played a very significant role: it preserved a woman from harm, protected her from evil magic and stimulated a procreation function.

As such a headdress could he worn only by the woman abie to give birth, so it can be concluded that it depicts pagan Goddess Rozhanitsa - the mother of all Earth beings - who was celebrated in «Rigveda» hymns. This Goddess had been incarnated in the form of either a primordial cow, or a golden tree, or a woman in childbirth in the embroidery of the North Russian female headdress up to the turn of the 19th and 20th centuries.

Reflection of pagan beliefs in the ornamentation of North Russian female headdresses
(Using materials of the Vologda regional museum-reserve)

The female headdresses of Northern Russia had always been associated with fertility. This article of clothing was thoroughly decorated and often cost as much as a few milch-cows or a horse. The motifs and images of embroidered compositions can hardly be concerned with concepts of the Orthodox Church.

The embroidery of the North Russian female headdresses distinctly reflects the pagan cult of ancient deities-creators of the Universe named Rod and Rozhanitsa. Researcher Boris Rybakov proved that long before the Christianity was introduced, the eastern Slavs had had a developed cult of Supreme Goddess Rozhanitsa - the patroness of women and birth, and of God Rod - the patron of rams, storms, moisture on the whole, fertility and blood relationship.

On the northern female headdresses goddesses of Rozhanitsa are depicted as either zoo-anthropomorphic beings (which combine the features of both a human and an animal), or stylizing geometrical figures, or golden trees. It is notable that these images in their outline repeat the figure of a woman and childbirth, and all of them are horned. Moreover, some female headdresses were also sewn with horns.

In such a way a woman was compared to a cow or a goat that from ancient times had symbolized fertility.

The headdresses of the old-aged women of Northern Russia depicted God Rod as a horned bull always concerned with Water and the Moon cults.

Images of the water-fowl in Russian folk tradition
(Sources and genesis)

The images of the water-fowl - ducks, gooses, swans - played an exceptional role in the Russian folk tradition. The gooses-swans were always mentioned in the songs of a ritual character. Their connection to the other world, the world of the departed, is traced in Russian fairy-tales, riddles, spells and rituals invoking fertility.

In the old Aryan mythology a goose-swan was identified with the sky, the sun, the universe, the light, and a universal and individual soul, universal music. The great Water Goddess from the Veda epoch named Sarasvati was always accompanied by a goose, which stood for the all-embracing sky. In the Indo-Iranian (Aryan) mythology the water-fowl accompanied the Goddess-Mother of water who was often depicted as a world tree with birds sitting on it. And in the tradition of all Indo-European nations, a pair of ducks had always symbolized a conjugal love. The worship to the sacred goose-swan and duck in the ancient Indo-European epoch are recorded in the hymns of «Rigveda» and «Avesta». The archaic Eastern-Slavonic traditions trace an identical worship.

The author is convinced that this cult originates from the native land of Indo-Europeans - the polar territory - and dates back to the oldest antiquity. It is confirmed by the petrogliphs of the 5th-ivth millennia B.C., which were encountered on the crags of the White Sea and Onega Lake and which depicted goose-swans in the scenes of a mythological ritual character. On the northern rivers and lakes this water-fowl has heen hatching out and fledging its chicks, here these careful and cunning birds, the fowling for which was quite difficult in ancient time, became most helpless when moulting. Moreover, at the most difficult for ancient northern people time - in famine spring and summer, the water-fowl was the main source to feed them. And this fact to a great extent promoted the development of the cult of gooses, swans and ducks. This ancient cult had heen preserved in different forms in the folk culture of the Russian North up to the early 20th century.

Possible sources of the image of a horse-goose and a horse-deer in indo-Iranian (Aryan) mythology

Of the ancient Aryan mythological images, the image of a horse-goose and a horse-deer seems to be the most interesting and enigmatic. The outward similarity of the bird's flying to the horse's running is not sufficient to explain this phenomenon. The image of a horse is compared exactly to the images of a goose and a swan but not to any other species of hirds. The explanation of it can be found in the old mythology of Indo-European nations as well as in ancient artifacts of art and religious cult. The archaeological finds of the Mesolithic (7th-5th millennia B. C.) made in the polar regions of the Russian North testify to the existence of the developed cult of the water-fowl and an elk at that distant time. This cult is reflected in the petrogliphs which

331

were found on the crags and which dated from the ivth -3th millennia B. C. Here appeared the image of a goose-elk combining the features of a bird and a deer.

While analyzing the archaeological and historical materials the author concludes that in the deep Indo-European antiquity an elk was used as a saddle and carriage animal. The fact that it was an elk but not a reindeer is obvious today.

As the Eurasian and North American wild reindeer had turned out to the untamable, so the people had to tame the disappeared today Sayany deer. So in the territory of the European North the domesticated reindeer appeared not earlier than in the 13th century. There are many facts confirming that before the Aryans came to steeps, they had used an elk as a carriage animal. And only later having already the experience in treating carriage elks, the Aryans managed to domesticate a wild steep tarpan-horse.

The images of a horse on the one hand and of an elk-goose on the other were united in the mythology and rituals and resulted in a complicated synthetically image of a horse-goose and a horse-deer, which is perpetuated in the Russian embroidery, weaving and casting.

Reflection of Vedas' mythological topics in Eastern-Slavonic calendar rites

The heliefs of northern Russian peasants preserved up to the turn of the 19th-20th centuries, especially the stable calendar-ritual cycles, evidently reflect the relics of the archaic Indo-European calendar that has deep-going roots. The Eastern-Slavonic pre-Christian picture of the world differentiated two temporal cycles: the period from winter solstice (December 22) till summer solstice (June 22) and the period from summer solstice till winter one. The

332

beginning of either cycle was marked by the calendar ritual actions: winter Christmas-tide and summer John Baptist's Day. The author thinks that the explanation of the correlation of these ritual actions with these calendar cycles lies in the depth of millennia. According to the Veda tradition, the time periods of the alive, of the died and of the gods were different: the Period of ancestors was a lunar month (or 28 days), the Period of gods was a year, where the Day was the sun's movement northwards (December 22-June 22) and the Night - the sun's movement southwards (June 22-December 22). The analysis of the Eastern-Slavonic calendar rites based on the dates of summer and winter solstice shows that the same philosophic concepts and the same mythological ideas are recorded in the old Aryan texts («Rigveda», «Makhahharata» and «Avesta»):

1. On the Day of gods (from December 22 till June 22) all died get an everlasting life m the world of gods and so cannot be subjected to the incarnation in the world of people. They can visit their relatives on a special day of the Christmas-tide.

2. In the Night of gods (from June 22 till December 22) all died must return to the world of the alive in the form of dew, rain or snow in order to be reincarnated into a newborn child. Both the Feast of the Dew, antedating John Baptist's Day, and the rite itself opening the marriage season imply the incarnation process.

3. As the souls of the other world were represented as twinkling lights, so on the Christmas-tide and on John Baptist's Day the alive people join m the world of the died through all three fire hypostasis: fire itself (the sun and a bonfire), water (that potentially bears fire) and a tree (from which rubbing a ritual fire was made).

The ancient ritual notions of dividing the year into two parts (the day of the gods and the night of the gods) date back to a distant historical period when the ancestors of all Indo-Europeans (partially Indo-Iranians and Slavs) lived in the polar territories, in the north of Eastern Europe.

Along the way of myths
(Alexander Pushkin and Russian fairy-tale)

The author compares the subjects of the poem «Ruslan and Ludmila» by Alexander Pushkin to the old Indian epos «Legend about Rama» («Ramayana») and reveals a complete coincidence of them.

1. In «Ruslan and Ludmila» a wizard kidnaps a beauty named Ludmila, the wife of prince Ruslan, and takes her away up to the clouds. In the «Legend about Rama» a demon kidnaps a beauty named Sita, the wife of tsar's son Rama, and takes her away up to the clouds.

2. Both Ludmila and Sita escape from their kidnapper's in a magic garden.

3. Ruslan is helped by sorcerer Finn and the head of wizard Chemomor's brother. This head is possessed of a magic sward. Rama is helped by sorcerer Vibhishana, a brother of demon Ravana. Moreover, the demon sacrifices one of his ten heads to get immortality and power equal to the divine. To compare, wizard Chemomor cuts of Fhis brother's head but lets it live.

4. Both Chemomor and Ravana can be killed only with definite magic arms: one with a sword, another with an arrow.

5. Both Chemomor and Ravana cannot force the beautiful capt4es to be their w4es.

6. Chemomor is helped by witch Naina, who offended by Finn's refusal of her love, calls Chemomor to fight with Ruslan. Demon Ravana is called to fight with Rama by

female demon Shurpanakha, offended by Rama's refusal of her love.

7. Cbemomor deludes Ludmila with a ghost of wounded to death Ruslan. Demon Ravana tries to delude Sita with a ghost of Rama's bloody head.

8. Both Ruslan and Rama first perish but then they recover with the help of magic water from the remote mountains given them by a sorcerer (Finn in the first case, and Vibhishana - in the second).

As at the moment when Alexander Pushkin was writing his poem, there was no European translation of the «Legend about Rama», the author surmises that both works are based on the identical very ancient subject, which was perpetuated both in the old Indian and North Russian versions. Moreover, some details from «Ruslan and Ludmila» convinced that the source used by Pushkin is older than the «Legend about Rama» dating from the late 2nd -early 1st millennia B. C.

Veda means knowledge.

In 1903 in Bombey appeared the book «Arctic nat4e land in Vedas» by B. G. Tilak, the prominent Indian researcher and public figure. Having studied the ancient texts for many years the author comes to the conclusion that the nat4e land of Aryans occupied northern Europe - some territory near the Polar Circle. On that very territory the most ancient texts of the Aryan sacred books: «Rigveda», «Makhabharata», «Avesta» - were being written. According to these books the knowledge of their creators was enormous for that epoch.

«Makhabharata», for example, describes different aircrafts and calls them «flying chariots» or «d4ine birds». They were used by the epic's personages for going spaceward. The fly of such a «flying chariot» described in a very realistic way is on the whole reminiscent of the fly of a nowadays spaceship.

The epos describes different kinds of weapons of mass destruction, from nuclear to psychotropic. Not by chance, at the first experimental explosion of an atomic bomb R. Oppenheimer cited «Makhabharata»'s description of the «space arms of gods».

The ancient Aryans knew the smallest spaces of time, which the contemporary c4ilization has discovered only over recent decades.

The old texts describe in detail the formation of the Universe and the primary self-organization of the matter, which lasted 25, 92 x 1012 years. In «Makhabharata» the fundamental principle of the Un4erse is called the eternal Brahma-creator, or a genuine light. This idea of some super light as the base for building the material Universe was likewise adopted by ancient Egyptians.

Some relics of these concepts could be found in the Eastern pre-Christian world-perception. According to them the seventh day of a week was dedicated to a «light» when people worshipped not to the sun but to the invisible light that was identified with the divine essence.

The discoveries of the 20th century have corroborated the wisdom of the ancients. The ubiquitous streams of invisible neutrino (a genuine light called by ancient wise men «eternal Brahma»), g4ing birth to everything in the Universe, penetrate everything around like water pierces a sieve.

S. V. Zharnikova
Сборник научных статей. Вологда. Издательство «МДК». 2002

The ancient secrets of the Russian North

The Russian North - its forests and fields were not trampled by the hordes of conquerors, its free and proud people for the most part did not know serfdom, and it was here that the oldest songs, fairy tales, were kept clean and inviolable, were in Russia. It is here, according to many researchers, that such archaic rites, rituals, traditions that are more ancient than not only ancient Greek, but even recorded in the ancient Indian "books of knowledge" - the Vedas, the most ancient cultural monument of all Indo-European peoples, have been preserved. A. N. Afanasyev wrote about the significant proximity of Slavic and Vedic mythology back in the 19th century, who attached great importance to the convergence in mythological subjects and ritual practice among the Eastern Slavs and the ancients.

These convergences and visible parallels are noted in the works of Russian historians and linguists of the 19th and early 20th centuries; it is enough to recall the works of A. Kh. Vostokov, I. I. Sreznevsky, Vs. Miller, V. V. Bartold, N. M. Galkovsky and others. The idea of the unity of the sources of folk culture of the Slavs and Aryans is a red thread in the work of V. A. Gorodtsov "Daco-Sarmatian religious elements in Russian folk art." Recently, scientists began to raise the question of the possible presence of an ancient Indo-Slavic community, which was distinguished not only by significant linguistic similarities, but also by its exceptional cultural and economic proximity that developed under conditions of a very long cohabitation.

Since most modern historians believe that at the turn of the 2nd - 1st millennium BC the Aryan tribes were already in the northwestern part of the Hindustan Peninsula and Iran, it is natural to assume that similar religious ideas and the mythology of the Aryans and Slavs should have developed much earlier.

The idea of many scholars was aimed at searching for the source lands of the Aryans, their ancestral home (this name should be understood as those lands where disparate tribal groups formed tribes, developing, over the course of centuries, similar mutually intelligible dialects and languages that became one of the main signs of emerging ethnic groups).

"The Slavic language is an Indo-European language that has generally preserved an archaic type." The domestic linguist B.V. Gornung believed that the ancestors of the Aryans (Indo-Iranians) settled in the north-east of Europe at the end of the 3rd millennium BC and were somewhere near the middle Volga, and another prominent linguist V. I. Abaev writes: "Through a row centuries the Aryans carried the memory of their ancestral home and its great river Volga. "

Back in the 20s of the 20th century, Academician A.I. Sobolevsky said that in the vast expanses of European Russia, up to the northern regions, names dominate, based on some kind of ancient Indo-European language. He wrote in his work: "The starting point of my work is the assumption that the two groups of names (water sources) are related to each other and belong to the same language of the Indo-European family."

In the 2 millennium BC, tribes of cattle breeders and farmers, calling themselves Aryans, come to northwestern India and northern Iran from their East European "ancestral home".

Some of the Aryans left East Europe east in search of a better share, but it is difficult to imagine a situation in which the entire population of a significant part of the lands of their original settlement would have left them. Most likely,

338

such a situation is simply impossible, because no historical reasons have been identified that could have caused their (aryas) to leave their "ancestral home". Probably, part of the Aryan tribes remained at home, in the vastness of Eastern Europe, to become the ancestors of some future peoples of this land.

And there is nothing surprising in the fact that the historian P.N. Tretyakov quotes the words of academician N. Ya. Marr, who believed that the ancient basis of Slavism was not limited, for example, to the Volga region, but stretches far north, "to those places that lately they were considered by no means Slavic and occupied Slavs already at the dawn of the so-called historical time."

The ancient ethnic groups of the East European north, preceding the migration of Finno-Ugric groups here because of the Urals, N. Ya. Marr sometimes called "northern Sarmatians" or "Russes." Aryan tribes left from southeastern Europe, from the Black Sea lands (as almost all historians believe the drought was due) millennia ago to find a new homeland in India and Iran (right: Aryana - "Aryan Land"). They left and carried away with them their traditions, tales, myths, beliefs, rites, their songs, their ancient gods.

In 1903, a book with the strange and intriguing title "The Arctic Homeland in the Vedas" was first published in Bombay. Its author, the wonderful scientist Bal Gangadhar Tilak, devoted his whole life to the study of the culture of his native people. Tilak has long and carefully studied ancient legends, legends and sacred hymns, born in the depths of millennia by the distant ancestors of the Indo-Aryans and Iranians. And so, summing up the strange phenomena that were described in the sacred books of the Indians (Vedas) and Iranians (Avesta), B. Tilak came to the conclusion that stunned his contemporaries: the homeland of the ancestors of the Indo-Iranians was in northern Europe, somewhere near the Arctic Circle.

The book impressed many contemporaries of the writer as an exploding bomb. Someone considered this a bona fide delusion, someone - a fairy tale, and some and falsification. And it really didn't fit in my head how the north of Europe could be a "blessed land", and in fact his hymns of the Rig Veda, the most ancient of the Vedas, described it that way.

The results were not slow to affect, and after Tilak's book another work was published in 1910 - the book of the Russian scientist E. Elachich, "The Far North as the birthplace of mankind".

As in the work of B. Tilak, the book of E. Jelacic contains numerous excerpts from the ancient texts of the Rigveda and Avesta, which could be explained only by the "northern" hypothesis of their origin.

Created in ancient times by the common ancestors of the Slavic and Indo-Iranian peoples, the hymns of the Vedas, along with the ancient Iranian Avesta, are considered one of the oldest monuments of human thought.

So what are the many facts stored in myths, traditions, prayers and hymns that testify to the fact that they were created in the far north of Europe? In particular, these are descriptions of those natural phenomena that, of course, could not have arisen in India. Only in the polar latitudes during the polar night is it possible to see how the stars describe their diurnal circles near the motionless North Star, creating the illusion of a circle of sky above the circle of the earth, fastened like wheels by a fixed axis.

In the hymns of the Rigveda and Avesta it is said that in the homeland of the Aryans six days a day and half a night last, and "the human year is one day and one night of the gods."

Naturally, life away from the North Pole could not give rise to ideas about a long polar night and about a day lasting six months. How could people living far from the north sing the dawn with these words:
In truth, it has been many days
During which until sunrise
You, oh dawn, were visible to us!
Many dawns did not enlighten to the end,
Oh, give, Varuna, we dawns to dawn to live.

Here, the singer of the ancient Aryan anthem addresses the powerful lord of the heavenly ocean, the keeper of cosmic law and truth on earth, the god Varuna with a request to help survive the long multi-day dawn and survive until the day. He asks:
Oh give us a long dark night
See your end, oh night!

It is interesting that in the Vedas and in the Avesta, memories of the polar night, which lasts 100 days a year, have been preserved. So, in the Indian service there is a rite of reinforcing the warrior god and thunder Indra with the ritual drunken drink "Soma" during his struggle to free the sun from captivity, which lasts one hundred days. In the ancient Iranian Avesta, which also tells about the struggle of the warrior god Tshitris for the sun, the priests reinforce it with a drink for one hundred nights. It must be said that the legend of the struggle to free the sun from long captivity, the idea of which could be inspired only by a polar night, is often found in the entire mythology of the Vedas.

It is interesting that in the Vedas and in the Avesta, memories of the polar night, which lasts 100 days a year, have been preserved. So, in the Indian service there is a rite of reinforcing the warrior god and thunder Indra with the ritual drunken drink "Soma" during his struggle to free the sun from captivity, which lasts one hundred days. In the ancient Iranian Avesta, which also tells about the struggle of the warrior god Tshitris for the sun, the priests reinforce it with a drink for one hundred nights. It must be said that the legend of the struggle to free the sun from long captivity, the idea of which could be inspired only by a polar night, is often found in the entire mythology of the Vedas....

It is interesting that in the Vedas and in the Avesta, memories of the polar night, which lasts 100 days a year, have been preserved. So, in the Indian service there is a rite of reinforcing the warrior god and thunder Indra with the ritual drunken drink "Soma" during his struggle to free the sun from captivity, which lasts one hundred days. In the ancient Iranian Avesta, which also tells about the struggle of the warrior god Tshitris for the sun, the priests reinforce it with a drink for one hundred nights. It must be said that the legend of the struggle to free the sun from long captivity, the idea of which could be inspired only by a polar night, is often found in the entire mythology of the Vedas....

Compare this ancient description with what S.V. Maksimov writes about the aurora at the end of the 19th century: "I was riveted on my eyes by a wonderful, unprecedented spectacle that now opened from a dark cloud. It burst instantly and instantly shone with dazzling colors, whole a sea of flowers that poured from one to another, and as if sparks streamed endlessly from above, sparks from below, from the sides ... That will pour over the whole roundabout with azure, green, purple, all the colors of a beautiful rainbow, topaz, yachts, emeralds will sparkle. "

Are these descriptions surprisingly similar, shared by many millennia? Probably, it's just as an incomprehensible, miraculous manifestation of the supreme deity to the people who bowed to him, the inhabitants of the polar regions of Europe, where you can only see such a bright and

342

multicolored spectacle on the coast of the White and Barents Seas, as the northern lights are more monotonous closer to the pole, and to the south - in general the phenomenon is extremely rare. S.V. Maximov notes that on the shores of the White and Barents Seas, "flashes" are accompanied by a piercing sound. Such a phenomenon is characteristic precisely for these latitudes and does not occur anywhere else. This indication is repeatedly found in descriptions of travelers and explorers of the Arctic regions.

But not only for continuous night, but also for continuous day, there are indications in the Vedas.

Near the pole it is observed how the sun, rising to a certain height above the horizon, stops, stands still and then goes back. The Vedas say: "The sun god stopped his chariot in the middle of the sky." This image cannot be explained otherwise than by the fact that the movement of the sun was observed in the northern latitudes.

N.R. Guseva, in a number of his works, emphasizes that: "Since the time the Aryans stayed in the Arctic, the lunar calendar has played a decisive role in calculating the months ... In the polar regions, the moon on the days of the full moon passes through the" point of the north "13 times a year, which means the whole the year is divided into 13 lunar months ... In the Rigveda and other monuments of ancient literature, the moon is devoted to so many hymns and so many prescriptions are connected with it that so far in the minds of the inhabitants of this country (India), the cult of the moon takes precedence over the cult of the sun - even thousands of years of farming could not shake this ratio ... "

Among the amazing phenomena of the land of the Aryans, described in the Vedas and Avesta, there is one, extremely important, which for almost a century has attracted the closest attention of researchers - these are the sacred mountains of the ancestral home of the Aryans: Meru in Indian traditions, Hara in Iranian.

Here is what ancient legends told about them:

In the north, where there is a "clean, beautiful, gentle, desirable world," in that part of the earth that "is more beautiful, cleaner," live the great gods: Kubera, the god of wealth, the seven wise sons of the creator god Brahma, embodied in seven stars of the Big Dipper, and, finally, the Lord of the Universe Rudra-Khara himself, "wearing light braids", "reed-haired, brown-bearded, lotus-blue-eyed of all creatures Ancestor." In order to reach the world of gods and ancestors, it is necessary to overcome the great and endless mountains that stretch from west to east.

Around their golden peaks the sun makes its annual journey, above them in the darkness seven stars of Ursa Major sparkle and the star of Dhruva located motionless in the center of the universe.

All the great rivers of the earth rush down from these mountains, only some of them flow south to the warm sea, while others flow north to the white ocean. On the tops of these mountains forests rustle, marvelous birds sing, wonderful animals live. But ordinary mortals were not allowed to enter them, only the most wise and courageous crossed this limit and left forever in the blessed land of their ancestors, the shores of which were washed by the waters of the Milky Ocean.

The mountains that separate the north and the White Sea from all other lands are called Meru ridges in the hymns of the Veda, and the greatest of them is the Mandara. In the Avesta, these are the Hara Mountains with their main peak, Mount Hukarya. And just as over the Meru mountains, over the High Hara sparkle seven stars of the Big Dipper and the North Star, set in the center of the universe. From here, from the golden peaks of the High Hara, all earthly rivers originate and the greatest of them is the pure Ardvi River, flowing with noise into the white sea of Vorukash, "having wide bays, widely indented." Over the mountains of High Hara the "fast-moving" sun always circulates, half a day lasts here for six months and night. And only the most courageous and powerful in spirit can go through these mountains and get into a happy country of the blessed, washed by the waters of the white sea-ocean.

Ancient Greek authors also wrote about the great northern mountains, who believed that these mountains, which they called the Riphean Mountains, stretched from west to east throughout northern Europe and were the northern border of Great Scythia. Herodotus wrote about the distant Northern Mountains, stretching from west to east.

Doubting the incredible, fantastic magnitude of the Riphean mountains, Aristotle nevertheless believed in their existence, he was convinced that the earth rises to the north, since the sun is lower there than in the south, and all the largest rivers of Europe flow down from these mountains except the Istra Danube.

This conviction was reinforced by the very logical conclusion that rivers always flow down from the mountains and never flow up into the mountains. Behind the Riphean Mountains, in the north of Europe, the ancient Greek and Roman geographers placed the Great Northern, or Scythian, ocean.

The question of where these mountains are located has not been resolved for a long time. It was suggested that the creators of the Avesta and Rigveda sang the ridges of the Urals in their hymns. Yes, indeed, the Ural Mountains are in the north with respect to India and Iran.

Yes, the Urals is rich in gold and gems; it stretched far to the freezing North Sea. But only Avesta and Rigveda and ancient historians constantly repeated that the sacred Hara and Meru, the Riphean mountains stretch from west to east, and the Urals are oriented strictly from south to north. All - and the Avesta, and the Vedas, and Herodotus, and Aristotle argued that the Great Northern Mountains divide the land into north and south, and the Urals - the border of west and east. And, finally, neither the Don, nor the Dnieper, nor the Volga originates from the Urals; the spurs of the Urals are not the border where the earth's waters are divided into the current and white-fronted northern sea and flowing into the southern sea. So the Urals, apparently, did not solve the ancient riddle. However, everything is so simple here.

The fact is that the common Ural ridge that we are used to today began to be called, as many people think, only from the middle of the 18th century (from the Bashkir name of the southern Urals - Uraltau). The northern part of the Ural Mountains has long been called the Stone or the Earth belt.

Unlike the South Urals, which stretches from north to south in the meridional direction, the polar Urals, where individual peaks rise more than 1800 m above sea level, and the total width of the mountain strip reaches 150 km. (at 65 ° north latitude), has a north-east latitudinal direction. Timan Ridge, which lies at the same latitude and, which is extremely important here, departs from the so-called "three stones," combines with the Northern Uvals, a hill stretching from west to east. It is here, on the Northern Uvals, that the main watershed of the basins of the northern and southern seas is located.

The outstanding Soviet scientist Yu. A. Meshcheryakov called the Northern Uvals an "anomaly of the Russian Plain" and, saying that the higher elevations (Central Russian, Volga) give them the role of the main dividing line, he made the following conclusion: "Central

346

Russian and Volga Uplands appeared only in the newest (Neogene-Quaternary) time when the Northern Uvals already existed and were the watershed of the basins of the northern and southern seas." And even more than that, during the Carboniferous period, when the ancient sea splashed on the site of the Urals, the Northern Uvals were already mountains. "

The Northern Uvals - the main watershed of the rivers of the north and south, the basins of the White and Caspian Seas - are located where on the map of Ptolemy the Hyperborean (or Ripeyan) mountains are located, from which the Volga, called ancient Avestan name Ra or Rha. But according to the ancient Iranian tradition, the source of this sacred river is on the mountains of High Hara, on the "golden peak of Hukarya". And here it is worth quoting the message of the Arab scholar Al-Idrisi (12th century) about the Kukaya mountains, which he places in the extreme northeast of Europe and which are similar to the Riphean mountains of ancient geographers, as well as Mount Hukarya Avesta. Al-Idrisi, referring to the Kukaya mountains, from which the Rusiyya river originates, notes that six large rivers flow into the mentioned Rusiya river, the sources of which are in the Kukaya mountains, and these are large mountains stretching from the Sea of Darkness to the edge of the inhabited land. .. these are very large mountains, no one is able to climb them because of the severe cold and the constant abundance of snow on their peaks. "

Let us turn to the dictionary of Brockhaus and Efron (vol. VII, 1892). It is said here that on the north-eastern outskirts of the Vologda province, mountain ranges do not reach the eternal snow line, but due to their northern position, often the snow does not leave them all year round. On the northern slopes, snow thickness reaches 3.5 - 4 meters by the end of March. And if the sacred mountains of Khara and Meru, and the Northern Uvals (in combination with the polar Urals) are the same thing, then it is not difficult to find the six rivers that Al-Idrisi wrote about. Large rivers: the Kama, Vyatka, Unzha, Kostroma, Sheksna, really flowing into the Volga (Rusiyu) really flow into the Uvals. And if you consider (as the ancients considered) the source of the Volga Kama, then the Volga-Rga (Rha) of Ptolemy and the Avesta actually begins from the Northern Uval. From them also originates the greatest of the rivers of the Russian North - the mighty and full-flowing Northern Dvina, which flows into the White Sea and has about a thousand tributaries.

There is a hymn in the Avesta, glorifying the sacred river of the Aryans Ardvisura, which flows into the White Sea. The following is a fragment of this hymn:

Pray great, glorious
Equal to
To all the waters taken together
Current on earth.
Pray current powerfully
From the height of Hukarya
To the sea of Vorukash.
From edge to edge worries
The whole sea of Vorukash,
And the waves in the middle
Heave when
Pours its own water
Falling into it, Ardvi
The whole thousand ducts
And a thousand lakes.

What river is chanted in the Avesta under the name Ardvi-Sura Anahita? Some see it as the Amu Darya, but this

348

river is always muddy, and it is said about Ardvi-Sura that it is transparent, pure ("anahita") and healing. So the Amu Darya is not suitable. Others believe that this is the Volga. There are many reasons for this - the latitude, the abundance of waters, the vast delta, as well as the fact of finding sources on high mountains. But, although all this applies to the Northern Dvina, no one paid attention to two factors that "play" in favor of this particular river.

Firstly, its upper part is formed from two rivers - the South and Sukhona, from where its name "Dvina", which means "double", comes from. The name "Ardvi" is also translated. So why should it relate to the Volga? The Volga has many tributaries, but the merging of two streams into one at a short distance does not create the Volga. So the name "Ardvi-Sura", "double merging (flowing, flowing)", most likely coincides with the Northern Dvina.

Secondly, in Avesta jail 5, it is said that there is a strange phenomenon: along with descriptions of frost, snow or hail plumbing the waters of Ardvi-Sura, it is mentioned "one duct of Ardvi flows through seven karshvars, flowing evenly in summer and winter". The Volga does not have a channel that would not freeze in the winter, and the Northern Dvina has it - it is the Yemen River, one of the large tributaries of the Dvina, which does not freeze in winter, since sources called here bumps blow from its bottom all year round.

If we take into account the above arguments, the coincidence of Ardvi-Sura with the Northern Dvina will be another confirmation of the Arctic theory, which defines the Polar region as the oldest initial territory of the initial formation of the Indo-European tribes, including the ancestors of the Aryans and Russians.

To all this, we can add that, being at 60 degrees north latitude, the Northern Uvaly is not only the main watershed of the Russian Plain and the borders of the north and south, but here you can already see the year, delimited by the light and dark half, you can see high, almost zenith the North Star and Ursa Major, and going down to the sea, and the aurora.

It has long been mined for gold until the 19th - early 20th century along the Vishera River, in the upper reaches of the Pechora. In the Vologda province, gold is noted in the upper reaches of Sugora and Ilych. The dictionary of Brockhaus and Efron informs that the banks and channels of the rivers Mer, Volga (near Kostroma), Unzhi and their tributaries abound in pyrite (gold blende) so much that it is enough for industrial development, and peasants at the end of the 19th century they collected pieces of rock washed by the rivers and took them to local factories. The Wurlam River, also flowing from the Northern Uvals to the south and its tributaries carry their waters in floodplains containing golden sand. In the area of the circumpolar Urals, Timan Ridge and Northern Uvals, a huge amount of minerals, many of which were well known and were used in ancient times. Rivers "flowing in the golden channels" and mountains "rich in precious stones" are not a myth, but a reality.

Thus, the mysterious sacred mountains of Aryan myths, Scythian ancestors and stories of ancient writers have very real outlines, as well as everything that is said about Hara and Meru, the Riphean mountains, which can be associated with the Northern Uvals and the polar Urals.

Among all that has been said about the sacred mountains of the Aryans (Riphean Mountains of the Scythians) and that we have not yet connected with the Northern Uvaly, there remains one important detail - the height of the mountains. Indeed, the Khara, Meru and

Riphean mountains are described as very high, but the height of the Northern Uval (unlike Timan and the northern Urals) does not exceed 500 meters above sea level. But here one should take into account such moments: when describing the peaks of Hara and Meru, the ancient singers constantly noted that they were covered in forest, abound in animals and birds, that is, they could not be very tall. Do not forget the fact that the low northern sky, the specific position of the sun, and also the fact that from here the rivers flowed both south and north (rivers flow from top to bottom, and not vice versa) - all this testified to ancient observers about one thing: the earth rises to the north and there are the highest mountains on earth.

It should also be taken into account that the height of the mountain ranges is not something absolutely stable; for millennia, the elevations rise and fall. It is worth recalling that the whole continent - Antarctica - sank 900 meters under the weight of ice. The Scandinavian glacier was no less and no less pressing on Europe, but here its pressure was balanced by the rise of the adjacent parts of the platform. Under such conditions, what could be the height of the Northern Uvalov, at the western end of which the glacier stopped?

The Scandinavian ice sheet finally melted to 8 thousand BC. e., and began the slow rise of Scandinavia and the lowering of the Russian North, which continues now. But this process is spasmodic, and we have no reason to doubt that the Northern Uvala is 10–9 thousand BC were higher than these days. And finally, in ancient myths it is said that beyond the mountains of Hara and Meru, on the shores of the Milky Sea, there is a happy country with a warm climate, free from cold winds and giving birth to abundant fruits. In the groves and forests of this particular country, where the sun rises and sets once a year, happy people live. It is in this country that the Avesta, Rigveda and Mahabharata place the land of their ancestors, the habitat of the gods and heroes.

All this taken together indicates that the north was indeed a sacred ancient ancestral home for the Aryans, whose memory they preserved in hymns, prayers and traditions. Millennia passed farther south and southeast, to the west and southwest shepherds and farmers settled. Well, north? Have all the Aryans left their native land in search of a better life? Probably not!

Look carefully at the map of the north of Eastern Europe, in the names of rivers, lakes, settlements. All these names are saved in the event that there are people who remember them. Otherwise, a new population comes and calls everything in a new way. In the Russian North to this day, one can find the names of rivers that are clearly associated with Sanskrit, explained only with the help of the ancient language of the Aryans - Sanskrit, as well as the names of many villages and villages.

It was in those places where these ancient names of villages and villages were preserved, in the weaving and embroidery of Russian peasants until the end of the 19th and beginning of the 20th centuries the tradition of ancient geometric ornaments, which can be found in the ancient cultures of Eurasia 6-2 thousand BC e. And first of all, these are the ornaments, often very complex and time-consuming, which were the "calling card" of Aryan antiquity.

"The people do not remember that he would ever invent his mythology, his language, his laws, customs and rituals. All these national foundations have already deeply entered into his moral being, as the life itself, which he lived through many prehistoric centuries, as past "on which the real order of things and the whole future development of life firmly rests. Therefore, all moral ideas for the people of the primitive era constitute its sacred tradition, great native antiquity, the holy covenant of ancestors to descendants." These words of the outstanding Russian folklorist of the 19th century F. I. Buslaev, uttered by him at a ceremony in Moscow University in 1859, have not lost their relevance today.

And plunging into the depths of millennia in search of answers to the question: "So what is this sacred tradition, what is this holy covenant of ancestors to descendants of?", We take with us, as a guiding thread, that memory of the past that has been preserved in our songs, bylins, in our rites, rituals, beliefs, in language and folk art.

According to a number of researchers, the Russian language possesses, when translating the Vedas, "a number of undoubted advantages over Western European languages." These advantages are associated with better preservation in Russian archaism than in Western languages.One of the largest modern American linguists P. Friedrich believes that the Pre-Slavic language better than all other Indo-European languages has preserved the ancient Indo-European system of tree names, from which he concludes that the ancestors of the Slavs lived in the general Slavic period in such a natural and climatic zone that corresponds to the ancestral home of the Indo-Europeans , and "after the general Slavic period, the carriers of various Slavic dialects continued to a significant extent to live in a similar area."

In 1911, an outstanding researcher of the Russian North A. Zhuravsky wrote: "In the" childhood "of mankind is the basis for the knowledge and direction of the future paths of mankind. In the eras of the" childhood of Russia ", it is the path to the knowledge of Russia, to the control knowledge of those historical phenomena of our modernity that seem to us fatally complex and not subordinate to the ruling will of the people, but roots that are simple and elementary, like the initial cell of a complex organism ... And we are obliged to make full use of the experiences of the gray-haired past, and the closer we get to the embryos of this past, the more consciously, more truly and more confidently we will go "forward" ... It is the history of the "childhood of mankind", namely ethnography, that will help us to know the logical laws of natural progress and consciously, and not blindly, go "forward" by ourselves and move our people "forward", because ethnography and history are the ways to know that "past", without which cannot be applied to the knowledge of the future, the knowledge of the present. "Humanity" consists of "nations", and, first of all, it is logically necessary for a nation to be a definite mutual whole, so that it does not appear to us in the third person plural - "they", but in the first "we". Russia ... cannot know itself without the help of knowing the roots of its past; but, without knowing oneself, it is impossible to know others and take into account one's position among others, how, without correcting oneself, it is impossible to correct others ... The embryos of many beliefs and ideals perished - we will search for their prints on objects until they perish forever. It's not only "interesting" or "curious", but also vital, necessary. "

We do not have a thousand-year history, as is customary now to write and speak, but many thousands of years. One thousand years can be discussed only in relation to the adoption of Christianity. Indeed, until this year, our ancestors did not live in caves and did not dress in skins. Not suddenly in the European world the word Gardarik ("Country of Cities") came into use as the name of Russia. These lands were on our lands, and they were not born in one day, but developed and developed over many centuries, since a city is not just a cluster of houses, but also a way of life, established industrial relations, centralization of trade and economic relations and a place the concentration of social structures that have developed over many centuries.

Gradually, over the course of centuries, technology changed, improving, but the themes of images, drawings and signs applied to craft objects were protected by tradition. They were not changed, because they all carried a semantic load, had a certain meaning, often magical, spellbinding, and were a reflection of the concepts of life and death, of acquiring offspring, of preserving property, breeding livestock, and ripening crops. It was scary to change them, since magic played a leading role in the beliefs of the Gentiles, and these drawings and signs had to be sacredly protected, as evidenced by at least the simple fact that they survived in folk art to the present day.

The plot language, the language of symbols, in this art aroused great interest, but the main attention in the works of scientists is devoted to identifying and explaining images of the female and male deities found even in later Russian embroideries - this is a clear relic of paganism.

It is interesting that such a female deity (and perhaps this is a praying woman) is almost exactly repeated in Russian embroideries, and on Indian fabrics and ritual objects, which is not a mere coincidence. Since ancient times, there have been many geometric motifs in Russian and other Slavic embroideries, which, along with other themes, also lead us to ancient times, which mean that some lines of history can be traced from them.

For more than a century, Russian folk embroidery has attracted the attention of researchers. At the end of the last century, a number of brilliant collections of this type of folk art were formed, and the first attempts were made to read complex "plot" compositions, especially characteristic of the folk traditions of the Russian North. There were many interesting works devoted to the analysis of the plot-symbolic language, features of technology and regional differences in Russian folk embroidery. However, most of these works focus on anthropomorphic and zoomorphic images, archaic three-part compositions, which include, as already mentioned, a stylized and transformed image of a person - a female (more often) or male (less often) pre-Christian deity.

The geometric motifs of the North Russian embroidery are somewhat separate, accompanying, as a rule, the main unfolded plot compositions, although very often in the design of towels, belts, hem, wounds and mantle shirts it is the geometric motifs that are the main and only ones that are extremely important for researchers. By the way, the analysis of patterns of local traditional lace also deserves much attention from this point of view.

Academician B. A. Rybakov repeatedly wrote about archaic geometry in Russian ornamental creativity and the need for its careful study. And in his works of the 1960s-1970s, and for the first time in his deep work on paganism of the ancient Slavs, the idea of the immeasurable depths of folk memory that preserves and carries through centuries in images of embroidery wood carvings, toys, etc., the most ancient worldview patterns, rooted in the unexplored distant millennia.

In this regard, the collections of the museum of the Russian North are very valuable, that is, those places where, one might say, the eternal remoteness from state centers, as well as a relatively peaceful existence (the Vologda region, for example, in its northeastern part practically did not know wars), the abundance of forests and the protection of many settlements by swamps and impassability - all this contributed to the preservation of an immeasurable number

356

of centuries of the most ancient forms of life and economy, careful attitude to the faith of fathers and grandfathers, and, as a direct consequence of this, the preservation of the oldest mvoliki encoded in embroidery ornaments, patterns in fabrics and lace.

Of particular interest are embroideries that "survived" to the turn of the 19th and 20th centuries, which originate from the northeastern regions of the Vologda and neighboring regions of the Arkhangelsk regions. Many scholars wrote that these were lands of the Finno-Ugric tribes, but these toponyms indicate completely different - the vast majority of place names here are Slavic, and many of them are very archaic. So, in the Tarnogsky District of the Vologda Oblast, out of 137 settlements, both large and small, only 6 have non-Russian names. It is in these areas that the traditions of ornamental patterns of the most ancient origin, as we will see below, have the best preservation.

Ornamental compositions, which will be discussed and which were reproduced in Vologda embroideries until the 1930s, adorned only sacred things. B. A. Rybakov very accurately speaks about this process: "The deposition in embroidery of very early layers of human religious thinking ... is explained by the ritual nature of those objects that were covered with an embroidered pattern ... Such are the wedding kokoshniks of brides, shirts, wraps for wedding carts and many other things. An especially ritual object that had long been separated from its household counterpart was a towel with rich and complex embroidery, bread and salt were brought on a towel, towels served as reins of a wedding train, and a coffin was carried on towels okoynikom and lowered it to the pit. Towels are hang red angle on the towel "religionists" placed icons. "

It is precisely such sacred ornaments that are presented in the Vologda Museum of Local Lore, and they will continue to be the main comparative material in our attempt to identify ornamental parallels between the oldest patterns of North Russian embroidery and ornaments created by those peoples who lived later in various historical eras on the vast territories of the Eurasian steppes and forest-steppes and spoke Indo-European languages, including those related to the Indo-speaking and Iranian-speaking branches of the pra-Indo-Iranian language (or unified m certain number dalektov tribes included in science under the name Aryan).

So, one of the oldest motifs of geometric type ornaments was the rhombus or rhombic meander among the peoples of Eurasia (many explained the meander as a conditional image of the top of a wave wrapped at right angles). The meander is even found on things dating from the Paleolithic, for example, on various bone products found at the Mezin site in the Chernihiv region. Paleontologist V. Bibikova in 1965 suggested that the meander spiral, torn meander stripes and rhombic meanders on objects from the Mezin site arose as a repetition of the natural pattern of mammoth tusks of dentin. From this, she concluded that a similar ornament for people of that era was a kind of symbol of a mammoth, the main object of hunting. This could have a magical spellbound meaning, aimed at the success of the hunt, and at the same time reflect in itself people's ideas about abundance.

The meander pattern in its various combinations and modifications continues to exist for many millennia, spreading ever wider among the neighboring Indo-European peoples and diverging beyond their territories in the process of the movement of the Aryans to the southeast. We find it as a symbol of good luck and a kind of ward from misfortune on cult objects and ceramics (i.e., on the storages of food and drink very important for people's lives) and in later cultures. It should be noted that already on the bone products of the aforementioned Mezinsky site, one can trace how outlines of a swastika — another characteristic ornament for all Indo-Europeans — grow from the strip of double meander, shown in movement from right to left. This element is also depicted in its main form - in the form of a cross with ends bent at right angles, and being complicated by new elements in the form of additional processes.

The swastika took one of the leading places in the ornament. If you place a dot in its four "departments", it will be a symbol of the sown field and at the same time a prayer for a good harvest. By the way, if you put two swastikas on top of each other with the top turning 45 degrees, you get the old Slavic sun sign "Kolovrat", that is, a spinning wheel (colo) with eight spokes with clockwise bent ends.

The sign of the swastika, dating back to antiquity, among the ancestors of Russians and Aryans began to be designated the light of the sun as a source of life and prosperity. This sign can be traced from Arkhangelsk to the lands of India, where it is visible everywhere - they decorate temples, houses, clothes and, of course, many items related to the wedding.

All the ancestors of the Indo-European peoples developed in ancient times in the process of historical contacts a certain amount of similar vocabulary, but the ancestors of the Germans and other European peoples belonged to the western group of Indo-Europeans, while the ancestors of Russians and Aryans belonged to the eastern, much more mutually close. The so-called Aryan swastika can still be seen in handicrafts of Russians, especially northern ones: it adorns many works of folk art, including patterned knitted mittens.

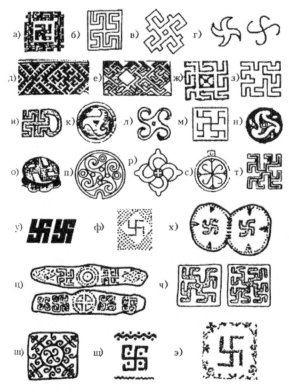

Swastika motive:

a-h) traditional motifs of embroidery and lace. Vologda, 19-20 century;

i) Novgorod. 13th century;

k) Chernihiv. 12-13 century;

k) Russia 13-15 century;

m) Ryazan;

n / a) Tripoli culture. Eneolithic;

Pt) Scythian-Sarmatian products. I thousand BC e. - beginning of n. e .;

u-f) Andronovo culture. The era of bronze;

hc) North Caucasus. The era of bronze;

h) Zap. Caspian littoral. The era of bronze;

sh) India;

u) drawing on a wedding vessel. North India;

e) embroidery motif, Tajikistan, 20th century.

360

A peculiar transformation of the meander motif is typical for Tripoli ceramics ⌐ - shaped ornament, consisting of the so-called "geese".

On the whole, we can determine the circle of ornamental basic motifs with which, focusing on Tripoli as their kind of arch, we will compare the materials of subsequent cultures. This is a meander and its varieties, a meander spiral, a hard-drawn cross, a swastika, "geese".

In search of the closest analogies in time, we naturally turn to the ceramic complexes of those cultures that existed at different times in Eastern Europe and the Urals with the Ural lands. We find the traditions of ceramic ornamentation, which includes an amazing variety of variations of meander and swastika motifs, among the closest neighbors of the "Srubniks" - the Andronovo culture created by Indo-Iranians and genetically related to the Srubnaya. Synchronous in time, these two cultures existed for a long period in the very vast territories of the steppe and forest-steppe zones of our country.

We have every reason to talk about the distribution among the Russians of the ornamental patterns described here. As in the entire Andronovo ornament, in North Russian folk embroidery and brane weaving, the composition is divided into three horizontal zones, the upper and lower often duplicating one another and the middle bears the most important patterns from their point of view in importance. We don't know what the forms of ornaments were on things made by people in the era of the most ancient Indo-Iranian (All-Aryan) unity, but we believe that the described elements of ornamental patterns were hardly born overnight in the minds of the same Andronovites, but are

361

rooted in genetically related the culture of their common ancestors.

Ornament on the vessels of Sintashta

The mentioned middle strip of the horizontal composition can carry the most diverse combinations of the indicated elements of the ornament, which are absolutely identical to the North Russian, Trypillian and much more eastern and southeastern cultures, consistent in time for different cultures. Of particular interest is the legitimacy of such analogies, traced in archaeological East Slavic materials. For example, a buckle in the shape of complex crosses, found in Novgorod in the 1960s, dating from the mid-13th century, found a repetition of its pattern in embroidery recently made on a towel by a Vologda peasant woman. The find of the slate spindle-frog published by G. Polyakova in the Slavic settlement near Ryazan, which dates from the 11th-13th centuries, is interesting because the figure in the form of a six-pointed Orthodox cross surrounded by meander spirals and swastika motifs is scratched on the spindle-wheel. Similar examples could be continued. It remains for us to state the following: similar ornaments may arise without mutual connection among different peoples, but it is difficult to believe that among peoples separated by thousands of kilometers and millennia, if these peoples are not ethnogenetically connected, they can appear so completely independently complex ornamental compositions, repeated even in the smallest details, and even performing the same functions: charms and signs of belonging to a family or family.

It is impossible to deny the inevitability of the emergence of ethnogenetic ties between the ancient ancestors of the Indo-Iranian tribes and the indo-speaking and Iranian-speaking branches that stood out from their community, and, accordingly, those ethnic groups that took shape in close proximity to them for millennia, up to the formation of the large and close in their culture logging and Andronovo communities. With their addition, the process of their partial disintegration, expressed in the resettlement of individual tribes or even their groups, both to the west and to the east, should also have taken place. The departure of the Aryans, for example, ended, as recognized by science, by the second half of the 2nd millennium BC. The ancestors of the Slavs, territorially close to them for such a long time, partially moved to the west, forming groups known as the Western Slavs, and the main massif, called the Eastern Slavs, settled on the lands of Eastern Europe.

Leaving east and south, the Aryan tribes carried away with them traditional forms of culture - established production skills, types of ornaments (and understanding of the symbols reflected in them), customs and beliefs.

On their way to India and Iran, the Aryans entered into contacts with the peoples of the countries through which they passed, settling there for different periods of time and partially mingling with this population. Therefore, we are also interested in those motifs of patterns that are close to the Russian ones that are revealed among peoples living, for example, in the Caucasus or Central Asia (although it should be remembered that part of the land was part of the Andronovo culture before the Urals and before Afghanistan).

Unfortunately, scientists only in the last 25-30 years began to trace racial, linguistic, cultural and other Arya-Slavic parallels in their writings, and such studies significantly expand the boundaries of our knowledge about our own past. Here we refrain from far-reaching conclusions and only note in conclusion that the scope of this analysis is limited by the borders of the polar, steppe and forest-steppe zones of our country. Undoubtedly, the involvement of Indian and Iranian materials would greatly expand this framework. In our deep conviction, the hypothesis of the Indian historian B. Tilak about the probability of the oldest unification of the ancestors of the Aryans (in the distant era of their common language) in tribal and tribal unions in the polar regions convincingly proves not only the possibility, but also the full likelihood of this fact by numerous descriptions of the Arctic nature, preserved in the monuments of ancient Indian literature.

The most ancient ancestors of the Slavs, judging by the many rapprochements of various sides of the sources of their culture with the ancient Aryan, and then with the culture of the peoples of the Eurasian steppes, native speakers of the Indo-European languages (such as Andronovites who once stood out from the Indo-Iranian community), were apparently so close to the Aryans, who transmitted to their descendants both many common elements of the language, and general motifs of ornaments. Both language and ornaments were means of mutual communication and evidence of genetic proximity, and possibly signs of membership, joining the same clans, the same tribes.

Literature:

1. Третьяков П. Н. Некоторые вопросы этногенеза восточного славянства. Краткое сообщение института истории материальной культуры. № 1. 1940.
2. Махабхарата. Вып. V. Ашхабад. 1984.
3. Максимов С. В. Год на севере. Архангельск. 1984.
4. Гусева Н. Р. Русские сквозь тысячелетия. М. 1998.
5. Махабхарата. Вып. V. Ашхабад. 1983. Глава 280.
6. Геродот. История в девяти книгах. Л. 1992.
7. Мещеряков Ю. А. Рельеф СССР. М. 1972.
8. Гусева Н. Р. Славяне и арьи. Путь богов и слов. М. 2002. Приложение III.
9. Карамзин Н. М. История государства Российского. Т. 1. М. 1989.
10. Рыбаков Б. А. Язычество древних славян. М. 1981.
11. Бибикова В. О. О происхождении мезинского палеолитического орнаменте. Советская археология. № 1, 1965.
Меандровые и свастичные орнаменты представлены в работе:
Жарникова С. В. Архаические мотивы северорусской народной вышивки и их параллели в древних орнаментах населения евразийских степей.

S. V. Zharnikova
2003

Rivers - storage facilities

The river of times in its aspiration
Carries out all the affairs of people.
G. R. Derzhavin

Among the many legends preserved by the memory of mankind, the ancient Indian epic Mahabharata is considered the greatest monument of culture, science and history of the ancestors of all Indo-European peoples. Initially, it was a story about the civil strife of the Kuru peoples, who lived more than 5 millennia ago between the Indus and the Ganges. Gradually new ones were added to the main text - and Mahabharata came to us containing almost 200 thousand lines of verses in 18 books. In one of them, called "Forest", sacred sources are described - rivers and lakes of the country, ancient Aryans, i.e. the land on which the events unfolded in the great poem unfolded.

But speaking of this country, named in the epic Bharata, we note that the final event of the narrative was the grandest battle on Kurukshetra in 3102 BC. However, according to science, Aryan tribes on the territory of Iran and Hindustan at that time did not exist yet, and they lived in their ancestral home - quite far from India and Iran.

But where was she, where all these grandiose events were unfolding? This question worried researchers back in the last century. In the mid-19th century, the idea was expressed that the territory of Eastern Europe was such an ancestral home. In the middle of the 20th century, the German scientist Scherer returned to the idea that the ancestral home of all Indo-Europeans was on the lands of Russia, based on the fact that, judging by the texts of the Rigveda and Avesta, in 3 thousand BC Aryans lived in

Eastern Europe. As you know, the great river of our country - the Volga - up to the 2 century bore the name by which the holy book of the Zoroastrians of Avesta knew her - Ranha or Ra. But the Ranha Avesta is the Ganga River of the Rigveda and the Mahabharata!

According to Avesta, on the shores of the Vorukash Sea (the Milk Sea of Mahabharata) and Ranha (Volga) there were a number of Aryan countries from Aryanam Vaedzha in the far north to seven Indian countries in the south, beyond Ranha. The same seven countries are mentioned in the Rigveda and Mahabharata as the land between the Ganga and the Yamuna, on Kuruksetra. They are said about them: "The glorified Kuruksetra, all living beings, you just have to come there, get rid of sins", or "Kurukshetra - the holy Altar of Brahma; there are holy brahmanas - sages. He who settles on Kuruksetra will never know sadness. " The question naturally arises: so what kind of rivers are the Ganges and the Yamuna, between which the country of Brahma lay? We have already found out that the Ranha Ganga is the Volga. But ancient Indian traditions call the Yamuna the only large tributary of the Ganges, flowing from the south-west. Let's look at the map, and it will become clear to us that the ancient Yamuna is our Eye with you! Is it possible?

Apparently, yes! It is no accident that during the Oka river, here and there, rivers with names come across: Yamna, Yam, Ima, Imyev. Moreover, according to Aryan texts, the second name of the Yamuna River was Kala. So, still the mouth of the Oka is called by the locals the mouth of the Kala.

Other large rivers are also mentioned in the Rigveda and Mahabharata. Thus, not far from the source of the Yamuna (Oka) was located the source of the Sindhu River

367

flowing east and south and flowing into the Red Sea (Red Sea) in Sanskrit - stream, sea). But remember that in the Irish and Russian annals the Black Sea was called the Black Sea, that is, the Red. So, by the way, a section of its water area in the north is still called. On the shore of this sea the Sindh people lived and the city of Sindh (modern Anapa) was located. It can be assumed that the Sindhu of the ancient Aryan texts is the Don, whose sources are not far from the source of the Oka.

There are many rivers in the Volga-Oksk interfluve, over whose names millennia have not been dominated. No special effort is required to prove this. It is enough to compare the names of the Pochye rivers with the names of the "sacred krinits" in Mahabharata, more precisely, in that part of it, which is known as "Walking through the Krinitsa". It is in it that a description of more than 200 sacred reservoirs of the ancient Aryan land of Bharat in the basins of the Ganges and the Yamuna (as of 3150 BC) is given.

It is also surprising that we are dealing not only with the almost literal coincidence of the names of the sacred krinits of the Mahabharata and the rivers of Central Russia, but even with the correspondence of their relative positions. Thus, in Sanskrit and in Russian, words with the initial "F" are extremely rare: from list of Mahabharata rivers, only one has a "F" at the beginning of the name - Falguna, which flows into Sarasvati. But, according to ancient Aryan texts, Saraswati is the only large river flowing north of the Yamuna and south of the Ganges and flowing into the Yamuna at its mouth. Only the river Klyazma located to the north of the Oka and south of the Volga corresponds to it. And what? Among hundreds of its tributaries, only one bears a name beginning with "F" - Falyugin! Despite 5 thousand years, this unusual name has practically not changed.

Another example. According to the Mahabharata, to the south of the sacred Kamyaka forest, the river Praveni (that is, the Pra-river) flowed to the Yamuna, with Lake Godavari (where "vara" is a Sanskrit circle). What about today? As before, south of the Vladimir forests, the Pra River flows into the Oka and Lake Gode lies.

Or another example. Mahabharata tells how the sage Kaushika during a drought flooded the river Paru, renamed for it in his honor. But further the epic reports that the ungrateful locals still call the river Para and it flows from the south to the Yamuna (Oka). And what? The river Para still flows from the south to the Oka River and, like many thousands of years ago, the locals call it.

The description of the krynitsa of five thousand years ago speaks, for example, of the Pandye River, flowing near Varuna, the tributary of Sindhu (Don). But the Panda River today flows into the largest tributary of the Don - the Vorona River. Describing the path of the pilgrims, Mahabharata says: "There is Jala and Upajala, the rivers flowing into the Yamuna." Is there now anywhere near the Jala river ("Jala" - the Sanskrit river) and Upa-jala? There is. This is the river Zhala (Tarusa) and the Upa River, flowing nearby into the Oka. It was in Mahabharat that the river Sadanapru (Great Danapr), the Dnieper, flowing west of the headwaters of the Ganges (Volga) was first mentioned.

But if the names of the rivers have been preserved, if the language of the population has been preserved, then the peoples themselves must probably be preserved? And, indeed, they are. Thus, the Mahabharata says that to the north of the country of Pandya, lying on the banks of

Varuna is the country of Martiev. But it is to the north of Panda and Crow on the banks of Moksha and Sura that the land of Mordva (Mortva of the Middle Ages) lies - the people who speak the Finno-Ugric language with a huge number of Russian, Iranian and Sanskrit words.

The country between Yamuna, Sindh, Upajala and the Couple was called A-Vanti. Exactly so - Vantit (A-Vantit) called the land of Vyatich between the Oka, Don, Upa and the Pair Arab travelers and Byzantine chronicles.

Mahabharata and Rigveda mention the people of Kuru and Kuruksetra. Kurukshetra - literally "Kursk Field» and it is in the center of it that the city of Kursk stands, where the "Word of Igor's Campaign" places the Kursk - noble warriors.

An ally of the Kauravas in the Great War with the Pandavas was the people of the Sauvirs who lived in the country of Sindhu. But just like that - until the 15th century they called the Russians-northerners Sauvirs, from where Prince Igor Svyatoslavovich, the hero of the "Tale of Igor's Campaign" was born. This people is mentioned - Sauvirs Ptolemy in the 2nd century.

The Rigveda reports the warlike people of Krivi. But Latvians and Lithuanians even call all Russians - "Krivi", by the name of the neighboring Krivichi ethnic group, whose cities were Smolensk, Polotsk, Pskov, and present-day Tartu and Riga.

Speaking about the history of Eastern Europe, archaeologists and historians in general, the period from 10 to 3 thousand BC not particularly detailed. This is the Mesolithic-Neolithic, with their archaeological cultures. But the archaeological culture in a certain sense is abstract, and after all there were real people who were born and died, loved and suffered, fought and were related, and somehow appreciated themselves, their lives, they called themselves by some specific names. That past, far from us, was present for them. And it is the ancient Aryan sources that make it possible to shed light on some of the dark pages of these seven millennia (from 10 to 3 thousand BC).

In one of the tales of Mahabharata it is said: "We heard that when Samvarana, son of Raksha, ruled the land, great calamities came for the subjects. And then from all kinds of calamities the kingdom destroyed by hunger and death, drought and disease was destroyed. And the troops of the enemies defeated the descendants Bharat. And, bringing the earth into a concussion on his own, consisting of four military branches, the king of the panchals quickly went through the whole country, subjugating it. And with ten armies he defeated that battle. Then the king of Samvaran and his wife, advisers, sons and clan he fled in great fear, and began to live by the great river Sindhu (Dona) in a grove located near a mountain and washed by a river. So the descendants of Bharata lived for a long time, settled in a fortress. And when they lived there for a thousand years, the great descendants of Bharata visited the sage Vasishtha. And when he lived there for the eighth year, the king himself turned to him: "Be our home priest, for we are striving for the kingdom." And Vasishtha gave his consent to the descendants of Bharata. Further we know that he appointed the descendant Puru the autocratic king over all kshatriyas (warriors), according to her land. And he again took possession of the capital, which was previously inhabited by Bharatha and forced all the kings to pay tribute to him. The powerful lord of the country Ajamidha, having taken possession of the whole earth, then made sacrifices. "

This is what Mahabharata tells about the affairs of bygone days. But when and where did this happen? The reign of Samvaran refers, according to the chronology adapted in the Mahabharata, to 6, 4 thousand BC. e. Then, after the defeat and exile, the people of Samvarana live in the river basin. Don in the fortress of Ajamidha for a thousand years, up to 5, 4 thousand BC. e. All this millennium in their native lands is dominated by other conquering people and alien's panchals. But after 5,4 thousand BC the kauravas conquer their homeland from the Panchals and again live on it.

It would seem that the veracity of this ancient tradition is impossible in our days neither to confirm nor deny. But this is what modern archaeological science tells us. L. Koltsov writes: "Butovo culture was one of the major cultural manifestations in the Mesolithic of the Volga-Oka interfluve. Noteworthy is the localization of the described monuments of Butovo culture in the western part of the Volga-Oka interfluve. The absolute chronology of the early stages of the Butovo culture is determined by the framework from the middle 8 millennium BC until the second half of 7 millennium BC (i.e. before us is the reign of King Samvarana - 6400 BC). In the second half of 7 millennium BC the Volga-Oka interfluve invades another gron a Mesolithic population, which resides in this region, in the western part, leaving archaeological culture, which we call ienevskoy. With the introduction of alien population of Butovo culture initially moves to the east and south of the region. Under the pressure of the Yenev culture, the Butovo population probably split into several isolated groups. Some of them, apparently, even left the Volga-Oka basin, as evidenced by the facts of the appearance of typically Butov elements in other neighboring regions. Such are the monuments with Butovo elements in the Sukhona basin or the Borovichi parking in the Novgorod region. "As for the displaced Butene's Yenevites, their origin seems to the archaeologists" not quite clear. "They note that: " Apparently somewhere in the second half of the Boreal period (6.5 thousand BC) a part of the population of the Upper The Dnieper region moved to the northeast and populated a part of the Volga-Oka interfluve, displacing the Butovo tribes. "But" the isolation of the Yenev population, the absence of peaceful contacts with the cultures surrounding it, ultimately led to the decline of culture and its crowding out by the "Butovo people" who had become stronger by the end of the existence of the "Yenevites". Thus, at the end of 6 thousand, "the Late Butovo population again begins to" reconquest "- the re-capture of its original territory."

So, "the Yenev culture, which was in a hostile relationship with Butovo and lost touch with the" mother "territory, apparently degenerated, which subsequently led to an easier movement of the Butovo people back to the west and their assimilation of the remnants of the "Yenevites" in any case, in the Early Neolithic Upper Volga culture, which was formed in the region in the 5th millennium BC., we almost no longer find elements of the Yeni culture. Butovo elements are sharply dominant. "

When comparing the text of the epic and the data of archeology, the coincidence of the chronology of the whole event and its individual episodes is striking. And a logical question arises: are the descendants of the Puru-Paurava not hiding behind the "Butovites", and their enemies Panchals behind the "Yenevites"?

Especially since it is not strange, but time was not dominant over these events. And today, at the source of the Don (near the Donets River), near the cities of Kimovsky and Epifanyu, on a hill there is a tiny village that has retained its ancient name - Ajamki. Maybe someday archaeologists will find here the ruins of the ancient fortress of King Samvarana - Ajamidha.

But in this case, we can assume that the names of other settlements of the ancient Aryans have survived to this day. And so it is.

So at the confluence of the Upa and Plava rivers is the city of Krapivna (nettle). But one of the books of Mahabharata tells about the city of Upaplava - the capital of the Matsyev people who lived in the kingdom of Virata. And the word "virata" in Sanskrit means "bast plant, nettle."

The greatest of the seven sacred cities of the ancient Aryans was the city of Varanasi - the center of learning and the capital of the kingdom of Kashi that is, "shining." The epic claims that Varanasi was founded in ancient times, under the grandson of the great-ancestor of the people of Manu, who escaped from the flood. According to the astronomical chronology of Mahabharata, Varanasi as a capital existed already 12 thousand 300 years before our days. Its name is produced either from the word "monitor", which means "forest elephant" (mammoth), or from the name of the rivers Varana and Asi, on which this city stood, or it is possible that it also comes from the combination of "vara-us", which means "our circle (fortress)."

But is there a city with that name on the Varana River today? If you look at the banks of the river Crows, then we will not see such a city there. However, we recall that until the 18th century, the present Voronezh River was called the Great Voronoy, was navigable and even fuller of the upper Don. On this river today stands the largest city in the south of Russia - Voronezh. About when it was founded, we do not have any exact data. Voronezh is mentioned both under 1177 and in 1237. It is believed that the fortress of Voronezh was restored in 1586. In the 17-18 centuries, the city was wooden, but as early as 1702 there were ruins of some stone buildings called locals "kazarsky" within its boundaries. Now on the territory of Voronezh there are at least four ancient Russian settlements. There are also monuments of preceding eras. But could Voronezh be ancient Varanasi?

This question should be answered positively. Firstly, the name Voronezh is closer to the ancient Aryan Varanasi (Varanashi) than the modern Indian Ben-Ares (the city of Ares), especially since in the 16th century the fortress was called Voronets.

Secondly, the ancient Aryan epic indicates in the Varanasi region a number of geographical objects that are absent in India. In addition to the Varana River (Great Vorony), Asi, Kaveri, and Deva rivers flowed near Varanasi. But near Voronezh itself the rivers Usman, Kaverie, Devica still flow. Not far from Varanasi were the Vay-duryia pond ("duryia" - a mountain) and the Deva-sabha mountains ("sabha" - a hill). But even now, in the Voronezh and Lipetsk regions, the Baygora river flows (Bai is a mountain), and the hills south of Voronezh, near the Sosny and Don rivers, are called Devogorie.

One of the books of the Mahabharata speaks of Varanasi as a city in the Videha region. But the epic country of Videha, with the capital Mithila, was located at the edge of the seven estuaries of the Ganges (Volga) and thousands of lotus lakes and, as Sanskrit commentators believed, had nothing to do with the Kashi kingdom. (By the way, now there are many lotuses growing in the Volga delta, and 5-6 thousand years ago the level of the Caspian Sea was 20 meters lower than the modern one and the Volga delta merged with the Terek and Ural deltas into one huge lake region).

This apparent contradiction is simply explained. At Voronezh, the Veduga River flows into the Don, by whose name, apparently, the Videha region was named.

Near the city of Varanasi, as Mahabharata testifies, the city of Hastin was located, which became the capital of the Aryans after the Battle of Kurukshetra (Kursk Field) in 3102 BC. And what? Next to Voronezh is the village of Kostenki (a city in the 17th century), famous for its archaeological sites, the oldest of which date back to 30 thousand BC. e. The cultural layers of this village come from ancient times to our days without a break, which indicates the succession of culture and population.

So, we think, it can be argued that Voronezh and Varanasi, like Kostenki and Hastin, are one and the same.

On the Voronezh River there is also another large city in the south of Russia - Lipetsk. This name is not in the Mahabharata. But there is the city of Mathura (Mathura), also one of the seven sacred cities of the ancient Aryans. It was located on Kurukshetra (Kursk field) east of the Yamuna (Oka). But even now, the Matyra River flows into the Voronezh River near Lipetsk. Epos says that in order to capture the city of Matura, Krishna had to first master the five hills in its vicinity. But today, as well as many thousands of years ago, the five hills north of Lipetsk continue to dominate the valley.

It is possible that the numerous information on ethnogenesis stored by Mahabharata will help archaeologists in the identification of those archaeological cultures of Eastern Europe, which still bear their conventional archaeological names. So according to the Mahabharata in

376

6.5 thousand BC "all these panchals are descended from Duhshanta and Paramestkhin." This confirms the emergence of a tribe or people called by the archaeologists "Ienevites", immediately before their invasion of the Volga-Oka interfluve, since Duhshanta directly preceded Samvaran.

Once Gavrila Romanovich Derzhavin wrote: "The river of times in its aspiration takes away all the affairs of people."

But we were faced with an amazing paradox when real rivers seemed to stop the flow of time, returning to our world those people who once lived along the banks of these rivers and their affairs. They returned our Memory to us.

S. V. Zharnikova
2010
Content

Alexander Bykov
Should we be afraid of climate change?
A. A.Seibutis
Indo-Europeans: Paleoecology and Natural Plots of Myths
S. V. Zharnikova
Rigveda about the northern ancestral home of the Aryans
S. V. Zharnikova
Plants of the Indo-European Motherland
(Based on materials by V. A. Safronov, T. V. Gamkrelidze, Vyach. Vs. Ivanova)
S. V. Zharnikova
Fauna of the Indo-European ancient homeland
Alexey Artemyev
Why did mammoths go awry?
Grigory Maksimovich Bongard-Levin, Edwin Arvidovich Grantovsky
From Scythia to India. Mysterious Beast Sharabha
A. A. Tyunyaev
Home moose known from the Mesolithic
S. V. Zharnikova
The oldest domesticated animals and the image of the goose horse and the deer horse of ancient Aryan mythology
S. V. Zharnikova
Possible origins of horse-goose and horse-deer images in indo-iranian (Aryan) mythology
Anatoly Ekhalov, Svetlana Zharnikova.
Non-black earth granary of Russia?
S. V. Zharnikova, A. G. Vinogradov
Reconstruction of a possible climate change in the Indo-European ancestral home

378

S. V. Zharnikova

Hyperborea and the Aryan ancestral home
(Natural--scientific aspects)

Edito A. G. Vinogradov
Technical Editor S. Ukhanova
The original layout S. Hromov
Formatted by S. Hromov

WP IP «General electronic books" (CI-USA)
(p.h. "Academy")

Printed in Great Britain
by Amazon

59026156R00215